Commercial Transitions and Abolition in West Africa 1630–1860

Studies in Global Slavery

VOLUME 9

The titles published in this series are listed at *brill.com/sgs*

Commercial Transitions and Abolition in West Africa 1630–1860

By

Angus Dalrymple-Smith

BRILL

LEIDEN | BOSTON

This research was funded by the Netherlands Organisation for Scientific Research for the project "Is Poverty Destiny? Exploring Long Term Changes in African Living Standards in Global Perspective" (NWO VIDI Grant no. 016.124.307).

Cover illustration: *Gezicht op de Westafrikaanse kust van Elmina tot Mouri en aanzicht van kasteel St. George te Elmina* (Prospect of the Coast from El Mina to Mowri and Prospect of St. Georges Castle at El Mina). Cf. Koninklijke Bibliotheek, Den Haag, inv. nr. 693 C 5 dl III, to. p. 497 en 693 C 5 dl III, to. p. 461 en 61 B 25, na p. 156.

Library of Congress Cataloging-in-Publication Data

Names: Dalrymple-Smith, Angus, author.
Title: Commercial transitions and abolition in West Africa 1630-1860 / by Angus Dalrymple-Smith.
Description: Leiden ; Boston : Brill, [2020] | Series: Studies in global slavery, 2405-4585 ; volume9 | Includes bibliographical references. |
Identifiers: LCCN 2019037974 (print) | LCCN 2019037975 (ebook) | ISBN 9789004363458 (hardback) | ISBN 9789004417120 (ebook)
Subjects: LCSH: Slavery--Africa, West--History. | Africa, West--Commerce--History. | Africa, West--Economic conditions.
Classification: LCC HT1331 .D35 2019 (print) | LCC HT1331 (ebook) | DDC 306.3/620966--dc23
LC record available at https://lccn.loc.gov/2019037974
LC ebook record available at https://lccn.loc.gov/2019037975

Typeface for the Latin, Greek, and Cyrillic scripts: "Brill". See and download: brill.com/brill-typeface.

ISSN 2405-4585
ISBN 978-90-04-36345-8 (hardback)
ISBN 978-90-04-41712-0 (e-book)

This book is printed on acid-free paper and produced in a sustainable manner.

To my wonderful family
Mirjam, Evie and Morris

Contents

PART 2
The Long-Term Roots of the Commercial Transitions: Case Studies

Figures, Maps and Tables

Figures

Maps

Tables

Appendices

Introduction: Historiography of the Commercial Transition

In 1807, the British parliament passed a Bill ending its participation in the transatlantic slave trade. The abolition movement responsible for this legislation went on to have a profound influence on Britain's foreign policy, ultimately leading to the end of this trade by the 1860s. In West Africa, regional exports gradually evolved from being dominated by captives destined for New World plantations, to commodities such as palm oil for European and North American industrial and consumer markets. This process became known in later literature as the 'commercial transition' and has become one of the key themes in West African historiography (Law 1995b, p. 1).

Contemporary campaigners against the slave trade were sure that Africans needed encouragement to make the switch from trading slaves and therefore assumed that abolition was a necessary part of the commercial transition.[1] This was also the starting point for earlier modern historians of the period whose focus was directed on the nineteenth century and the so called 'the crisis of adaption' faced by elites who had formally depended on slave exports.[2] However, more recent scholarship has recognised that trade in non-slave goods had always been an important part of West Africa's economic relations with the Atlantic world and that this trade had a strong influence over developments in the nineteenth century.[3] Furthermore, an analysis of the export trends along different parts of the West African coast shows marked differences both before and after 1807.

As will be discussed below, some regions almost immediately ceased their involvement in transatlantic slave trading while other continued to deal in captive Africans for another four decades. Secondly, exports of (non-slave) commodities were rising fast in some areas, falling in others and almost non-existent along some sections of the coast. Accounting for these differences is difficult as, so far, the literature has focused on particular areas or products.[4]

1 Thomas Clarkson (1789), a leading eighteenth century abolitionist stated that "…it is impossible that we can trade successfully in both of them (*i.e. slaves & commodities*) at the same time, (one of them having hitherto proven an insuperable impediment to the other)…" Another influential campaigner Thomas Buxton (1840, p. 309) believed "..legitimate trade.." with Africa was not possible without a permanent British presence to deter slave traders.

2 See for example, Dike (1956), Hopkins (1973), Austen (1987).

3 Northrup (1976), Eltis (1994), Behrendt et al. (2010), Law et al. (2013).

4 See below, ref. 18 for an overview of the relevant literature.

 | DOI:10.1163/9789004417120_002

Furthermore, there is relatively little quantitative data about West African commodity exports in the pre-abolition period, especially in comparison to the wealth of information about the numbers and characteristics of the export trade in people available through the Transatlantic Slave Trade Database (TSTD). What is currently lacking in the literature, and what this book aims to provide, is a long-term comparative analysis which can explain the marked variations in the speed and nature of the commercial transition across different areas of West Africa.

This book has two main aims. Firstly, to provide the most comprehensive analysis to date of the trade in commodities and products of commercial agriculture from West Africa's three most important trading regions – the Gold Coast, the Bight of Benin and the Bight of Biafra – from the late seventeenth until the first decade of the eighteenth century. Secondly to determine what, from a comparative perspective, were the most important pan-regional variables determining the very different reactions to abolition and the commercial transition in the case study regions.

The book is organised into two parts. Part 1 will present a range of both new and published quantitative data on the commodity trade in the first and second halves of the eighteenth century as well as analysis of exports of commercial agriculture for the provisioning of slave ships. As this study is largely focused on the export trade from West Africa, the data is based on the records and accounts of European slave and commodity traders as virtually no quantitative data from African sources exists for this period. This approach has been criticised by scholars who have argued that relying on non-African sources, which are themselves not always entirely reliable, risks underestimating or even misunderstanding the impact and significance of the Atlantic trade on African societies.[5] However, data from the TSTD, in combination with region specific studies based on qualitative sources, has led to a greater understanding of the social, political and economic development of the states and societies of pre-colonial West Africa.[6] This book aims to provide similar insights by using the results of the quantitative analysis to argue that the patterns of trade established in the late seventeenth and eighteenth centuries were crucial in

5 A particularly thorough and engaging summary of such arguments can be found in Green (2011), pp. 4–14.

6 For studies that rely heavily on the TSTD, see for example Klein (2010, pp. 105–131) for an overview of the African organisation of the slave trade, Shumway's (2014) study on the impact of the transatlantic slave trade on the Fante along the Gold Coast or Nwokeji's (2010) analysis of the development the Aro commercial organisation in the Bight of Biafra and its impact on society, culture and economic life in the region.

determining the nature and speed of the commercial transition in these regions.

Part 2 takes a case study approach looking at the three case study regions through a newly developed model of analysis to explain patterns of external trade in West Africa in the pre-colonial era from a comparative perspective. These chapters will argue that regional variations in the speed and timing of the commercial transition can be explained by five key factors: (1) the nature and duration of long-term trade relations; (2) the identity of the principal European trade partner; (3) certain aspects of the ecology of the different regions; (4) the regional political contexts; and (5) the development of institutions that either encouraged or discouraged elite participation in non-slave exports.

This is the first study that has used a long-term, comparative analysis to explore West Africa's trade over the long eighteenth-century in relation to the nineteenth-century commercial transition. It therefore provides a unique perspective and generates fresh insights into the political and economic development of three important regions and their relationship to a changing Atlantic world.

1 From Slaves to 'Legitimate Commerce': Different Places, Different Times

In 1842, the author of a British Parliamentary Report on West Africa and the state of the slave trade[7] stated that: *"…a trade in produce has been gradually growing up and gaining upon the Slave Trade in proportion as the enterprise of the British merchant pushes on the one and the vigilance of the British cruiser checks and cripples the other…"* The report was written 35 years after the passing of the 'Abolition Bill' by parliament in 1807, which outlawed participation in the transatlantic slave trade for British merchants. This trade had begun in the late fifteenth-century by the Portuguese, who required labour for their expanding Atlantic and American empires. By the late eighteenth-century it had reached its apogee in West Africa[8] with thousands of captives embarked annually onto European and American vessels and sent to labour in the plantations and mines of the New World. At first, Britain was the only major slave trading

7 Parliamentary Papers 1842 (551) (551-II) Report from the Select Committee on the West Coast of Africa; together with the minutes of evidence, appendix, and index. Part 1.–Report and evidence. Dr Madden's Report p XX.

8 The trade in the West Central region of Africa, what is now Congo Brazzaville and Angola, was to expand into the nineteenth-century.

nation to cease their involvement in the traffic of African captives to the Americas.[9] They were eventually joined, often unwillingly, by the French, Dutch, Spanish and Portuguese/Brazilians following a long diplomatic and military campaign which finally halted the traffic by the 1860s.

The 1807 Bill was the result of a sustained campaign by what became known as the abolitionist movement. This had begun in the eighteenth century and was a product of a changing intellectual and religious climate. Writers such as Montesquieu and Rousseau argued that slavery was in principal contrary to human nature,[10] and Adam Smith argued in the 'Wealth of Nations' (1776) that wage labour was more economically productive to society than coerced labour. In fact, Klein (2010, p. 190) has argued that it was this, rather than humanitarian concerns for the African victims of the trade, that drove the movement: "*The anti-slave-trade campaign was based fundamentally on a belief in free labour as one of the most crucial underpinnings of modern society and the institution that guaranteed mankind's progress out of its medieval past.*" However, the campaign did have a profoundly moral side, especially for dissenting Protestant movements, such as the Quakers and Methodists who were among the first to actively campaign for the trade to end (Jennings 2013).

The extent to which abolition was a moral or an economically rational decision has been fiercely debated. Some historians, most famously Eric Williams (1944), have argued that plantation slavery in the Americas was already in decline and therefore British withdrawal from the transatlantic slave trade represented nothing more than the abandonment of a failing sector of the economy. Others, most notably Drescher (2004, 2010), Eltis et al. (2005) and Davis (2006) have instead made the case that the slave plantations of the New World were flourishing at the beginning of the nineteenth century and remained an economically dynamic model of production until the institution of slavery itself was outlawed. When seen in this light, the Bill of 1807 would have been contrary to the economic interests of Great Britain, although realistically it is

9 Denmark had abolished its own trade in 1802, although its merchants were never a major carrier of slaves. The French had temporarily ceased their involvement after 1794 in the wake of the revolution and Haitian rebellions but resumed trading in 1803. The United States did officially prohibit its citizens from engaging in the transatlantic slave trade, but this prohibition was easily circumvented, especially given anti-British sentiment (Thomas 1999, pp. 523, 545–548, Brooks 1970, p. 115).

10 In the "Spirit of the Laws" (1748), Montesquieu writes that "*The state of slavery is in its own nature bad. It is neither useful to the master nor to the slave.*" (Book 15, Chapter 1). However, in the same Chapter he goes on to argue that "*It is impossible for us to suppose these creatures* (Africans) *to be men…*" In the opening Chapter of "The Social Contract" (1762), Rousseau begins by stating "*Man was born free, and he is everywhere in chains*" arguing that society should not constrain the freedoms of its citizens.

unlikely that its merchants or traders suffered much as a consequence of the decision (Inikori 2009, p. 171, Klein 2010, p. 190).

In the eyes of abolitionists, the shift towards commodity exports was a fundamental component in the strategy to undermine the slave trade and bring 'civilisation to Africa'. Campaigners against the slave trade in the 1790s, such as Thomas Clarkson (1789, pp. 8–9) and the former slave Olaudah Equiano (1794, p. 357), were already arguing that promoting alternative forms of commerce was the most effective means by which export slavery might be undermined. This was to become dogma amongst abolitionists in the nineteenth century (Law 2013, p. 4), most famously articulated by David Livingston's linking of 'Commerce, Christianity and Civilisation'.[11] It was for this reason that the trade in commodities came to be known as 'legitimate commerce', being perceived as a means of weaning Africans away from export slavery and towards the kinds of productive activities viewed as morally acceptable by Europeans (Buxton 1840, p. 264).[12]

Among historians of West Africa, the impact of this change from slave to commodity exports has been a key debate since the 1950s (Law 1995b, pp. 1–3). Dike's (1956) study of the Bight of Biafra argues that, as the region started to produce more palm oil and export fewer people, the power of the traditional ruling elite was undermined, leading to increasing levels of social disruption. This reasoning was later developed and extended by Hopkins (1973) who argued the ending of transatlantic slavery created a severe economic shock which weakened elites by removing their main source of income. This 'crisis of adaption'[13] fuelled conflict and instability, eventually creating conditions of vulnerability which enabled the partition of West Africa by European powers in the 1880s and 1890s. However, this crisis also marked the beginning of what he argued was the 'modern economic history' of the continent, dominated by

11 '*...by guiding our missionary labours so as to benefit our own country, we shall thereby more effectually and permanently benefit the heathen.... We ought to encourage the Africans to cultivate for our markets, as the most effectual means, next to the Gospel, of their elevation*'. Livingston (1858, p. 720).

12 The term is objectionable on many levels; Law (1995, p. 26) argues that it is both Eurocentric and obscures the fact that Africans had always exported non-slave products. Furthermore, all of the commodities exported during the nineteenth-century were at least partly produced by some form of coerced labour. The expansion of 'legitimate commerce' thus led to a huge increase in slave ownership within Africa (Lovejoy 2011, p. 161).

13 The term was used in a 1968 article about the endemic warfare in Yorubaland in the later nineteenth-century. Hopkins argued that the rise of palm oil exports led to a severe crisis for elites who had previously based their power and wealth on raiding and slave exports. This in turn led to social disruption, violence and increasingly frequent interventions by Britain which ultimately led to colonisation (Hopkins 1968).

small scale producers rather than elites. Hopkins' thesis has attracted both support and criticism. Lovejoy (2011, p. 184) has argued that the development of 'legitimate commerce' led to West African societies establishing, not a more modern economy, but instead a slave mode of production.[14] This process was to separate Africa from the dominant capitalist economies in the rest of the Atlantic, which had largely abandoned slavery by the end of the nineteenth century.

Eltis (1987) and Eltis & Jennings (1988) have argued that external trade, with some exceptions, had very little impact on the majority of the inhabitants of West Africa and therefore only modestly affected long-term development. However, this argument does not apply to the areas from which most slaves were exported – Biafra, the Gold Coast / Asante, Dahomey and Yorubaland (Eltis & Jennings 1988, p. 958).[15] These were areas of relatively high population density containing, according to recent estimates, around 15 million people (Frankema & Jerven 2014). In these areas, the Atlantic trade had a substantial impact on many coastal societies, but less so on the savannah states of the interior. A more substantive criticism of Hopkins comes from studies which, like Manning, (1990, p. 142) argue that "*The merchants, warlords, and monarchs who dominated the capture of slaves also dominated the exploitation of slaves within the continent*". This was also argued by Latham (1973) for the Biafran port of Old Calabar and later applied more generally by Austen (1990, pp. 101–102). In addition, Austin (2013, p. 259) has argued that Hopkins' analysis underestimated the extent to which the elites from the period of the slave trade maintained their wealth and power during the era of 'legitimate commerce'.

However, these studies fail to account for the fact that the impact of abolition and the commercial transition varied considerably across both the time and space of West Africa (Law 1995b, p. 5, Law et al. 2013, p. 23). Figures I.1a., I.1b and I.1c show the number of slaves exported from West Africa's most important regions of embarkation. On the Gold Coast, the sale of captives fell to

14 This is when "*...the social and economic structure of a particular society included an integrated system of enslavement, slave trade and the domestic use of slaves....,*" in contrast to societies with a "*lineage or domestic mode of production,*" where slaves exist either as a marginal feature or an institution but where the social and political systems are based on ethnicity and kinship. Lovejoy 2011 (pp. 10–12).

15 They might in addition have included the Senegambian region, which although a minor region with regards to slave exports was heavily involved in commodity trading throughout the eighteenth and nineteenth Centuries (Searing 2003). Sierra Leone, as the base of British abolition efforts and the destination of a resettlement programme for thousands of Africans captured in other regions was also profoundly impacted by contacts with the Atlantic (Wyse 1989).

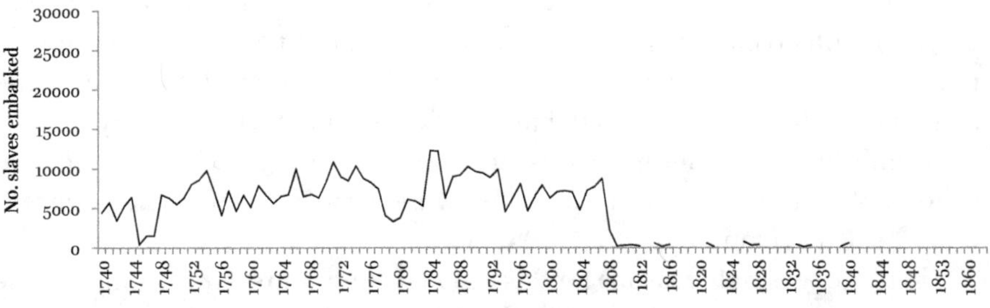

FIGURE I.1a Number of slaves exported from the Gold Coast, 1740–1860

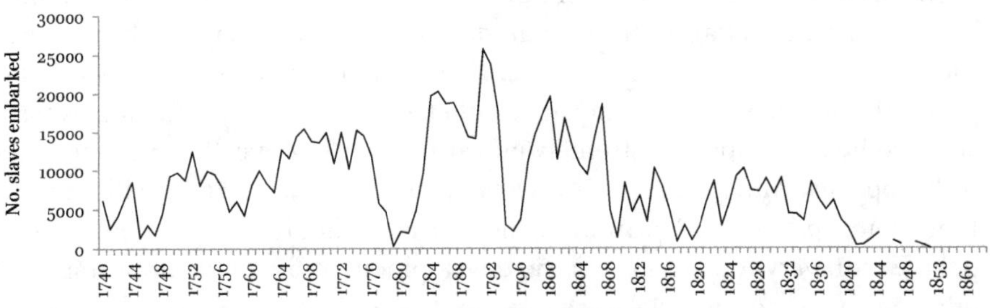

FIGURE I.1b Numbers of slave exported from the Bight of Biafra, 1740–1860

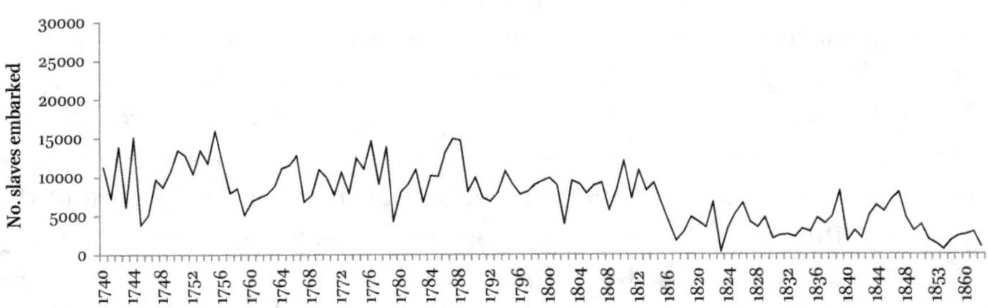

FIGURE I.1C Numbers of slaves exported from Bight of Benin, 1740–1860
Note: (All data in this book from the Slave Trade Database were downloaded on 01/06/2016)
Source: slavevoyages.org

negligible levels immediately after 1807. In the Bight of Biafra, there was also a post-abolition recovery but this was followed by a steady decline from the late 1820s, and by the 1840s the export of captives had more or less ceased. Lastly, in the Bight of Benin, there was a similar dramatic fall in slave exports but only after 1815, after which time exports recovered and continued up to the 1850s.

The patterns of commodity trading were also strikingly different. On the Gold Coast, the nineteenth century saw an increase both in gold and palm oil exports (Garrard 1980, p. 163, Lynn 1997, p. 39). The Bight of Biafra became the biggest exporter of palm oil in the first half of the nineteenth century, exporting significant quantities by at least the 1820s (Lynn 1997, p. 19). By contrast, exports of commodities from the Bight of Benin were virtually non-existent until the 1840s (Manning 1982, p. 52).

There are two main reasons for this gap in the literature. Firstly, much of the work cited above on the impact of abolition and the rise of 'legitimate commerce' within Africa fails to analyse the commercial transition in the context of the long historical development of Africa's non-slave trade.[16] This is in part because the transatlantic slave trade dominated commercial exchange with the Atlantic during the late seventeenth and eighteenth centuries. More importantly, its scale and the horrors it inflicted upon millions of captives have since come to occupy an extremely powerful place in the collective memories of Europeans, Americans and Africans (Thomas 1999, pp. 10–11, Hilton 2010, Klein 2010, pp. xv–xix). Accordingly, most research has focussed on the trade in people with very few studies on the development and relative importance of other forms of commercial exchange, and how these influenced the nature and speed of the commercial transition. The focus on the trade in people has had the additional effect of making British abolition efforts against transatlantic slavery deemed to be the most important driver of West African economic and political change. Other studies of West Africa and the slave trade have recently concluded that to explain inter-regional differences, scholars must give far greater weight to factors that were endogenous to the region, rather than limiting their search to the decisions and actions of Europeans.[17] This book will apply this reasoning to the commercial transition. Secondly, most of the studies on this period of West African history generally target single case study regions.[18] The resultant literature has focussed on explaining how factors specific to individual areas influenced patterns of historical change.

16 This was noted by the editors of a recent volume on the commercial transition (Law et al. 2013, pp. 8–10) and investigated by two contributors to the same volume (Eltis 2013, Austin 2013a).

17 For example, the debates on the high levels of mortality experienced by both slaves and crew during the middle passage (Hogerzeil & Richardson 2007, Klein & Engerman 1997, Eltis 1984, 1989) and the impact of African resistance (Behrendt et al. 2001, Richardson 2001).

18 These include, but are by no means limited to; Bight of Benin: Manning 1982, Reid 1986, Law 1991, Bay 1998, Law 2004, Mann 2007, Monroe 2012, Norman 2012; Gold Coast: Reynolds 1974, Wilks 1975, Wilson 1991, DeCorse 1992, Wilks 1993, McCaskie 2003, Perbi 2004,

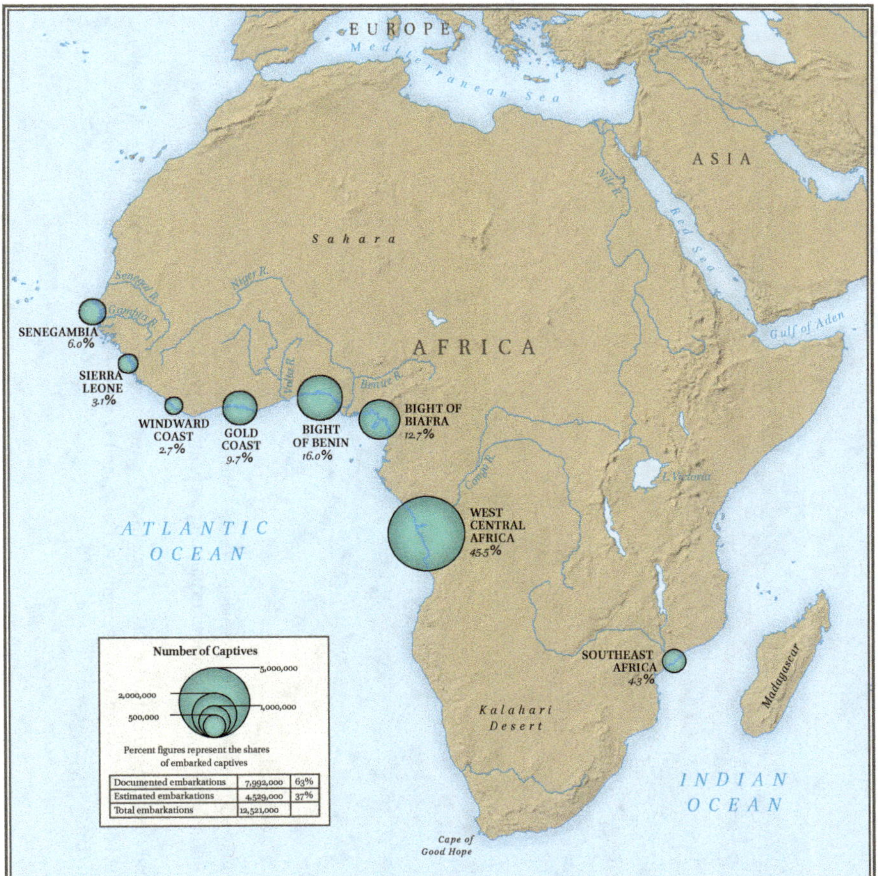

West Central Africa was the largest regional departure point for captives through most of the slave trade era. As voyage length was determined as much by wind and ocean currents as by distance, routes were not necessarily quicker from regions closer to the Americas and Europe. Regions west of the Gold Coast generated a relatively small share of the total slaves carried across the Atlantic.

MAP I.1 Major coastal regions from which captives left Africa, all years
Source: http://www.slavevoyages.org/assessment/intro-maps (accessed 16/01/2017)

This book will take a different approach by applying a long-term, comparative historical analysis to West Africa's three most important slave regions which

Austin 2005, Shumway 2014, Sparks 2014; Bight of Biafra: Latham 1973, Northrup 1978, Martin 1988, Dike & Ekejiuba 1990, Lovejoy and Richardson 2004, Nwokeji 2010. Two edited volumes on the commercial transition, Law (1995) and Law et al. (2013) also, with some exceptions, look at individual regions / states in isolation and do not use a comparative perspective. In addition there have been studies on specific commodities such as gold – Garrard 1980, kola – Abaka 2005, Lovejoy 1980 and palm oil – Lynn 1997.

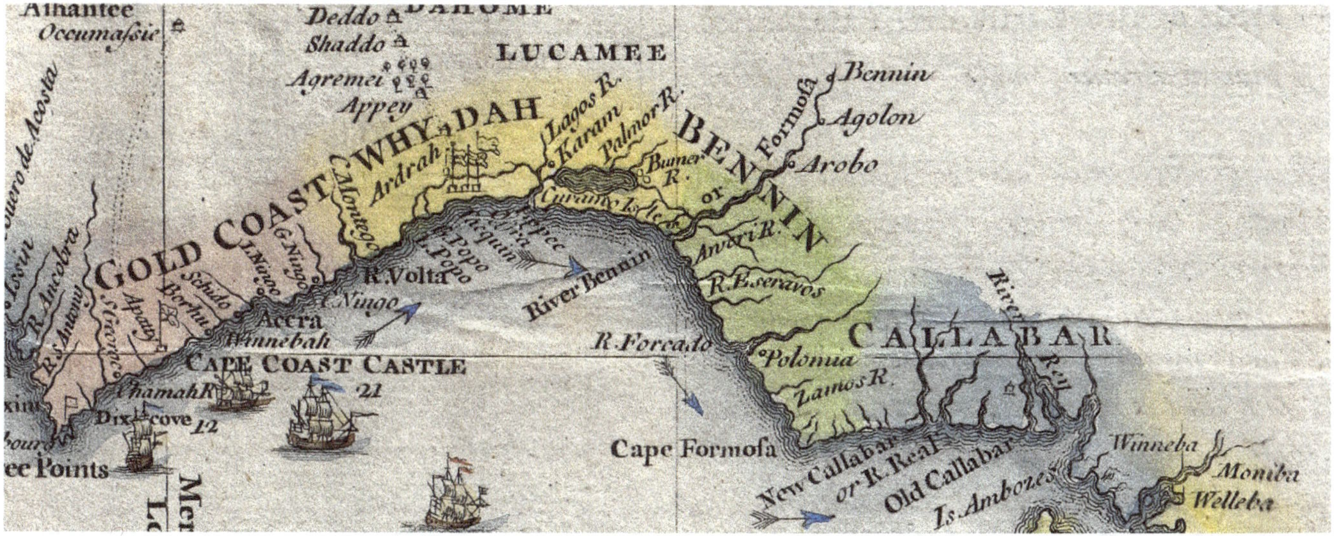

MAP I.2 Enlarged section from Postlethwayt's 1755 map showing the three case study regions. Postlethwayte was a vocal supporter of slavery, an advocate of the Royal Africa Company and was strongly in favour of expanding trade and British influence within Africa (Brown 2010, pp. 88–89)
Source: Postlethwayte, M. (1755), "A new and correct Map of the Coast of Africa from Cape Blanco Lat. 20°, 40'. N. to the Coast of Angola, Lat. 11°. S. With Explanatory Notes of all the Forts and Settlements belonging to the several European Powers." Mr. Postlethwayte's Universal Dictionary of Commerce, Vol. II, (London), p. 945

together accounted for around eighty percent of the region's embarkations from the seventeenth to the nineteenth centuries; the Gold Coast, the Bight of Benin and the Bight of Biafra.[19] These trading zones were used by European traders from at least the early eighteenth-century as a way of referencing different parts of the coast. Within these regions, the bulk of slaves came from just a few ports with sophisticated trading networks connecting Europe and the Americas to internal suppliers of captives (Eltis et al. 1999, Klein 2010, pp. 106–107).

The Gold Coast roughly corresponded to modern day Ghana and ended at the Volta river. The three ports of Elmina, Cape Coast Castle and Anomabo, located in territory controlled by the Fante, handled the majority of slave embarkations in the eighteenth century. From the 1740s both slaves and gold came almost exclusively from the Asante empire, which had become the dominant power in the region and will be the focus of the first case study. The Bight of Biafra extended from Cape Formosa to Cape Lopez in Gabon, but the almost all of the trade, both in captives and commodities, was conducted through the ports of Bonny, Old Calabar and Elem Kalabari which were supplied from the interior Igbo and Ibibio regions (see Chapter 5). These areas, and the trading network that connected this interior region with the coast, will be the focus of the second case study. The Bight of Benin began at the Volta river and continued to Cape Formosa in modern day south east Nigeria. In the 1720s the main areas through which slaves were traded and the most important port, Whydah, were conquered by the Dahomean empire. As this region then essentially controlled the supply and marketing of the majority of the region's captives until the early nineteenth-century, it will be subject of the final case study.

The temporal scope of the book covers the 200 years from roughly the middle of the seventeenth century to 1860s. This covers the period from when north European nations, in particular Britain, the Netherlands and France, began to expand their American possessions, demanding ever increasing numbers of coerced labourers to work the plantations of the new world (Eltis 2000, pp. 61–62, Klein 2010, pp. 31–33) and continues until the transatlantic slave trade finally ended.

19 In this context West Africa refers to the area from modern day Senegal to Cape Lopez in Gabon. Further south, the region known in the slave trade database as West Central Africa, covered two other slave-trading zones. Firstly, the Loango coast, which stretched to the river Congo and Angola (Da Silva & Sommerdyk 2010, pp. 80–84) and secondly Angola. Portuguese / Brazilian merchants had a near monopoly on the slave trade in Angola and, while north European merchants were dominant in Loango in the eighteenth century, they were entirely displaced by the Portuguese after abolition (Lovejoy 2011, p. 53).

2 West African Trade with the Atlantic World

The first part of the book argues that the nature of the commercial transition in the different case study regions in the nineteenth century was a continuation of existing long-term patterns of trade. In the Bight of Biafra, the transatlantic slave trade stimulated substantial growth in both commercial agriculture, for the provisioning of ships for the middle passage, and commodity production for slave merchants in the period before abolition. The subsequent rise of the palm oil industry can therefore be regarded as the continuation of an existing trend, including the market institutions that were developed to facilitate the commodity export sector. Over the long term, non-slave products dominated output from the Gold Coast region except for a relatively short period in the eighteenth century. Exports of captives were already falling from the 1780s, so the abrupt ending of transatlantic slavery in 1807, and subsequent increase in gold production and forest products should be interpreted as a reversion to the earlier, and long established form of trade. Finally, the area of the Bight of Benin that came to be controlled by the kingdom of Dahomey focused exclusively on slave exports. In contrast to the other two regions, there was no response to the demand for slave ship provisions, nor to increasing demand for other export commodities during the eighteenth century. The relatively late transition to commodity exports should thus be seen in the context of the region's long history of specialisation in slave trading.

Having established the stylised facts of these regional patterns of trade, the second part of the book presents a new interpretation of the commercial transition. In the Gold Coast and the Bight of Biafra particular institutions developed in the seventeenth and eighteenth centuries to manage trade, control and monopolise violence and extend the power of certain elite groups. These institutions allowed powerful families and individuals to profit (both financially and socially) at least as much from using slaves in the internal economy to produce export commodities, as they could from selling captives into transatlantic slavery. In the Gold Coast, elite status was highly dependent on the production and possession of gold. Demand for gold guaranteed a strong domestic market for coerced labour, which could effectively compete with export of captives to the Americas. In the Bight of Biafra, trade with the Atlantic world provided the wealth that underpinned the power of powerful groups, families and individuals across the region. However, there were no ideological or economic barriers to trading in commodities as opposed to slaves. This meant that when demand for African commodities in European markets began to rise at the end of the eighteenth century, households could respond by using their free and coerced labour to increase production of other commodities, due to the support of groups who could trade and market these goods to foreign merchants.

By contrast, the Dahomean state developed in a late seventeenth and eighteenth-century context where a militarised, slave raiding institutional model enabled the monarchy, with the support of elite families and lineage groups, to monopolise wealth and power. The transfer of large amounts of labour to other forms of economic activities, such as palm oil production, directly threatened this power. It was only under extreme pressure in the late 1840s, due to the increasingly effective abolition efforts of the British, the rise of regional competitors and military setbacks, that it became worthwhile for elites to invest in the development of a commodity export sector. The following section will set out which factors were relevant, and which were not, in the development of institutions that were either accommodating to the commercial transition or which encouraged a focus on the export of captives.

3 Accounting for Regional Differences

3.1 *Shared Factors that cannot Explain Regional Variation in the Commercial Transition*

There are two factors that were common across all major slave exporting areas in West Africa and, as such, cannot provide a satisfactory explanation for the varying ways in which African societies responded post-1807 to abolition. First, the efforts undertaken by the British to prevent other nations from continuing the slave trade. Second, changes in either the African supply of slaves, or the demand for slaves from New World plantation owners. After first substantiating these claims, the chapter will continue with an overview of explanatory factors that account for the observed variation.

3.2 *British Slave Trade Patrols*

The decision by the British parliament to withdraw from the transatlantic slave trade, and to dedicate a good deal of military and diplomatic effort to abolishing the traffic in coerced labour to the Americas, ultimately led to the end of the trade by the 1860s (Klein 2010, pp. 188–211). However, abolition efforts in the period up to the 1830s, although not entirely unimportant, did not have a decisive impact on the commercial transition in the three case study areas. The particular case of the Gold Coast will be dealt with in greater detail in Chapter 4, but this chapter will provide a broad overview of the military and diplomatic efforts of British attempts to halt transatlantic slavery before the late 1830s to underpin the claim that if African merchant elites had wanted to continue the export of slaves, they had ample opportunities to do so.

Table I.1 shows the areas where the British concentrated the activity of their anti-slave patrols during the first 30 years of the abolition era. Until the 1820s the vast majority of ships captured were in the Sierra Leone region of Africa, and the Caribbean, where the British had permanent settlements and harbours. The patrols then switched their focus to the Bights of Benin and Biafra, the centres of most of the slave trading in West Africa during this period. Defying the fact that the squadron was based in Freetown, the Gallinhas region down the coast was able to develop a new, thriving market in slaves, mainly to Cuba (Jones 1983). In the period when the navy began to concentrate its efforts in the 'Bights' there was a resurgence in slave numbers from this region, probably driven by more competitive prices of captives compared to other major slave markets further down the coast in Angola (Lovejoy & Richardson 1995a). There were three principal reasons for the lack of effectiveness in British abolition efforts: a lack of financial commitment to upscale navy patrols, anti-British hostility and the illegality of boarding foreign vessels or attacking African territory without due cause.

The British government was initially unwilling to support its enthusiastic anti-slavery rhetoric with any significant expenditure on a military force capable of deterring slave traders. Until the establishment of an official anti-slavery patrol in 1818 under Sir James Yeo, the navy relied on an ad hoc

TABLE I.1 Ships captured and condemned by the Royal Navy 1808–1839 by region of capture

	Bight of Benin	Bight of Biafra	Sierra Leone	Gold Coast	West Central Africa	Atlantic	Caribbean
1808–1815	9	15	48	2	2	2	38
1816–1820	7	4	25	3	0	1	2
1821–1825	11	35	8	4	0	0	2
1826–1830	34	44	15	2	0	1	22
1831–1835	6	33	4	1	0	2	16
1836–1839	28	48	33	10	9	1	25

Source: TNA – FO315 (data from Grindal 2016, pp. 761–783)

squadron of vessels based around Sierra Leone (Wills 2012). Even then the patrol consisted of only 6 ships covering some 2,000 miles of coast and, although this figure was to rise it was never sufficient to seriously deter slavers.[20] Furthermore, many of the vessels in the patrol in its earlier days tended to be older vessels, which could often be outrun by slave ships (Brooks 1970, p. 111). Anti-British sentiment also hampered the cause, especially in France and America. After the war of 1812, the United States, despite being on paper an ally of Britain in the fight against the slave trade, made no serious efforts to limit the involvement of their nations. Even when slavers were caught they were rarely punished in American courts (Brooks 1970, p. 115).

Perhaps the biggest difficulty was establishing an acceptable legal framework for stopping and searching foreign vessels without risking an international incident (Ryan 2011). Boarding the vessel of another nation constituted a violation of sovereignty and was therefore a legitimate reason to declare war. This was something Britain was anxious to avoid after the conclusion of the Treaty of Paris in 1814, which finally brought peace to the continent after the Napoleonic Wars. In practice this meant that it was relatively easy for ships to evade being captured by simply flying the flags of nations, such as the United States, whose vessels were off-limits to the British (Brooks 1970, p. 62). Law (2010) supports this, noting that boarding vessels was often contrary to international law. In addition, he notes that international maritime law also recognised that each sovereign nation controlled the 3 miles of water from their shores (essentially a cannon shot). British ships following slavers into the lagoons and rivers of Africa were therefore violating this widely accepted principle.[21] This legal argument was used by Africans to protest against British actions, such as the destruction of slave barricoons at Gallinahs by a British officer in 1840. A review of these actions by a parliamentary committee endorsed the opinion of the local rulers and the commander was later sued by

20 The number remained under ten during the 1820s, and began to increase in the 1830s and by 1848 there were 27 naval ships. However even this was far from enough as admitted by a naval officer during the 1842 parliamentary enquiry into West Africa. When asked *"Is it your opinion that the trade could effectually and permanently put down by ships of war?" he replied "No, I do not think it could; it would take all our navy to do it, I should think, to watch the coast,"* Parliamentary Papers 1842 (551) (551-II) Report from the Select Committee on the West Coast of Africa; together with the minutes of evidence, appendix, and index. Part 1.–Report and evidence, Clegg to enquiry, paras 1599–1604. While the French and the Americans were later to join in this effort their anti-slave patrols seem to have had even less impact (Brooks 1970).

21 Opposition to the character of British anti-slavery policy was also to be found in Britain. The Duke of Wellington publicly opposed the 1839 equipment act had a 'criminal character' (Thomas 1999, p. 658).

a Spanish trader for damages suffered by the destruction of his property. The eventual outcome of the case was to declare that British captains could not be held personally liable for their actions, which gave them an effective *carte blanche* to engage in military action in Africa, but this was not until 1848 (Law 2010, p. 155).

At the same time, reasons for the falling number of slave embarkations from West Africa may also have included the impact of trading south of the equator becoming a more attractive prospect for slave merchants. Eltis (2009) argues that abolition mainly affected the trade which sailed around the Northern Atlantic Gyre[22] which was dominated by North European trading nations. The bilateral trade between the Americas and Africa, which used the Southern Atlantic Gyre, was largely unaffected and grew considerably during the first few decades of the nineteenth century. During the initial negotiations with Spain and Portugal on the subject of the slave trade, Britain agreed that the slave trade south of the equator would be excluded from their abolition efforts. In addition, this region had remained unaffected by the conflicts in the second half of the eighteenth century in the north Atlantic and local slave supplies were more reliable. As West Central Africa had been the largest supplier of captives until the 1750s, the shift southwards could also be seen as a resumption of a more established long-term pattern of trading that had briefly been interrupted by the rise of West African export slavery (Eltis 2009, p. 128).

The slave trade patrols did eventually become more successful in the 1830s and this was, in the analysis of both Eltis (2009) and Law (2010), mainly the result of the British defying international law in the name of their humanitarian goals. The Equipment Act of 1839 authorised the British navy to seize vessels of other nations if they were simply equipped for the slave trade, without carrying any slaves (Thomas 1999, p. 658). Spain agreed to this measure in 1835 but the Brazilian parliament refused, leading the British to unilaterally impose this law in 1839 until Brazil reluctantly agreed to accept it in 1842 (Law 2004, p. 157, Martinez 2011, p. 92). The Royal Navy was also prepared to violate African territorial sovereignty, bombarding Whydah in 1841 (Law 2004, p. 190) and Lagos in 1851 (Mann 2007, p. 84). They expanded the remit of the patrol to Brazilian and Cuban waters in the 1850s and 1860s, which meant that slaves could no longer be imported in sufficient numbers for the trade to be profitable (Reid 1986, p. 282, Law 2004, p. 191, Klein 2010, p. 196). In the long term these efforts not only enforced the ending of the transatlantic slave trade but also set a

22 A system of ocean currents that rotate clockwise around the Atlantic north of the equator.

precedent which put Africa outside of the norms of international law and laid the legal foundations for the justification of colonialism (Law 2010).

In summary, in both the Gold Coast and Biafra the commercial transition was well under way before abolition efforts began to have a meaningful impact. In the case study chapters, it will be argued that certain aspects of British abolition policy are important for understanding the *timing* of the move away from export slavery, but they cannot explain the ultimate *causes* of different inter-regional transitions in export composition.

3.3 *Changing Demand for, or Changing Supply of, African Slaves*

Changes in the demand for or supply of African slaves are also unlikely to explain the intra-regional variation in patterns of the commercial transition. Austin (2013a, p. 249) suggests that, in some areas of West Africa, the supply of slaves came under strain towards the end of the eighteenth century because those bearing the brunt of slave raiding had learnt to defend themselves more effectively. This forced raiders to seek new sources of slaves at ever increasing distances from the coast which increased costs, forced up slave export prices and led to fewer slaves reaching embarkation ports (Klein 2001). Other literature has effectively argued that the violence attending the slave trade led to depopulation, which further restricted supply (Inikori 2011, p. 669, Nunn 2008, p. 142, Manning 1990, p. 171). However, the expansion of 'legitimate commerce' saw a corresponding rise in domestic slavery, since coerced labour was a prerequisite for any increase in West African commodity production (Austin 2008a, 2008b, 2009, Lovejoy 2011, p. 161). If slaves were simply transferred from one to another form of economic activity, a possible supply shortage cannot have been a leading cause of the retreat from slave exporting. Moreover, regarding the domestic African economy, studies by Austin (2005, pp. 43,130–133) and Lovejoy & Richardson (1995a & b) indicate that the internal market for slaves was fairly integrated. Their data is based on a limited number of observations from the interior regions and the coast, but it nonetheless reveals a significant degree of price convergence. So even if sources of supply would have dried up in some areas, the internal West African trade in slaves created a situation in which those who wanted to sell slaves to European vessels, would have opportunities to find supplies from elsewhere.

As for demand, some sources suggest that planters in the Americas had a preference for slaves from the Bight of Benin and the Gold Coast rather than from the Bight of Biafra (Eltis 2000, pp. 186–187). Ultimately, however, the priorities for slave traders were speed of embarkation and reliability of credit arrangements, enabling supply of the greatest numbers of captives as quickly and cheaply as possible (Eltis et al. 2007, p. 1339). When merchants in the

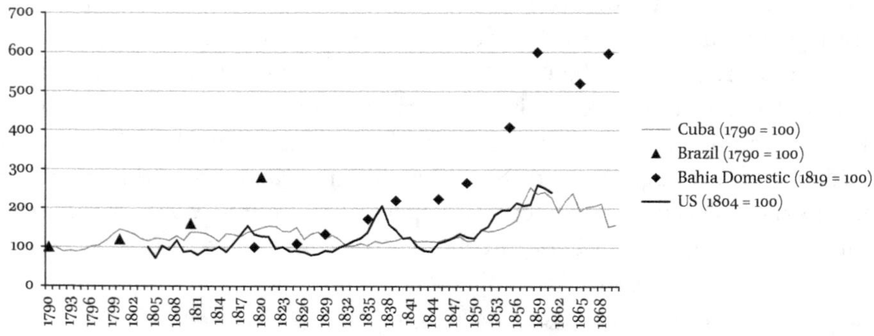

FIGURE I.2 Price indices of the average costs for slaves in Brazil, Cuba and the US 1790–1870
Sources: Bergard (1995), Miller (1986), Historical Statistics of the United States Table Bb209–214, de Queirós Mattoso, Klein & Engerman (1986)

Bight of Biafra, and particularly the port of Bonny, began efficiently embarking large numbers of captives, planters were happy to buy Biafran slaves (Lovejoy & Richardson 2004, p. 364, Nwokeji 2010, pp. 22,42). In other words, as long as demand remained high, local traders continued to have an opportunity to sell.

Demand for coerced labour from Atlantic and African markets remained high and evenly spread. Within the Americas, recent scholarship has generally supported the argument of Drescher (2004, 2010) that the plantation system was growing in the late eighteenth and nineteenth centuries.[23] The value of coerced labour continued to grow in all parts of the Americas, thus ensuring that there were still considerable profits to be made from the transportation of slaves across the Atlantic (Figure I.2). This was a consequence of the fact that, with the exception of some non-sugar producing states in the United States and the island of Barbados, no slave importing region was able to achieve a fully self-sustaining slave population (Tadman 2000, Curtin 1972, p. 60). This ensured that there was always, until at least the 1850s, a demand for slave imports from Africa. Thus, the variegated commercial transitions cannot be adequately explained by differences in internal market prices for slaves.

23 See for example Davis (2006) who argues that plantation system of the American south was run according to principles of mass production which would become standard working practices in the twentieth century.

3.4 *Factors that may Explain Regional Variation in the Commercial Transition*

The following five factors did have an impact upon the different paths of commercial transition in the three regions it explores. The first factor relates to certain aspects of region-specific ecologies. All regions were able to produce commodities for export to Atlantic markets. The Asante state either directly or indirectly controlled the areas where gold was produced and transported to the coast. In addition, it exercised a near monopoly on kola nuts. These were a kind of stimulant, which was not considered *haram* among the Islamic states of the savannah. Nonetheless, during the late eighteenth and early nineteenth centuries a series of jihads created a new, strongly Islamist empire which consumed increasing quantities of kola and whose only source for this product was in territories held by the Asante (see Chapter 4). The Bight of Biafra was particularly well endowed with both oil palms and riverine trade systems necessary to transport oil to the coast (Lynn 1997, pp. 61–62). In the Bight of Benin, despite the absence of palm oil exports in the period under study, the region was endowed with an ecology suitable for oil palms (see Chapter 6).

The eastern side of the Bight of Benin, partly controlled by Dahomey, was also suitable for palm oil production (Bold 1822, p. 62). In the second half of the nineteenth century, the focus of Dahomey's trade shifted eastwards towards the towns of Cotonou and Godomey. From this area, palm oil could be transported directly to these towns by rivers from the interior (Law 2004, pp. 228–230). After 1850, the production of palm oil and, from the 1860s, of palm kernels, increased rapidly. Manning (1982, p. 52) estimates that by the 1880s, around 5,000 tons of oil and about 7,600 tons of palm kernels were being produced yearly for ocean-bound exports from Dahomean territories.[24] Thus, this region's lasting focus on the slave trade was not because there were ecological constraints to the production of tropical forest commodities for export markets.

However, some aspects of each region's ecology were important due to their influence over the other factors outlined below. In the case of the Asante state, the presence of gold within its territories was crucial to state and societal development. Within the Bight of Benin two unique geographical features were significant. Firstly, a break in the rainforest belt, which contained more savannah-like conditions, also known as the 'Benin Gap' (Law 1991, p. 19); secondly,

24 To put this into context, according to the British customs' records, exports of palm oil from the Bight of Biafra did not regularly exceed 5,000 tons until the 1820s. In 1855 the port of Calabar was exporting around 4,000 tons of oil, the Cameroons 2,110 tons and Brass 2280 tons. Only the ports of Bonny and Elem Kalabari exported more (Lynn 1997, p. 21).

a system of interconnecting lagoons at the coast. These had important consequences for the regional political situation. In the Bight of Biafra, ecology also played an important role. The poor quality of the soil meant the coastal populations had always been dependent on importing foodstuffs from further inland in exchange for fish and salt (see Chapter 5). This commerce was important as it formed the basis of the trade in slave ship provisions during the eighteenth century and in palm oil during the nineteenth century.

The second factor is the duration and nature of external trade relations. From the sixteenth to the nineteenth centuries, the types of products exported and the nationality of the main trading partner remained fairly consistent in each region. Therefore, earlier developments in trade with the Atlantic strongly influenced the nature of the commercial transition. The presence of gold was of central importance for the Gold Coast region and the Asante. In fact, the first Europeans to go to West Africa in the fifteenth century went in search of gold (Shumway 2014, pp. 25, 51). For the first two centuries of contact with the Atlantic world, this region's trade output was dominated by gold which in turn had a powerful influence on the development of institutions and elite attitudes to external trade.

By contrast, in the Bight of Benin external trade expanded rapidly from the 1660s and, as already established, only slaves were traded to Europeans. Embarkations from the region were usually well under 1,000 a year in the 1640s but over 10,000 people a year were regularly being taken from the region by the beginning of the eighteenth century. The Gold Coast did not begin exporting so many captives until the 1750s.[25] This had a decisive impact on the development of the Dahomean state and, more importantly, on the development of an elite culture based on militarism, which was profoundly suspicious of other types of external trade. In the Bight of Biafra, the export of slaves only became significant from the 1740s onwards, although captives had been embarked there since the sixteenth century. In both the Gold Coast and the Bight of Benin external trade was a crucial factor in the development of centralised states in the late seventeenth-century. The relatively late expansion of external trade in Biafra meant that the region remained characterised by far smaller, decentralised political entities, often no bigger than villages. Trade was coordinated by a trading network under the control of the Aro people that allowed the region to export significant quantities of both captives and commodities. In this environment, power and wealth were entirely dependent on trade, not on military success or the maintenance of states.

---

25 www.slavevoyages.org.

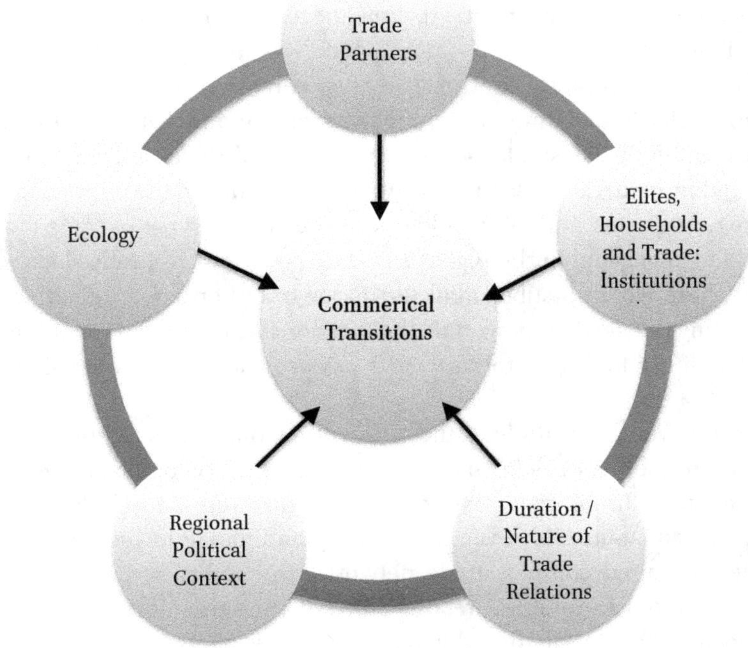

FIGURE 1.3 Explanatory model for region-specific commercial transitions

Related to the previous factor was the nationality of each region's main trade partners. Slave merchants along the Bight of Benin sold far more captives to the Portuguese and French than they did to the British, while slave merchants in the Gold Coast and Biafra did most of their business with ships from Bristol, Liverpool and London. As will be shown in Chapters 2 and 3, the British tended to buy far more commodities and food provisions in West Africa than other European traders. The extent to which national European trade preferences influenced regional trade specialization in Africa in the eighteenth century is unclear and ecology may have been central in determining the former's preferences as well, but the *identity* of the trade partner was important in explaining the nature of local commercial transitions.

Next, there is the regional political context. The Asante and Dahomean states were both militarily powerful, expansive empires under a centralised authority supported by powerful elite families and lineage groups. Furthermore, these states had their origins in the mid- to late seventeenth-century and established military superiority over their neighbours by the adoption and effective use of firearms. By the 1740s, the Asante had defeated all major rivals and achieved political and economic regional hegemony. However, Dahomey was never able to secure such a position, which was mainly due to regional ecological barriers to military control. The dryer conditions of the Benin gap allowed the cavalry-based armies of Oyo to threaten Dahomean territories until the 1800s, while the coastal lagoon system permitted the establishment of rival slave trading centres. These threats, in turn, strengthened the military ideology of the ruling elites, and this ideology also affected the types of trade they were willing to engage in. In the Bight of Biafra, the lack of centralised states meant that there were no substantial territories to either defend or attack, thus eliminating the need for powerful elite individuals or families to maintain permanent military forces, or to base their power or legitimacy on military success.

Finally, there was the attitude of the different regional elites to household participation in trade. As will be argued in the case study chapters, the main unit of production for all major export commodities were households, supported by coerced labour. However, transporting and marketing goods to Atlantic traders required complex trade networks, the ability to provide and guarantee credit and to establish relationships of trust with foreign traders. This was beyond the capacity of individual households and required the support of more powerful individuals or groups who had previously managed the sale and marketing of slaves. In the case of Asante and Dahomey external trade was managed by the state and aristocratic elites, while in the Bight of Biafra it was the Aro network working with coastal trading organisations and influential individuals in the interior. The literature indicates that in Asante territories and the areas around the Bight of Biafra the aforementioned groups were prepared to engage in both the slave and commodity trades (McCaskie 2003, p. 42; Wilks 1993, p. 127; Nwokeji 2010, pp. 183–185). In Dahomey, the monarchy, the elite families and lineage groups were, for the reasons outlined above, profoundly distrustful of all types of trade as a means of securing wealth (Law 1991, p. 344).

The model in Figure I.3 provides the framework for the analysis in Chapters 4, 5 and 6. This model illustrates the main argument, namely that the interrelated factors determining the initial patterns of trade with the Atlantic world that evolved over the eighteenth century, and sometimes even earlier, continued to influence the nineteenth-century commercial transitions, and that the exogenous shock of abolition in 1807 accelerated this transition, but did not put it in motion.

4 Organisation

As stated above this book is divided into two parts; the first (Chapters 1–3) sets out the patterns of trade between West Africa and the Atlantic world, the second (Chapters 4–6) examines these patterns in the context of the case studies.

Chapter 1 introduces the first part with a broad overview of regional patterns of trade. This chapter, looks at evidence from three different trading organisations working from around 1700 to the 1760s. This chapter argues that recognised regional patterns of commodity trading were already established in the eighteenth century and that these continued into the era of abolition. In particular, that the area of the Bight of Benin controlled by Dahomey never exported significant quantities of commodities in contrast to the Bight of Biafra and the Gold Coast.

Chapter 2 quantitatively examines regional patterns and European demand for slave ship provisioning in the long eighteenth-century, calls for a major downward adjustment of available estimates of the slave trade induced demand. However, there was also considerable variation in provisioning strategies among slave trading nations and, more importantly, across main regions of slave embarkation. Traders in the Bight of Biafra, and to a lesser extent the Gold Coast, provided considerable quantities of commercially produced foodstuffs, and in these areas the expansion of the slave trade did provide a boost to commercial agriculture. By contrast, in the Bight of Benin ships tended to bring the greater bulk of their food with them from Europe and/or stocked up with provisions from other areas along the coast.

Having examined exports of foodstuffs, Chapter 3 looks at West African exports of commodities such as gold, palm oil, dyewoods and ivory from the 1730s to 1807. It examines whether or not the trade in captives crowded out the exchange of other products and finds that while the volume of commodities from the West African coast grew there were considerable regional differences. In the Gold Coast exports of non-slave goods, most importantly gold, fell over the eighteenth century. In the Bight of Benin commodities do not seem to ever have been export in significant quantities. However, in the Bight of Biafra commodity exports rose in tandem with the expansion of slave exports.

Chapter 4 begins Part 2 with a study of the Gold Coast region and more specifically the Asante empire. This shows that the export of people was a relatively short interruption to a pattern of trade dominated by the application of coerced labour to the production of commodities and, more specifically, gold. Institutional developments made gold the most important marker of status and wealth within the region and more specifically Asante. This in turn meant that there was always a strong internal market for slaves as factors of production. A near monopoly of regional output through control of goldfields and lack of external threats meant the Asante state was far less dependent on slave exports to acquire crucial European imports. It also led to the Asante state, and economic actors within its territories, developing strong links to northern savannah markets, affording them the opportunity to rapidly develop an alternative export commodity, kola, to service the new Islamic states of the interior at the beginning of the nineteenth century. Crucially, both elites and households stood to gain from the end of transatlantic slavery, which explains why the withdrawal of the region's biggest buyer of slaves in 1807 was sufficient to effectively end the export of slaves.

In Chapter 5 it is argued that in the Bight of Biafra, the wealth and power of elite institutions, both in the interior and at the coast, was always dependent on trade, and not on the maintenance of more centralised states or the broadcast of military power. This was probably in large part due to the relatively late expansion of export slavery in the region, which meant that networks developed that did not require centralised states or large scale raiding to handle large numbers of captives. These networks always handled both slaves and commodities and, as with Asante elites, were not materially disadvantaged by the commercial transition. Households could harness the coerced labour that would otherwise have been exported to gain access to goods that enhanced their living standards. Consequently, when British abolition efforts finally became effective in the late 1830s, it was in the context of an already highly developed and expanded commodity export economy and was therefore sufficient to end the export of slaves.

By contrast in Chapter 6 the book shows that in Dahomey there were strong, path dependent reasons why a commodity export sector did not develop until transatlantic slavery was effectively over. Firstly, its institutional development was heavily influenced by a late seventeenth-century regional political context, in which slave exports formed the basis of wealth and power. This encouraged the development of a highly-militarised state, which enhanced the wealth and power of elites. It was also a necessary development, given the inability of any one polity to gain any kind of regional hegemony, meaning the state was always threatened, either militarily or economically, by other regional powers. The high labour demands of both the military and a more powerful elite meant that labour was always directed towards the goals of elites and not households. In that event, the development of a significant export commodity sector was only possible in the 1840s in the context of more effective British abolition efforts and domestic military setbacks.

PART 1

Trends in the (Non-Slave) Trade With West Africa Over the Eighteenth Century

CHAPTER 1

Regional Patterns of (Non-Slave) Trade in the First Half of the Eighteenth Century

> …the bowels and surface of Africa, abound in valuable and useful returns …
>
> OLAUDAH EQUIANO (1794 p. 357)

∵

Part 1 of the book will quantitatively examine the patterns of the commodity trade in the three case study regions and to reveal how they interacted with transatlantic slavery in the century before abolition. The current literature on West African trade in the century before abolition has focused almost entirely on the commerce in captives. There has been very little quantitative analysis of the development of the trade in commodities and commercial agriculture and how this interacted with transatlantic slavery. This contrasts with studies of earlier periods, when commodities played a far bigger role in the trade between Africa and the Atlantic. Non-slave products, especially gold and ivory, initially attracted Spanish and Portuguese traders to the region (Lovejoy 2011, p. 36, Thornton 1998, p. 26). The initial rise in demand for coerced labour for the Iberian empires of the Americas from the 15th to early seventeenth Centuries was largely met by the West Central African region (Lovejoy 2011, p. 47). Until North European nations began to acquire sugar producing Caribbean Islands in the 1630s, they generally focused their trading efforts on the acquisition of commodities.

Even after by states such as England and the Dutch Republic began to expand their plantation economies, commodities were still an important part of their overall trade with Africa. Supporting earlier work by Van den Boogaart (1992), Den Heijer's (1997) research into Dutch West India Company (WIC) accounts shows that between 1674 and 1740, 64% of the goods dispatched to Africa for trade were intended for non-slave commodities. Of these, ivory and gold made up by far the largest percentage (around eighty seven percent gold, ten percent ivory) in terms of value, but other products were still bought in

 | DOI:10.1163/9789004417120_003

large quantities.[1] Even though the British were buying ever more slaves from the 1650s, it wasn't until the last decades of the seventeenth century that their value passed that of commodities (Eltis 1994). However, after the 1680s there was a huge expansion in the transatlantic slave trade and by the beginning of the eighteenth century captive labour had become West Africa's most important export. This has led many scholars to devote insufficient attention to the growth and development of other African exports (Eltis 2013, pp. 31–32). This neglect has meant that important long-term patterns have been ignored, and these patterns are crucial for understanding the nature of the commercial transition in the nineteenth century. Some have argued that the export of captives undermined and crowded out other forms of commercial exchange (Inikori 2007, 2011, Rodney 1972). By contrast, the following chapters will show that export slavery, in some areas, greatly stimulated trade in other products.

During the period under study, the different regions of West Africa generally exported the same kinds of commodities, even if the relative quantities changed over time. Along all parts of the coast, slave ships could buy food to feed themselves and their cargoes of captives in advance of the middle passage. Eltis (2013) suggests the scale of this trade in provisions was not exceeded by 'legitimate commerce' until the 1850s. The extent and regional variations of this trade will be examined in Chapter 2. In addition, some agricultural products were bought with the intention of selling back in Europe. Pepper had been purchased since the sixteenth century but from the 1770s palm oil, which had previously only been bought to provision slave ships, became increasingly sought after for its industrial applications in Europe. Many regions also exported sylvan products from the tropical rainforests (the most important being dyewoods,[2] hardwoods and beeswax) and ivory. Most of the region's gold came from the Gold Coast but some was also available along the windward coast in modern day Cote d'Ivoire. Finally, gum Senegal was purchased in large quantities from the Senegambian region in the east.

This chapter will provide a broad overview of West African patterns of trade to the mid-eighteenth century. The growth and development in the trade in these products from 1750, will be the subject of Chapter 3.

1 For example, while only consisting of 0.54% of the value of goods the WIC still imported 1,323,548 pounds of Pepper against 2,955,533 pounds of Ivory (Den Heijer 1997)

2 In particular, camwood from around Sierra Leone and the Windward Coast and redwood from the Bights of Benin and Biafra. See Chapter 4 for more details.

1 The Commodity Trade in the Early Eighteenth Century

This section will examine quantitative data on the commodity trade in the case study regions, for the period from around 1700 to the 1760s. The data comes from three sources. Firstly, the records of the British Royal Africa Company, which had been granted a royal monopoly over the trade with Africa in the 1670s. In the first three decades of the eighteenth century it gradually lost out to privately backed enterprises but was still an important carrier of both slaves and commodities (Hair & Law 1998, p. 259, 260). Secondly, data from private traders, operating out of Bristol, which was the largest slave trading port in England at the time (Richardson 1987, Vol II, p vii). Finally, the archives of the Dutch Middelburgsche Commercie Compagnie (MCC), which became the Republic's largest carrier of slaves after the Netherlands West India Company lost its monopoly in the 1720s (Postma 1990, p. 133), provide valuable and detailed information.

The Royal Africa Company sent out two types of ship to Africa; one for slaves and the other for commodities (Tables 1.1 & 1.2). What is striking is that while the Bight of Benin took in thirty percent of their slaving ships, only seven percent of commodity vessels sailed there. By far the most important regions for non-slave items were Senegambia and the Gold Coast, where the British also kept the majority of the trading forts.

In terms of exactly what was bought we can turn to the invoice books of the Royal Africa Company.[3] These are a series of accounts of all the goods that

TABLE 1.1 Royal Africa Company commodity ships by destination 1679–1752

	1679–1689	1690–1699	1700–1709	1710–1719	1720–1731	1732–1752	Total	% Total
Senegambia	8	9	4	3	12	25	61	40
Sierra Leone	8	0	2	7	12	1	30	20
Gold Coast	0	0	3	5	26	11	45	30
Bight of Benin	0	0	0	0	9	1	10	7
Bight of Biafra	0	0	0	0	0	0	0	0
West Central Africa	0	0	0	0	5	0	5	3

Source: Database of commodity vessels to Africa: Eltis (2013)

3 It should be noted that the RAC's patterns of trade were probably exceptional during this period. The directors of the RAC were actively following a policy of increasing their investment

TABLE 1.2 Royal Africa Company slave ships by destination 1679–1752

	1679–1689	1690–1699	1700–1709	1710–1719	1720–1731	1732–1752	Total	% Total
Senegambia	40	12	13	1	14	0	80	15
Sierra Leone	9	7	4	0	3	0	23	4
Gold Coast	22	11	49	21	18	0	121	23
Bight of Benin	90	22	29	7	11	0	159	30
Bight of Biafra	66	7	2	0	0	0	75	14
West Central Africa	42	11	6	0	6	0	65	12

Source: slavevoyages.org

were returned for sale in their vessels from 1721 to 1741 (see Table 1.3). By value, gold and ivory from the Gold Coast were by far the most significant items of trade.[4] The Bight of Benin also exported ivory, which almost certainly came from the Volta regions around the western Slave Coast or from the Kingdom of Benin, and not from the area around Whydah (Strickrodt 2015, p. 115, Den Heijer 1997, p. 134, Johnson & Feinberg 1982, p. 437). Gold was a significant item of trade along the Bight of Benin, and especially at Whydah, until around the 1760s although it was brought from Brazil by Portuguese vessels to be either re-exported to other European nations or exchanged for slaves (Law 1990b, pp. 107–12, Den Heijer 1997, p. 134).

We now turn to the records of private traders. The data in Table 1.4 is taken from Richardson (1986, 1987) and shows 63 slave ships from the port of Bristol 1720 to 1734. The figures in brackets in the second column indicate the total number of ships sent from Bristol during the period. This sample shows ships which recorded bringing back African commodities, although none mentioned gold. The sample does not indicate exactly where the commodities were bought, only where the majority of slaves were purchased. This means that it is very possible that ships bringing back wood from the Gold Coast had first purchased it in Sierra Leone or the Windward coast (where dyewoods were more common).

in 'articles of home return' (i.e. commodities) to compensate for their inability to actively compete with independent traders after they lost their legal monopoly on slaves in 1698 (Law 2013, p. 129).

4 Over the period the total value of commodities per region was: Gold Coast £84,030, Senegambia £28,588, Bight of Benin £17,529, Sierra Leone £10,169

TABLE 1.3 Value of commodities (£) bought by RAC ships by region of trade 1721–1741 and number of observations (Obs) in the sources

	Beeswax	Gold	Gum	Hides	Ivory	Mallaguetta	Palm Oil	Wood
Region	Value (Obs)	Value (Obs)	Value (Obs)	Value (Obs)	Value (Obs)	Value (Obs)	Value (Obs)	Value (Obs)
Bight of Benin		15,372 (7)			2.146 (12)			11 (1)
Gold Coast	1.271 (9)	61,696 (16)	23 (4)		17,336 (47)	1.379 (5)	354 (9)	1.97 (10)
Senegambia	17,051 (17)	433 (3)	1.882 (9)	15 (5)	9.168 (34)	1 (1)	23 (1)	15 (3)
Sierra Leone	2.58 (3)	2 (1)			2.827 (8)		11 (1)	4.75 (5)
Total Value	20.902	77.503	1.905	15	31.477	1.38	388	6.746

Source: TNA T70/957, T70/958, T70/959, T70/960

Whilst limited, the sample does at least indicate that voyages to most regions bought a range of commodities in addition to slaves. The single ship shown going to the Bight of Benin followed the same strategy as RAC vessels in only purchasing ivory. By contrast, traders were picking up a far greater range of products in the Bight of Biafra and the Gold Coast. Richardson (1986 Vol 1, p xvi) has noted that of the 594 vessels which left Bristol for Africa from 1698 to 1729 only 20 were specialist commodity ships but "*....most Bristol slave ships returned home from the New World with some African products, and the quantities involved were sometime large.*" Dyewoods, bought from the Cross River region around Calabar, the Loango coast and Sierra Leone, were particularly important for the textile industry in South West England (Behrendt et al. 2010 pp. 84–85). While Bristol merchants bought less ivory than the RAC, it was still an important product and most was traded through the ports of Bonny and Calabar (Behrendt et al. 2010, p. 83).

Next, we address the records of the *Middelburgsche Commercie Compagnie* (MCC). These have some weaknesses for the purposes of this study, as the company's main regions of slave trading were the Windward Coast and the Loango coast of West Central Africa (Vos 2009, Sommerdyk 2015). However, their ships did trade in all the areas relevant to this study and most importantly their records detail exactly where they traded. Up until the 1750s the MCC was still

TABLE 1.4 Average quantities of commodities purchased / Bristol ship by region 1720–1734

Region	No. of voyages: sample (total)	Dyewood (lbs)	Guinea grains (lbs)	Ivory (lbs)	Gum Seneca (lbs)	Bees wax (lbs)
Bight of Benin	1 (3)			3.528		
Bight of Biafra	33 (89)	5.741	5.683	3.177		672
Gold Coast	9 (48)	6.669	1.661	4.629	1.512	
Senegambia	9 (10)	2.242	364			1.004
West Central	12 (24)	23.494	10	3.024		2.129

Source: Richardson (1986, 1987)

sending specialist commodity ships to Africa, called 'Retour schepen'. A sample of 7 of these ships from the 1730s to the 1750s, includes details of exactly which products were bought in different parts of Africa.[5] The ships began trading around the Windward coast, in particular Cape Lahou, and then moved down to the Gold Coast and onto Popo on the Bight of Benin. In these areas they bought gold and ivory, before proceeding to the area around modern day Gabon / Cameroon to buy beeswax, redwood and more ivory. There are no records of any 'retour schepen' stopping at Whydah.

Qualitative and secondary sources together with quantitative data all reliably suggest that there were well established regional patterns of trade by the mid-eighteenth century. African merchants in the Bight of Biafra and the along the Gold Coast were exporting both captives and commodities. However, there is no evidence that the area of the Bight of Benin controlled by Dahomey was engaged in the production of any substantial quantity of export commodities for the Atlantic market.

2 Trade in Africa in the Eighteenth Century

Both internal and regional trade will be discussed in greater detail in the case study chapters, but it is worth noting here that there were both similarities and significant differences between the three regions with regard to their involvement in trade within West Africa. In all three areas, there was always a trade

5 Africaanse Galey MCC 173, Guinese Galey MCC 500, Groot Prooijen MCC 483, Prins Willem de Vijfde MCC 964, Philadelphia MCC 893, Vrouw Johanne Cores MCC 1204, Mercurius MCC 754

between the coast and the interior in salt and fish due to the relative paucity of natural sources of protein and salt in the forest regions.[6] Likewise salt, mined or extracted from brine lakes, and cattle/meat were traded south from the savannah. Within the region around the Bight of Biafra, fish and salt from the coast and salt from Urburu Lake on the savannah were traded for yams, iron and brass in the forest zone, as well as slaves (Northrup 1978, p. 73, Lovejoy 1985, p. 686). Along the Bight of Benin, a trade in fish and salt from the coast to the interior was noted from the seventeenth century and likely increased in tandem with the expansion of the slave trade which had a "*multiplier effect upon trade even in purely indigenous commodities*…" Law (1989a, pp. 220–221). There was also a thriving trade along the coastal lagoons and rivers between the slave and gold coasts and which eventually allowed goods to be traded with the Oyo empire in what is today south west Nigeria. Trade goods from the Gold Coast could be exchanged for high quality Yoruba cloth or jewellery and again it is likely that European trade did stimulate this commerce (Law 1989a, pp. 213, 214, Law 2004, p. 28). Along the Gold Coast fishing and salt production were one of the key (non-agricultural) industries (Shumway 2014, p. 27) and was noted as an important item of trade with their northern neighbours (Bowdich 1819, p. 334).[7]

However, long-distance trade was very different. The Akan region in what is today southern Ghana, had a long history of commercial exchange with the interior savannah markets in Hausaland and Borno. Gold, salt and kola nuts were exchanged for manufactured goods such as textiles, leather, ironware (Lovejoy 1985, p. 683). The Dahomeans seem to have developed regular trade links with other African polities, at least by the nineteenth century. The explorer Clapperton reported meeting traders working for the Dahomean king at the town of Kiama in Borgu, which sat on the trade routes between both Dahomey and Asante to Hausaland. They reportedly exchanged European trade goods for around 200 slaves in the area and boasted that the "*….it is from Dahomey that the people of these countries receive all their rum and European articles.*" (Clapperton 1829, pp. 83, 84, 123, Law 1989b, p. 58).[8] However, all of this trade was dependent on transatlantic commerce, and there is no evidence

6 Protein sources were few due to the presence of the tse-tse fly which limited the number of animals that could survive (Alsan 2015) and salt could only be obtained through pot-ash which was a far inferior product to imports from the coast or the savannah (Lovejoy 1986, p. 1)

7 In the nineteenth-century Wilks (1975, p. 68) notes that the Asante state allowed its coastal vassals to pay their tribute in salt.

8 While Clapperton was prepared to accept this statement, it cannot have been true given the rising importance of the port of Lagos at the time (Mann 2007, p. 40) and the fact that slaves from Yorubaland had been traded for European goods via such ports as Porto Novo throughout the eighteenth century (Law 1989b, pp. 55–56).

that the Dahomeans, unlike the Asante, were engaging in the exchange of commodities / products which they had themselves produced. Long-distance trade between the regions around the Bight of Biafra and Hausaland never seemed to have developed, perhaps as suggested by Nwokeji (2010, pp. 167–168) due to political instability in the areas separating the forest regions from the north. This instability may have discouraged Hausa merchants from investing in the trade for products such as kola, especially when they were available via the Asante (see Chapter 4).

CHAPTER 2

Commercial Agriculture and Slave Ship Provisioning 1680–1800

> The most common cheapest, and most commodious diet is with vegetables, horse beans, rice and indian corn.... One or other is boiled on board at constant times, twice a day into a Dab-a-Dab (sometimes with meat in it) and have an overseer with a cat-o-nine tails to force it upon those that are sullen and refuse.
>
> JOHN ATKINS 'A Voyage to Guinea, Brazil and the West Indies' (1737), p. 171

This chapter considers the provisioning strategies followed by the slaving ships of different European nations and the varying responses from West African regions.[1] Historians have recently begun to explore the potential effects of the slave trade on the development of commercial agriculture in Atlantic Africa (Law et al. 2013). The introduction of New World crops, such as maize and manioc, enlarged the cultivation choice-set of African farmers and became important to the organisation of the slave trade, in similar ways as African food crops (e.g. black rice) may have underpinned the organisation and expansion of New World plantation economies (Carney 2001, 2009, Carney and Rosomoff 2011, see Eltis et al. 2007 for a critical review). Large numbers of captives needed to be fed during their journey to the coast, their stay at the coast before embarkation, their time on board before departure and during the ocean crossing. Captains taking in insufficient stocks put their cargo at higher risks of starvation and disease.[2]

The provisioning strategies of slave traders have remained understudied though. The literature generally assumes that the lion's share of food provisions required for slave voyages was produced in West Africa and sold by local

1 This chapter is based on an article co-written with Ewout Frankema (Dalrymple-Smith, A., & Frankema, E. (2017). Slave ship provisioning in the long 18th century. A boost to West African commercial agriculture?. *European Review of Economic History*, *21*(2), 185–235).

2 Miller (1979, pp. 95–102) and Newson (2007, pp. 72,85) argue that the poor diets of slaves from the Angolan port of Luanda, both during their stay at the coast as well as during the ocean crossing, raised mortality rates in comparison with other regions of embarkation.

 | DOI:10.1163/9789004417120_004

farmers or middlemen to the slave ships. Based on this assumption, David Eltis has argued that the increasing intensity of the eighteenth-century slave trade must have boosted West African food exports. In a first attempt to estimate the magnitude of the slave trade induced demand impulse, he reached the provisional conclusion that food exports approached a total annual value of one million British pounds (current prices) during the late eighteenth-century, which exceeded the total value of West Africa's commodity exports to Britain up to the mid-nineteenth-century (Eltis 2013).

Studying the Gold Coast, Klas Rönnbäck has argued that the demand for provisions by slave ships was too insignificant to generate any direct positive linkages for commercial agricultural development. Reasoning from a set of baseline assumptions regarding the size of the urban population in the seventeenth and eighteenth centuries, and the derived demand for marketable foodstuffs from the non-farming population, he estimated that slave ships and slave forts may have added ca. twenty seven percent to urban demand at the peak of the trade, and contributed ca. three to four percent to total agricultural production in the coastal regions (Rönnbäck 2015, p. 166). Rönnbäck, somewhat surprisingly, qualifies this contribution as 'rather marginal' (2015, p. 172). More importantly, however, Rönnbäck, like Eltis, fails to bring any new data to the table which might scrutinize his main assumptions, including the idea that slave traders bought their provisions exclusively at the Gold Coast.

This chapter has two aims. First, to estimate the comparative magnitude of the demand impulse to West African commercial agriculture, using primary sources on food sales from company account books, retrieved from a much larger and more diverse sample of slave voyages than hitherto has been compiled. This new dataset allows for deeper insights into the eighteenth-century development of provisioning strategies, which appear not as straightforward as many scholars have hitherto assumed. Second, to gain a deeper understanding of the commercialisation of agriculture in different parts of West Africa, by exploiting the temporal and spatial variation in slave ship provisioning.

This chapter uses primary sources on *actual provisions* taken on board in European ports of departure and along the West African coast from 187 British, Dutch, French and Danish slave journeys conducted between 1681 and 1807. The dataset includes voyages by private merchants and chartered companies, such as the British *Royal African Company* (RAC) and the Dutch *West-Indische Compagnie* (WIC). In addition, I analyse the instructions captains received for the provisioning of crews and slaves, as well as ships' logs and chartered company correspondence shedding light on the provisioning logistics. Journeys undertaken from the New World are excluded (e.g. Brazil, Cuba, US), as the current dearth of primary sources on this area of the trade warrants a separate study.

This study yields two major conclusions. First, there were substantial differences in the provisioning strategies of British, as compared to continental slavers and, more significantly, clear regional differences. British traders relied extensively on African provisions, although they began to stock up on food in increasing quantities in Liverpool and Bristol during the eighteenth century for reasons discussed below. These different provisioning strategies, of British versus continental traders, are due to the different positions the British held at the West African coast – especially the large range of fortified trading stations – as well as the more developed food markets in regions where British slavers conducted most of their trade; the Bight of Biafra and to a lesser extent the Gold Coast. In the Bight of Biafra, the provisioning trade was substantial enough to stimulate commercial agriculture. The data indicates that the Bight of Benin at no time engaged in a substantial provisioning trade. Agricultural commercialisation was thus a localized response to increasing slave trade induced demand for foodstuffs. However, on a broader plain, the eighteenth-century expansion of the slave trade had just a modest impact on commercial agricultural development along the Atlantic African coast.

Second, the data indicates that a growing proportion of the required calories and proteins for slaves were taken on board in European port cities over the course of the eighteenth century. This change in provisioning strategies was driven by declining relative prices of European provisions to slave purchasing prices, in combination with the increasing business risks faced by slave traders. Both the falling relative provisioning prices, and the rising share of European provisions, generate revised estimates of the slave-trade induced demand-impulse which are about seventy to eighty percent lower than those of Eltis. Since the economic weight of late eighteenth-century food exports was *considerably smaller* than previously assumed, the commercial transition from slave to commodity exports in the first half of the nineteenth century must have involved rather *modest losses* of food exports for most regions, and cannot have deepened the rupture of Atlantic Africa's international trade to any great degree. For the Gold Coast and the Bight of Biafra any loses in revenue from the provisioning of slave ships was compensated by the growth of other exports (see Chapters 4 and 5).

1 Did the Transatlantic Slave Trade Boost West African Commercial Agriculture?

The provisions slave ships took in from European ports typically included a few staples, principally wheat (often in the form of biscuits), beans, peas, rice and barley. For crew members, luxury items were added such as salted meat, stock-fish, butter, bread, cheese, suet, sweet oil, beer, wine and spirits. Provisioning of slaves and sailors on the slave ships was usually strictly segregated.[3] Moreover, throughout the eighteenth century special supply ships brought fairly large quantities of European provisions to the forts at the African coast, either to complement or replace consumption of local foodstuffs by European staff. In Africa, captains picked up foodstuffs common to the regions where they traded; rice from the Upper Guinea and Windward coasts, maize, millet or sorghum from the Gold Coast, yams from Biafra and Gabon and manioc from the Congo and Angola. Plantains, coconuts, limes, oranges and other fresh provisions supplemented these staple foods. West African palm oil served as an important source of unsaturated fat in slave diets (Harms 2008, pp. 112–119, Mandelblatt 2009, pp. 411–112, Klein 2010, pp. 94–96). Fresh water and firewood was also sourced from Africa in great quantities. As a rule, slaves were fed a kind of gruel comprised of whatever combination of the above had been bought, sometimes seasoned with salt and mallagueta pepper. Small portions of salted meat, stock-fish and tobacco were occasionally handed out to slaves, but most of this was reserved for crew members.

According to David Eltis, slave provisions constituted by far the biggest export market for commodities in the coastal areas of West Africa during the long eighteenth-century. Before 1650, sugar exports from São Tomé accounted for almost all of the cultivated crops exported, but the volumes of cash-crops traded in the eighteenth century paled in comparison to West Africa's nineteenth-century export boom (Eltis 2013, pp. 35–36, Frankema et al. 2015). Eltis made a first attempt to estimate the total value of West African food exports. Even though he acknowledges that his estimates are crude, and invites colleagues to improve upon them (2013, p. 45), his prime conclusion is nonetheless important: if annual food exports did indeed rise up to one million British Pounds in the late eighteenth-century, and exceeded the average annual value of West African commodity exports to Britain during the first half of the

3 For four MCC ships, surviving accounts of the daily quantities of food used show separate diets for sailors and captives, presumably also to emphasize social or racial hierarchy. These accounts were retrieved from the 'Consumptieboeken', which were separate to the 'Negotieboeken' which detailed purchases of food at the coast, from: Brandenburg 4e reis ZA: MCC290, Geertuda en Christina 4e reis ZA: MCC 420, Nieuwe Hoop 3e reis ZA: MCC 835, Zeemercure 1e reis ZA: MCC 835. For example, the consumption accounts of the *Nieuwe Hoop* from 1766 – 1768 report that the crew consumed bread, meat, bacon, blue & grey peas, salt fish, rice, sweet and rape oil, while slaves were given horse beans, barley, yams and African beans called *gobbegobsen*. French and Danish ships are also recorded as stocking separate food supplies for their personnel, who also ate at different times than slaves. Interestingly, the British sources do not speak to such a strict separation of slave and crew provisions, in particular regarding the consumption of staple foods.

nineteenth century, the abolition of the slave trade must have prompted a significant loss of non-slave export revenue and may have seriously distorted food markets, following an era of rapid growth up to 1807.

Eltis' estimates are based on two core assumptions. First, that most of the required provisions were sourced from Africa, and that European provisions constituted a negligible share, somewhere in the order of one to two percent, of the purchasing price of slaves (2013, p. 38). Second, following Curtin's (1973, pp. 168–169) classic study on the Senegambian slave trade, that slave maintenance costs constituted a fixed twenty five percent of their exchange value throughout the eighteenth century. Both assumptions, combined with an annual time-series of slave purchasing prices, thus allowed Eltis to estimate the average annual value of African-sourced provisions in the Atlantic slave trade during 1681–1807. Appendix 2.1 shows his estimates and explains his calculation procedure in greater detail.

The assumption that the lion's share of food provisions for the middle passage was produced by African farmers is repeated over and over again in the slave trade literature, but this has never been subjected to empirical verification.[4] The analysis of surviving account books of slave trade merchants indicates that, in the course of the eighteenth century, nearly half of all calories and proteins required to keep slaves alive on board European slave vessels – note that voyages from the New World are excluded – were sourced from European ports of departure. The slave trade may thus have stimulated commercial agriculture in the hinterland of some European port cities (e.g. Bristol, Liverpool, Nantes, Middelburg), as much as it stimulated commercial agriculture in West African regions of slave embarkation. This implication casts a different light on the relative magnitude of the slave trade induced demand for West African food exports, and raises new questions concerning the provisioning strategies of slave traders.

Furthermore, it is worth noting that the twenty five percent food share of slave purchasing prices is not the only figure one can select for this exercise. Curtin argued that the total costs of maintaining a slave was about half its market value per year. Obviously, food was a key component of those costs, but also a highly variable one depending on local harvest conditions, food prices and

4 This assumption informed the estimates of Eltis (2013), Klein and Engerman (1979) and Rönnbäck (2015) and is also put forth in other key studies such as Carney and Rosomoff (2011, p. 47) and Mandelblatt (2008, pp. 411, 421). In his study of the Danish slave trade on the Gold Coast Hernaes (1998, p. 337) even claimed that it was impossible to bring sufficient food supplies from Europe and that the 'millie trade' (maize) must therefore have given a major impulse to the local Gold Coast economy.

the time spent in captivity before embarkation.[5] Curtin stressed that during extensive waiting periods slaves were often put to work to contribute to their own maintenance (1973, p. 170). The insecurity about average time spent 'in store', the added value of slave labour and the market prices of slave food, all turn the twenty five percent estimate into a somewhat arbitrary choice. In an essay on the French slave trade Klein and Engerman (1979) state that "*the bulk of foodstuffs consumed by Africans in the crossing were purchased on the African coast, with rice and yams serving as the staples of the diet. The costs for these foods and for the water represented less than 5% of the total costs of outfitting the vessels and therefore offered little financial restrain on adding extra food.*" (p. 270). Although Klein and Engerman focus on the maintenance costs during a slave's time on board the ship, they do not attach much weight to food provisions within total outfitting costs.[6] It should be noted though that Klein and Engerman's estimate is based on just a single observation, a voyage of a French slaving vessel, *La Reine de France*, which appears in the dataset along with 27 other French slave voyages. The resultant analysis suggests that, although the twenty five percent estimate appears valid for the period up to the 1740s, this is far too high for the period 1750–1808, when the trade grew to its peak.

Rönnbäck (2015) has made the valid point that any measurement of effective slave trade related demand should be assessed against the *existing size* of domestic African food markets. Without bringing in any new data, but by adopting some baseline assumptions, he estimated the demand effect at the Gold Coast may have ranged between three to four percent of total agricultural production and twenty seven percent of total urban demand (2015, p. 166). However, in a sensitivity analysis of the main parameters, he reaches intervals

5 Curtin (1973) estimated the costs of feeding slaves around Saint Louis in Senegambia. He showed that prices of millet (the main staple) in the 1750s varied depending on rains and other harvest circumstances, from £2.60/ton in a good year to £19.50/ton in a very severe year. Curtin settled on an average of £6.80/ton. By asking how much millet a slave might need to live, he suggested a figure of £2.74 per year of millet, excluding costs for housing, clothing, guards and additional foodstuffs. As an average slave would sell for between £10 to £12, this implied that slave-owners had to pay maintenance costs between a quarter (in a very good year) to a half (in an average year) to four fifths (in a very bad year) of the eventual selling price. In Gajaaga, a kingdom on the upper Senegal, slaves could only be delivered once a year in the annual high season. This meant that slaves brought to this market had a price "*on a sliding scale, rising by 80% from a low point after the departure of the annual fleet to the high point just as the last boats prepared to sail at the end of the next high season.*" (1973, pp. 169–170).

6 The term 'outfitting costs' refers to the total expenses incurred to prepare a slave ship for the journey, including the exchange commodities required to purchase slaves, the provisions of crew members, ship maintenance costs and also the food rations reserved for slaves during their time on board the vessel.

from a nine to eighty percent contribution to urban demand in the final quarter of the eighteenth century (2015, p. 178). This indicates the pressing need for more precise estimates based on *new empirical evidence*. Before proceeding to offer such evidence, it should be added that whatever demand impulse the slave trade may have given to *commercial* agriculture in the coastal areas of West Africa, must have come at the expense of production in the raided areas. As most of the captives had been engaged in agriculture prior to capture, the Atlantic slave trade caused a relocation of food production, promoting the development of food markets in the areas of embarkation, but curbing both production and consumer demand in raided coastal or inland areas.

The conclusions in this chapter are based on a sample of 187 merchant accounts of slave voyages conducted by trade companies from four European nations between 1681 and 1807. Data on British slave voyages came from the account books of the RAC, which detail the cargoes bought in England and, in the 1720s, the provisions bought in Africa.[7] For the earlier period, (1680 to 1699) there is correspondence from the British forts on the West Coast of Africa, compiled by Robin Law (1997). Additionally, there are the records of five ships owned by a private trader, Humphrey Morice, who was involved in the trade in the 1720s.[8] These ships bought most of their slaves along the Gold Coast and in the Bight of Benin. For the post-1740 period there are two main sources: the papers of the Liverpool merchant, William Davenport, who sent around 20 vessels to Africa from the 1760s to the 1780s and specialised his commercial operations in the Biafra region;[9] and the Bristol Presentments, a weekly register of shipping from the port of Bristol which began in 1789 recording the cargoes and arrival and departure dates of 40 slaving vessels.[10] The latter concentrates on ships going to Biafra and the Cameroons, but like the Davenport papers also includes ships trading in other regions. The downside to these records is that they do not detail what provisions were bought in Africa, and this will be taken up this issue further later in this chapter.

The data on French voyages is from the private trading accounts of French slave merchants based in Nantes.[11] These sources offer quantities and values of food provisions taken on board at the start of the slave journey, but do not provide information on the provisions bought elsewhere in Europe or Africa. There is also Rinchon (1964)'s study of the voyages of one particular slaving

7 The principal source is the T70 series at The National Archives, London.
8 From the M7 series at the Bank of England, London.
9 The records are held at the Liverpool Record Office and Keele University and were accessed through www.britishonlinearchives.co.uk.
10 From the archives of Bristol Central Library.
11 From the Archives Départementales de Loire Atlantique.

captain, Van Alstein, who sailed on the Bight of Benin and the West-Central African coast (Congo and Angola). This source provides full details of both food purchases in Europe and Africa and also gives some African food prices. For the Danish trade there is the work by Svalesen (2000). It provides detailed information of only two voyages conducted by one ship, but does contain detailed instructions from the Royal Chartered Danish Guinea Company on provisioning logistics, and their orders on daily slave rations (2000, p. 112), which applied to all the ships the company sent out.

For the Dutch trade the archives of the Middelburgsche Commercie Compagnie (MCC) are the most important sources.[12] These records detail exactly what provisions were bought in Europe, what was bought in Africa, and in many cases exactly where. In addition, they provide prices of Dutch (Province of Zeeland) provisions and some scattered food price observations at the African coast. Most of the trade along the coast was conducted by barter, but the MCC converted all of the trade goods into either guilders or Flemish pounds, allowing for comparison of prices of individual items, which can be used for wider estimations of spending by other slave ships. Another advantage of this source is that the MCC traded regularly in all areas of Africa, with the exception of the Bight of Biafra.[13] The Appendix of Leo Balai's (2011) *Het Slavenschip Leusden* for the provisioning of three WIC ships in the 1720s, includes detailed information on the instructions for ships' captains from the company.

Table 2.1 summarizes the 'national' coverage of the sample. A distinction is made between the era when chartered companies and private traders were both active (1681–1740), and the later era of private trade (1741–1807).[14] The sample covers over one percent of all British, French and Dutch voyages and about zero point seven percent of Danish voyages in the private trade era. For 36 of the 187 voyages there is information on the total intake of foodstuffs in

12 From the Zeeuws Archief Middelburg.

13 When trade in the Biafra region reached its apogee the MCC was entering a period of crisis, suffering from rising insecurity in the Atlantic world and especially the 4th Anglo-Dutch war.

14 Until the early eighteenth century, most of the slave trade was a jealously guarded government monopoly. In Great Britain, the Royal Africa Company (RAC) and in the Netherlands the West-Indische Compagnie (WIC) were the sole permitted traders. The French government experimented with a series of chartered companies. Slaves to the Spanish empire could only be handled through the *asiento* contract. These companies were unable to prevent interlopers and smugglers from carrying slaves, partly due to fact that they couldn't meet the demand of their markets, but also because they operated notoriously inefficient business models (Thomas 1999, Klein 2010, Den Heijer 1997). By the 1730s most nations, with the exception of Spain, had abandoned the concept of chartered companies and left the trade to the private sector.

TABLE 2.1 Sample of slave ship voyages by nationality (flag), 1681–1807

	1681–1810 Share of total trade	1681–1740 Company era			1741–1807 Private trade era		
	%	No. of voyages	Sample	%	No. of voyages	Sample	%
Great Britain	47	3,840	34	0.89	7,384	84	1.14
France	14	873	1	0.11	2,557	27	1.06
Netherlands	5	544	2	0.37	705	37	5.25
Denmark	2	88	0	0	296	2	0.68
Spain/Uruguay	0	7	0	0	70	0	0
Portugal/Brazil	24	1,975	0	0	3,924	0	0
British America/US	8	185	0	0	1,781	0	0
Totals	100	7,512	37	0.49	16,717	150	0.90

Source: Transatlantic Slave Trade Database (TSTD); for the sample see pages 41–42 and Appendix 2.2a

both Europe and Africa (see Table 2.2). In 129 cases the European provisions are fully specified, while the African provisions are not. In 12 cases there is full information on African provisions, but not on European provisions.

While the coverage of British, French and Dutch voyages is good, the absence of similar coverage for voyages conducted from Portugal, Spain, Brazil and British America/US is a major limitation. Portuguese and Brazilian ships sailed mainly on West Central Africa (WCA hereafter), a region which played a major role in the eighteenth-century expansion of the trade, supplying roughly one-third of the number of slaves that crossed the Atlantic between 1681 and 1807. Although there is ample *qualitative* evidence that slave ships departing from Brazil were stocking up on large quantities of manioc flour in home ports such as Rio de Janeiro, it has proven impossible to retrieve quantitative estimates of the proportions of home-sourced versus Africa-sourced provisions.[15] This study excludes the southern part of present-day Angola, the focal area of

15 See for slave provisions from Brazil, Miller (1997, pp. 351–357); Curto (2004, pp. 132–133) and Newson (2007, p. 85).

TABLE 2.2 Average share of provisions from Europe and Africa in 36 'full data' voyages

	Obs.	1681–1740 Company era		Obs.	1741–1807 Private trade era	
		% Europe	% Africa		% Europe	% Africa
Great Britain	18	4	96	0	–	–
France	1	91	9	4	68	32
Netherlands	0	–	–	11	53	47
Denmark	0	–	–	2	76	24
Totals	19			17		

Source: see Table 2.1 and 2.2b

the Portuguese and Brazilian ships, but it does include the Northern part of the West Central African coastline, where trade was dominated by European vessels.[16] The implications of this omission are discussed later. A summary of the dataset is presented in Appendices 2.2a and 2.2b.

Although a coverage of around only one percent of the voyages made by British, French, Dutch and Danish slavers may seem small, nonetheless it is distinguishable as the first dataset able to serve as a starting point for a more systematic empirical investigation of food provisioning strategies by European slavers. There is a two-step approach to the data. First, the sample of 36 'full data' voyages is used to distinguish European from African provisions, and separate out provisions for crew members and fort personnel. Sailors and fort personnel were mainly fed on European provisions, which were separately recorded from 'Negro Provisions' in the account books of the slave trading companies. Next, all foodstuffs are expressed in metric weights (kilos), and convert all food types (rice, barley, corn, yams, beans etc.) into their caloric value (kcal) and protein content (grams), using FAO nutrition tables.[17] Appendix 2.3 lists the metric and nutritional conversion rates.

16 da Silva and Sommerdyk (2010) have argued for separating the West Central African Coast into a Northern region, referred to as the Loango coast, including Cabinda, Congo North, Congo River, Kilongo, Loango, Malembo, Mayumba, Mpinda and Rio Zaire, and a southern region in modern-day Angola concentrated around the ports of Luanda and Benguela. The Southern area was entirely dominated by Portuguese and Brazilian traders, whereas the North was mainly visited by Northern European vessels. The trade in the North was organised by small merchant networks in contrast to the much more centralised, state-run trade in the South.

17 http://www.fao.org/docrep/w0073e/w0073e08.htm#P14552_1185427.

Table 2.2 presents preliminary results based on the sample of 36 voyages. It demonstrates that the share of European provisions is, in many cases, far too high to verify Eltis' hypothesis that these constituted a negligible share of total food provisions.[18] Only the British ships observed operating during the company era sourced the lion's share of their provisions (ninety six percent) from West Africa. For other nations and periods the shares of provisions sourced from Africa and Europe are very different. Unfortunately, the 'full data' sample has a rather weak coverage, so it is important to be cautious when drawing further conclusions at this stage. Without any observations of British voyages in the 1741–1808 era, it remains unclear for instance, whether the different shares carried by British and continental vessels are due to different national provisioning strategies, or because of more generic changes during the eighteenth century.

Therefore, the second step is to use the information on total caloric intake of these 36 'full data' ships to derive a benchmark estimate of 'required' provisions per slave per day. This a deduction of how much of these day-rations was covered by European or African provisions in the larger sample of 151 voyages, in which only one of the two areas of food provisioning were observed. A subsistence diet with 2,000 kcal and 40 grams of protein per slave per day is assumed. These values are in line with the 'bare-bones subsistence diet' adopted in the comparative living standards literature (Allen 2001, Allen et al. 2011, see for an application to Sub-Saharan Africa; Frankema and van Waijenburg 2012) and sufficiently reflect the slave feeding instructions that captains received.[19] Even though 2,000 kcal is a bare minimum compared to current WHO recommendations of around 2,500 kcal for an adult male with a sedentary lifestyle, it suffices to keep people alive without losing muscle power.

The total number of required day-rations are obtained by multiplying the number of slaves embarked from the trans-Atlantic slave trade database (TSTD hereafter) with the average number of days the median slave spent on board. The estimate of required day-rations is not adjusted for slave mortality during the voyage, as captains would most likely have provisioned based on a best-case scenario (i.e. negligible mortality). Also included are a security margin as slave ship captains were well schooled in the unpredictability of their voyages (insecure slave supplies, adverse weather conditions, diseases, food rot, privateers and so on).

18 Note that Eltis suggests that non-African provisions are about 1 to 2% of slave purchasing costs. If total provisions constitute 25% of slave purchasing costs, the European share is 4 to 8% of total provisions.

19 Studies on British navy sailors show they consumed around 4,500 kcal per day, which seems a large difference, but it needs to be taken into account that slaves were confined for most of the day (Macdonald 2004, 177).

Factors of region and era-specific voyage duration are also accounted for. Embarkation times depended on the concentration of slave supplies, and the fact that middle passage (MP) took longer from some regions than from others. Shorter *expected* voyage lengths would have translated into lower provision requirements. The assume that provisioning strategies were based on the average number of days of the MP, plus one standard deviation as a security margin. Further, a linear slave intake rate is assumed. That is, for a slave vessel taking in 300 slaves in 100 days, and additional rations are added for three extra slaves per day. This is a conservative assumption, as slaves tended to be purchased in larger quantities towards the end of the TAC (Hogerzeil and Richardson 2007). 20–year interval means and standard deviations of the actual time spent at the coast (TAC), and on the MP, for the seven major West African slave trading regions (Senegambia, Sierra Leone, Windward Coast, Gold Coast, Bight of Benin, Bight of Biafra and West-Central Africa) are used. A check of the representativeness of the 'full data' sample on voyage duration revealed that in seventy one percent of these cases the observed ship remained within one standard deviation from the mean, with only one notable outlier. All the data on voyage length were taken from the TSTD and are presented in Appendix 2.4.

Figure 2.1 tests the accuracy of the estimation method for the 'full data' sample, and shows a scatter plot with the predicted number of day-rations on the x-axis, and the observed number of day-rations on the y-axis. The figure confirms the expectation that ships carrying more slaves for longer periods of time carried more supplies. Moreover, the procedure does not seem to systematically under- or overestimate the required number of day-rations. The slope of the regression line ($y = 1.03x$) is close to unity and the correlation is strong ($R^2 = 0.54$). A similar test for protein requirement indicates that the far majority of ships took much more than the 40 grams per day per person envisioned, especially in the form of beans and peas, but this is less relevant as calories posed the main constraint to storage space.

Even though the error margins to both sides of the regression line appear to be evenly distributed, there are quite a few ships carrying much more, or far less, provisions than the baseline model predicts. The likely explanation, supported by archival sources, is that 'overloaded' vessels took additional food supplies to African forts to alleviate local food scarcities.[20] Ships carrying far less

20 British forts at the coast, while buying provisions locally, also relied heavily on imported foodstuffs from Europe. For example, the Company of the Royal Adventurers to England Trading with Africa, who took over the management of the forts after the dissolution of the RAC, relied on regular deliveries of bread, flour and meat delivered on ships from England: TNA T70/928 – 932. The assumption is that the Dutch forts also bought food from visiting vessels, and speculated that this accounts for ships such as the Middelburgs

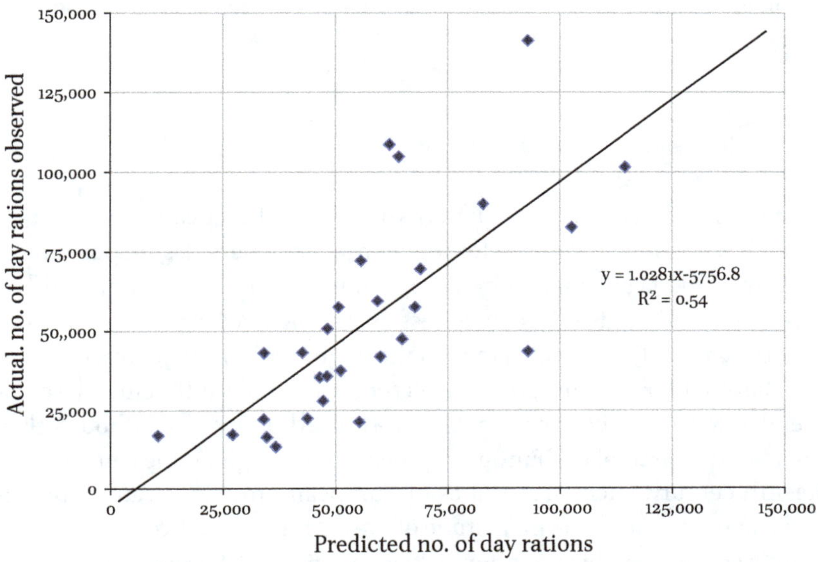

FIGURE 2.1 Scatter plot of required day-rations predicted by the new baseline model (horizontal-axis) *versus* actual observed no. of day-rations (vertical-axis)
Note: This sample includes English RAC, Dutch MCC, Danish and French ships as indicated in Appendix 2.2a. Two outliers were removed as they carried exceptional quantities of food from Europe – sufficient to make a double journey, and much more than recorded for any other ship. These traders probably sold part of their stocks to West African trading forts or other slave ships before heading across the Atlantic. This supports one of this chapter's central claims, namely that European provisions played a much larger role in the logistics of the transatlantic slave trade than hitherto has been assumed.
Source: See Appendix 2.2b

than the model predicts may have taken the risk to sail off without any safety margins.[21] Serious delays at the coast, or instances of food scarcity, often forced captains to take that course of action (Behrendt 2001, pp. 190–191). The bottom-line, however, is that the estimation model appears sound enough to

---

Welvaren (1755) and Vliegende Faam (1757) buying respectively 372% and 263% of required total provisions (see Appendix 2.2a and 2.2b).

21 In the full data sample of ships, 4 vessels (three RAC ships and 1 private vessel from France) sailed with under 50% of the required kcals to give their captives a sufficient daily quantity of calories. Sailing with insufficient provisions in order to free up space for more captives was apparently a common strategy on Portuguese / Brazilian vessels (Miller 1997, pp. 351–355). The impact on captives was described by a British sailor in Suriname in the 1770s who described a newly arrived group of slaves as "*…such a set of scarcely animated automatons, such a resurrection of skin and bones, as forcibly reminded me of the last trumpet.*" (Stedman 1796, p. 209).

be applied to the larger sample of voyages which have incomplete information.

2 Main Results

The first result is that the demand patterns of different European nations varied considerably. Figure 2.2 presents, for four consecutive periods, the percentage share of required kcal supplied by European provisions loaded onto British, French, Dutch and Danish slave trade vessels. This figure clearly shows that the French, Dutch and Danish ships took in the major part of the required kcal in Europe, but that for British slavers the picture is strikingly different. These slavers tended to rely much more on African-sourced provisions, although they too, increased their intake of European provisions throughout the course of the eighteenth century. Such large shares of European provisions cannot be neglected when estimating the magnitude of West African food exports.

There was considerable variation in the quantities of European provisions taken on board. The British RAC ships in the 'full data' sample took, on average, only four percent of their required kcal from England, although one ship, the Portugal, did take thirty six percent in 1729. Even though the French and Dutch reliably brought at least around fifty percent, or considerably more, of their kcal from Europe, there were also quite a few outliers. For example, the Dutch ship "Middelburgs Welvaren" bought a huge quantity of provisions in West Africa, totalling three hundred and twenty six percent of their caloric requirements, while still bringing substantial quantities of beans and barley from the Dutch Republic. It appears, therefore, that slave traders sometimes shipped food to or within Africa which wasn't required for the slaves on board. Nonetheless, despite the outliers, the overall trend is clear: over the eighteenth century the trade relied to a greater degree on European sourced provisions.

Why has the contribution of European provisions to the logistics of the transatlantic slave trade been overlooked for so long and by so many experts? The most likely explanation is that the literature has, repetitively, focussed on British slave ship records of the RAC, which are more complete and more readily accessible than most other slave-trade related sources. As noted above, the RAC obtained almost all its provisions from Africa. Indeed, one may easily conclude from written instructions on slave provisioning by the South Sea Company, the successor to the RAC, that food provisions were largely an African affair,

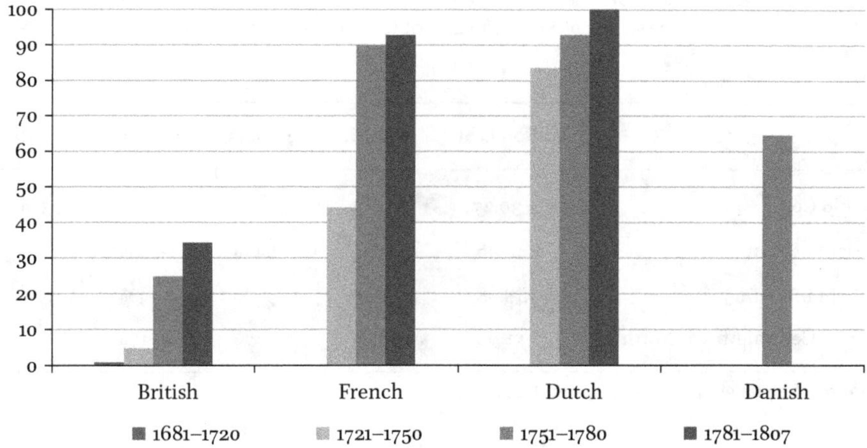

FIGURE 2.2 Percentage share of total required kcal supplied by European provisions, voyages by nationality, 1681–1807
Source: See pages 43–44 and Appendix 2.2a, available at www.aehnetwork.org

> The following account of a proportion of provisions for 100 Negroes to be taken in at Guinea: 80 chests corn at 5 ackeys per chest is 400 ackeys. 4 bushels of salt at 1 ackey per bushel is 4 ackeys. 20 gallons Palm Oil at 8 tacks per gallon is 13 ackeys 4 tacks. 50 ch Malaguetta at ackeys per is 4 ackeys. The above is according to the present usage of the Royal Africa Company.[22]

Nonetheless, whereas in the 1680s and 1690s European provisions constituted a negligible one or two percent in RAC voyages, this share, on ships of private British companies, rose to an average of thirty four percent during the apogee of the trade. The literature has also largely ignored the records of the Dutch and the French traders, whose provisioning strategies were fundamentally different.

Secondly, the results provide empirical support to the conclusions of Behrendt (2001, 181–184) and Eltis (2013, 44–45), who have noted that there were considerable regional differences in the type and quantity of provisions sold along different parts of the West African coast. Table 2.3 shows the average amounts of calories piled up at European ports for ships heading off to the Gold Coast, the Bight of Benin, the Bight of Biafra, and the WCA (North).

22 The South Sea Company: minutes of the Court of Directors 1713 (Donnan 1965, p. 157).

TABLE 2.3 Average European kcal taken to regions of embarkation (first column) and percentage shares of European kcal of total requirements by nationality, 1681–1807

	Million kcal	British	French	Dutch	Danish
Gold Coast	30.27	14%		99%	65%
Bight of Benin	40.46	9%	64%	89%	
Bight of Biafra	48.58	29%	73%	133%	
West Central Africa (North)	111.02	13%	98%	111%	

Source: See pages 43–44 and Appendix 2.2a

Firstly, the data shows that while British ships heading to the Bight of Benin took very few provisions with them, there is also no evidence that merchants in this region supplied significant quantities of foodstuffs to slave ships beyond fresh provisions while ships were loading (Law 2004, p. 192). To overcome this problem, RAC ships were instructed to take on rice along the Windward coast or 'corn' at the Gold Coast, before heading to ports such as Whydah or Jakin on the 'slave coast' of Benin. An analysis of the correspondence of British traders and officials in Africa in the last two decades of the seventeenth century indicates that ships were generally unable to sail to the Bight of Benin until they had acquired sufficient provisions in these regions.[23] This pattern continued into the private trade era, when similar provisioning strategies were adopted by the Dutch slavers of the MCC.[24] In 1789 a British slave ship surgeon who was familiar with West Central Africa stated that the "*....country finds no slaves*

23 The four-volume book of letters between British forts and slave ships compiled by Law (1997a) was analysed for all mentions of provisioning. Examples include an official writing from Dixcove fort on 13th November 1692 which complains of the fact that an RAC ship commanded by a Captain Jefferies "*..cannot move on* [to Ardah in the Bight of Benin] *for want of corn..*" Another letter from an official at Whydah on December 6 1686 notes that he was required to send canoes to Cape Castle to buy corn. Importantly, there were no references to the purchase of food supplies in the Bight of Benin in contrast to frequent discussions and reports of buying corn, yams and millet along the Gold and Windward coasts.

24 Later in the eighteenth century, the MCC records show that no African provisions were ever bought by MCC ships from the Bight of Benin. Instead, food purchases were made along the Windward or Gold Coasts.

provisions – we are therefore obliged to carry provisions partly from Europe and (when to be got) partly from the Windward Coast of Africa."[25]

Ships sailing to WCA took, on average, more than double the quantity of calories from Europe. This difference cannot be explained by greater voyage length, since the average time the median slave spent on board was not that much longer than that for the other regions of embarkation (see Appendix 2.4). A large part of the gap is explained by the fact that British slavers were much less active at the WCA coast[26] (TSTD). It would be misleading, however, to conclude from Table 2.3 that British slave ships would procure most of their provisions at the WCA coast (c. eighty seven percent). Slave ships did not necessarily buy their provisions at the same place they bought their slaves. The few British ships that traded at WCA probably first visited the British forts at the Gold Coast to stock up before continuing their journey further south, in a similar way as they would do when visiting the Bight of Benin (see below).

Slave captains recognised that they could not rely on local markets for provisions when trading along the Loango coast. Behrendt (2001, p. 184) suggests this was due to a more unforgiving climate which led to more frequent famines. Sommerdyk (2012, p. 121 and 137) agrees, but also points out that this trade in slaves involved smaller numbers and slower intake rates, with lower levels of market organization (e.g. merchant networks, credit facilities, etc.) than was common in the Gold Coast and the Bight of Biafra. Consequently, the region's slave traders may simply not have been able to manage the logistics of supplying sufficient quantities of food. That French and Dutch ships took along almost their entire required provisions from Europe suggests that they were more likely to sail straight on to the WCA coast than were the British. The sub-sample of French slave ships shows that the three ships bound for WCA in the 1760s to 1780s sourced, on average, ninety nine percent of the required calories from France, while the three ships sailing to Benin in the same period took a significantly lower forty nine percent from Europe. However, it is likely they made up the difference along the Gold Coast where the Dutch controlled the port of Elmina. Further south in Angola, there is also evidence that Brazilian slavers were unwilling to take the risk to depart with insufficient provisions, rather than paying the inflated prices charged during regular periods of drought (Miller 1979, p. 102). Carney and Rosomoff (2011, 68) quote a Portuguese governor of Angola who ordered that all ships coming from Brazil

25 John Knox (1789) *"Minutes of Evidence taken before a committee of the whole house To whom it was referred to consider the circumstances of the slave trade"* p. 93.

26 During the long eighteenth century, British slavers took only 13% of their slaves from WCA, compared to 42% for the Dutch and 46% for the French (TSTD).

should carry sufficient manioc flour to feed their slaves during the return voyage.

By contrast, the Gold Coast was recognised as an important area for provisioning, especially for ships going onto the Bight of Benin or West Central Africa (Shumway 2014, p. 54, Sparks 2014, p. 44). RAC correspondence compiled by Law (1997) shows repeated references to ships needing to 'corn' along the Gold Coast before proceeding to Benin (ref. 625, 904, 1349). The Danish ship, Fredericus Quartas, was required to stock up on corn at Annamabo before sailing to the Bight of Benin in 1700,[27] and the slave captain Phillips (1693, pp. 202, 205, 209) spent considerable time buying sufficient corn before moving on to Whydah. Accounts of British slaving voyages written in the eighteenth century also make regular mention of the need to stock up on provisions at British forts along the coast (Smith 1745, pp. 115, 126, 142, 164, Atkins 1735, p. 74, 99).

As noted in the introduction to this chapter, Rönnbäck's (2015, 166) study shows that demand from slave ships may have increased coastal production for the market by around three to four percent. This chapter offers new estimates of the annual quantities of food stuffs that may have been purchased during the apogee of the transatlantic slavery from 1760 to 1807. The sample includes full data for three ships, two Dutch and one English, which provisioned on the Gold Coast during this period.[28] The English ship took in the most provisions, which is used as a high estimate, while the Dutch ships took far less, and this is used as a low estimate: the number of ships visiting the Gold Coast during the period is multiplied with these estimates to find a median number (Figure 2.3). Thus, the region might have annually exported between 100,000kgs and 300,000kgs of corn/millet per year, which is a substantial quantity, although far less than was produced in the Bight of Biafra.

In the Bight of Biafra, the exchange of provisions produced by farmers in the interior for use as coastal commodities, such as salt, had been observed since the sixteenth century.[29] This internal trade was essential, as the coastal regions were unsuitable for large scale agriculture, making them dependent on imports, especially when the population grew during the eighteenth century (Behrendt et al. 2010, 102, Northrup 1978, 174). This exchange was made possible by the

27 Letter from the Governor Thrane of Christiansborg fort to the Directors of the West India and Guinea Company in 1700 (Justesen & Manley 2005, p. 95).

28 Prince Willem de Vijfde (1766, Voyage ID 10963, MCC 1005 + 960.3), Vergenoegen (1787 Voyage ID 11056, MCC 1089.1 + 1093), Ranger (1790, Voyage ID83272, Liverpool Record Office 147-zmisc).

29 This was noted by the explorer Duarte Pacheco Pereira at the beginning of the sixteenth century (Fage 1980, p. 71) and the Dutch physician and explorer Olfert Dapper in the later seventeenth century (Dapper 1676, pp. 136–137).

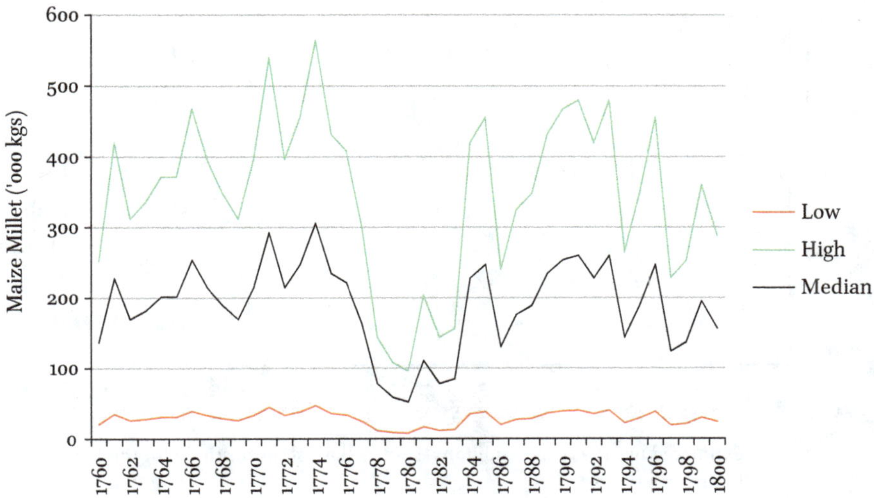

FIGURE 2.3 Estimated kgs of maize/millet ('000) sold to Gold Coast slave ships 1760–1800
Source: slavevoyages.org, see pages 54–56

many navigable rivers of the Niger Delta, and sophisticated inland trading networks, which will be explored in Chapter 6. For the purposes of this chapter, the key point is that the trade routes which had previously handled the exchange of agricultural produce in earlier periods, were now able to rapidly expand to handle considerable quantities of yams and palm oil for the provisioning of slave ships. The Biafran data is based on estimates by Behrendt (2001, p. 182) & Behrendt et al. (2010) that British ships were buying between 10,000 and 50,000 yams for the middle passage. This high and low estimate is multiplied by the number of ships which the slave trade database indicates as having the Bight of Biafra as their principal region of slave purchasing. The result shows that the region was probably exporting between 1.5 and 2 million yams a year, a far more substantial trade than the Gold Coast.

Thus, by the end of the eighteenth century, when British traders had shifted their focus to this region, we would expect that the transatlantic slave trade might have had an impact on commercial agriculture. Out of a total regional population of around 1 to 1,5 million,[30] around 14,000 slaves were exported each year in the peak period of 1781–1800 (TSTD). Assuming this trade required 225 day-rations per slave, and that eighty percent of this was sourced from domestic crops, this would have commanded around 7,000 year-rations of

30 Ballpark figures for the early nineteenth-century derived from backward extrapolations of the 1952 census, see Inikori and Daget (1988); Nwokeji (2000).

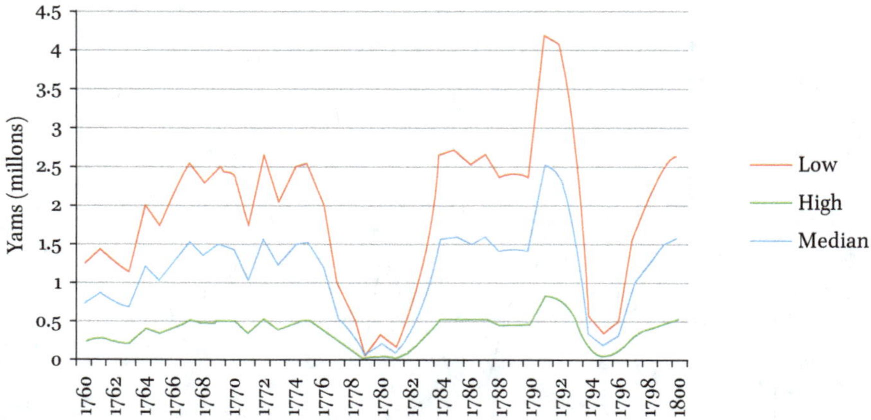

FIGURE 2.4 Estimated number yams (millions) sold to slave ships destined for the Bight of Biafra 1760–1800
Sources: slavevoyages.org, see pages 54–56

food. In view of the size of the total population, this only required a supply rise of zero point five to zero-point seven percent. Yet, if just ten percent of all staples were produced for the market, slave trade induced demand may have contributed some five to seven percent to market exchange of foodstuffs.

Table 2.3 also shows that Dutch slave ships piled up massive amounts of food when heading for the Bight of Biafra, but this must have been for a very different reason than scarcity of local food supplies, since food markets at Bonny and Old Calabar did adequately serve the much larger British fleet. The most likely explanation, which will be further elaborated upon later in the chapter, is that Dutch ships rarely visited the Biafran coast, and therefore lacked the connections with local merchants that the British had established during the second half of the eighteenth century. Stocking up in Europe may thus be interpreted as a precautionary measure against insecure market access in West Africa.

3 Changing Relative Prices and Trade Risks

Why did European slavers purchase more provisions in Europe as time wore on? One of the explanations is that the costs of food from Europe, as a share of total outfitting costs were declining sharply over the course of the eighteenth century, mainly due to a rapid rise in slave prices. Let's assume for the moment that European-sourced provisions were *no cheaper* than African-sourced provisions, meaning the price of a day-ration consisting of 350 grams of barley, 100 grams of horse-beans, 100 grams of rice and 0,01 litre of palm oil gives us an upper benchmark estimate of slave provisioning costs.

This ration offers just over 2,000 kcal and about 80 grams of protein. Consistent with Eltis' assumption that slaves spent on average 4.5 months waiting at or near the coast, and 3 months on board the slave ship, day-rations are taken as 225 per slave.[31] Annual British price-series of barley, beans and rice are taken from Clark (2006), with a thirty percent mark-up. Lacking price-series for palm-oil, a fixed average price per gallon based on scattered African price observations is added. To check the trend in British provisioning prices over the eighteenth century, there is also a newly constructed time series for barley, beans and rice for Dutch markets using Posthumus (1946). Although the Dutch price series have large gaps, the index-trend shows that Dutch staple food prices kept pace with British food prices (see Appendix 5). The slave prices are taken from the same source as Eltis (2013), which consists of a series for 1681–1700 from Eltis (2000) linked to a series for 1701–1800 from Richardson (1991), all in current prices.

Figure 2.5a shows the index-series of slave purchasing prices and slave provisioning prices (1701 = 100), and Figure 2.5b shows the slave provisioning prices (i.e. 225 day rations) as percentage share of slave purchasing prices. Together, these graphs help us understand why European slave traders may have increased their reliance on European provisions. In the mid-1750s slave purchasing prices started to rise from an index level of 114 in 1756, to a mere 535 in 1800. Slave prices experienced a temporary drop in the 1770s and 1790s, but never reverted to pre-1750 levels. Provisioning prices remained much more stable. Although there was a sizeable surge from 1770 to 1800, most of this was a price shock associated with the Napoleonic wars in the 1790s, when the index shot up from 103 in 1798 to 191 in 1800.

The implication of these diverging price developments is that the relative costs of food provisions fell over the course of the eighteenth century, from about twenty to twenty five percent of total outfitting costs in the early decades to about five to ten percent in the closing decades of the eighteenth century. Hence, if relative food prices had played a role in merchants deciding where to buy provisions (Europe or West Africa), the impact of this choice on the overall profit margin of slave trading companies decreased enormously.

31 Conceptually, it seems odd to consider food provisions for slaves waiting at the coast as part of West African food exports, since pre-embarkation maintenance costs will have been factored into the purchasing price of slaves. For reasons of comparability, however, the assumption of 225 day-rations required is maintained.

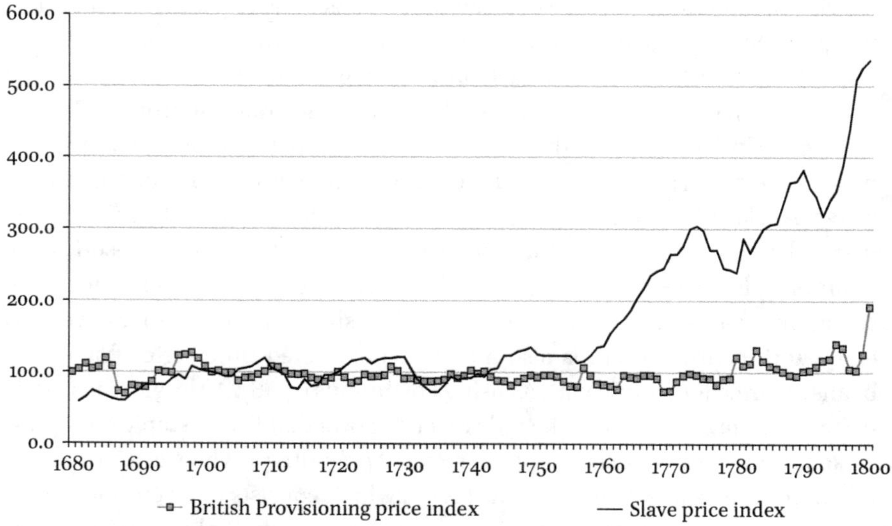

FIGURE 2.5a Index-series of slave purchasing prices (African coast) and slave provisioning prices (British staples), 1680–1800 (1701 = 100)
Source: Food price index based on Clark (2006); Slave price index based on Eltis (2005) and Richardson (1991)

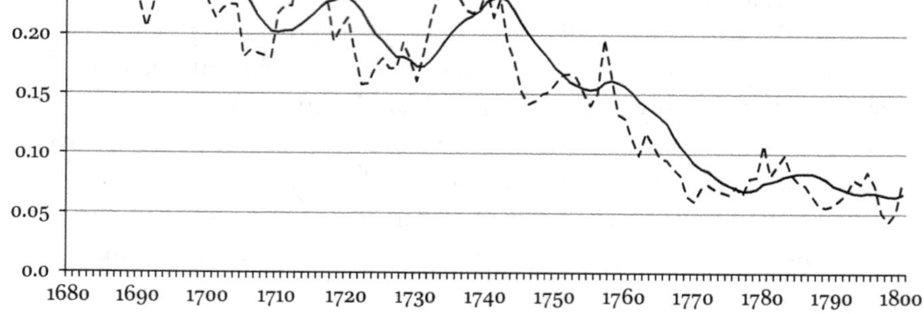

FIGURE 2.5b Slave provisioning price (225 day-rations) as percentage share of average slave purchasing price, 1680–1800 (10-year moving average in bold)
Source: Food price index based on Clark (2006); Slave price index based on Eltis (2005) and Richardson (1991)

Since no accurate information is available on the long-term price trends of African food staples, it is impossible to assess the long-term trend in European and African food price gaps – and an important topic for future research –, but scattered price observations of African rice, corn and yams presented later suggest that these gaps were not that large.

Given the declining relative cost of provisions, stocking up on food before departure became an increasingly attractive means to reduce voyage time and related business risk. As will be discussed in the following chapter, the trans-Atlantic slave trade, while potentially lucrative, was a highly insecure enterprise (Behrendt 2001, Morgan 2007, Haggerty 2009, McDade 2011), and the most successful merchants were those who best managed its risks. Moreover, as the eighteenth century progressed the risks increased due to rising competition among slavers, difficulties in finding the right cargoes to suit rapidly changing African consumer tastes and the need to protect increasingly valuable cargoes of slaves against disease, slave revolts and piracy (Haggerty 2009, pp. 819–822). This argument will be further elaborated later in this chapter.

4 Revised Estimates of West African Food Exports, 1681–1807

It is now time to revise Eltis' estimates. First the total number of slaves embarked in the period 1681–1807 are taken, according to nationality of the slaver (flag), and insert the new estimates of the share of European provisions in total provisioning requirements. This chapters' estimates of the share of European provisions in total provisioning requirements is inserted into the total number of slaves embarked in the period 1681–1807, defined by nationality of the slaver (flag). For British slavers, it is assumed five percent for 1680–1740 and a linear increase to forty percent during 1740–1807. For Dutch slavers, the assumption is eighty percent for the WIC era up to 1740, and ninety percent for the MCC traders after 1740. For French vessels, an assumption is made of fifty percent up to 1740 and seventy five percent thereafter, and for Danish ships fifty percent before 1740 and sixty six percent thereafter. Lacking any estimates for the Luso-Brazilian trade, it is conservatively assumed that ships departing from the New World sourced only twenty percent of food for the MP from their home ports, putting the revised estimates on the very safe side.

Next, there is a refinement Eltis' assumption of provisioning costs being a fixed twenty five percent share of slave purchasing prices, using the shares reported in Figure 2.5b. In so far as African provisions continued to offer a cheaper alternative, these shares represent an upper-estimate of the relative provisioning prices. This chapter maintain Eltis' assumptions for converting the value of exchange commodities f.o.b. to c.i.f. (multiplying f.o.b. series by 2), and the mark-up of three percent for the consumption of African provisions by slave ship crews.

Figure 2.6 compares the five year-interval estimates of the overall slave-trade induced demand impulse on West African commercial agriculture with the estimates offered by Eltis. The difference is found to be vast, although as already argued, the impact in the Bight of Biafra may have been substantial. In effect, the slave trade induced demand had a monetary value of around £60,000 in the first decades of the eighteenth century, increasing to c. £110,000 per year in the middle decades and c. £150,000 during the heyday of the trade in the 1780s to 1800s. The new estimates for the latter period are about seventy to eighty percent lower than those offered by Eltis. This difference has two causes. First, the non-African share in slave provisions was too significant to ignore. Second, Eltis' estimates were hugely inflated by assuming a fixed twenty five percent of rapidly rising slave purchasing prices after the mid-1750s. Yet, in the more likely scenario that provisioning prices remained stable, or rose to a much lesser degree, food provisions must have constituted a rapidly shrinking proportion of the total outfitting costs.

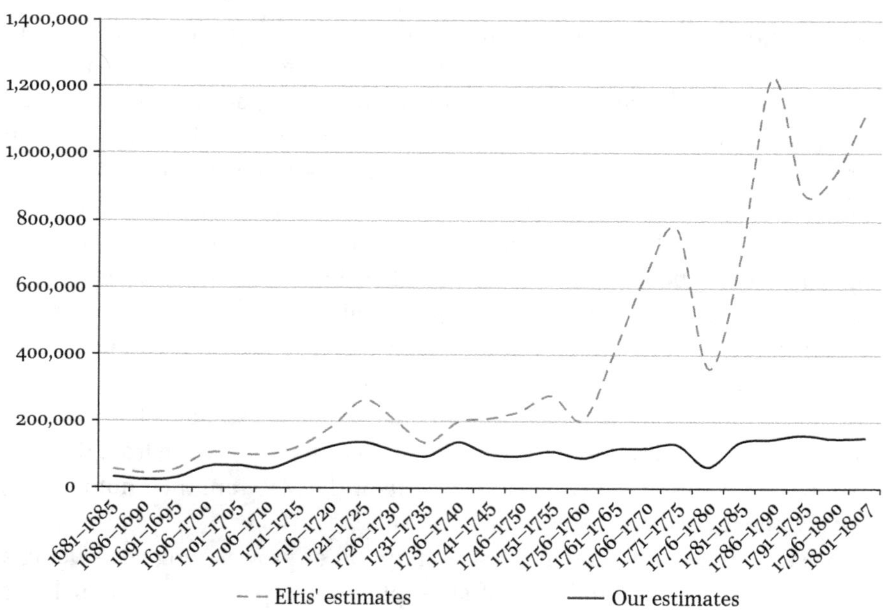

FIGURE 2.6 Estimates of the average annual value of African-sourced provisions compared to Eltis estimates, 1681–1807, in constant British £ of 1700
Sources: Eltis 2013; for new estimates see 59–61 and Appendix 2.6

5 Why did British Provisioning Strategies Differ and what were the Impacts on Different Regions?

The question that remains is why British slave traders adopted different provisioning strategies than continental slave traders, and how did this impact on different regions? This final section reviews four possible explanations, which are all in some way connected to the management of business risk: 1) differential access to West African food markets; 2) different price bids of African and European staple foods; 3) different sensitivity to slaves' dietary preferences; and 4) differential techniques to preserve food for ocean-bound journeys.

Beginning with the last two factors, it is generally acknowledged that techniques to prepare and conserve food improved during the eighteenth century, and fitted into a pattern of ongoing 'professionalization' of the slave trade (Behrendt 2001), one result of which was the declining mortality rates on board slave ships (Klein et al. 2001, p. 100). It is highly implausible, however, that the Dutch and French traders' greater reliance on European provisions could be explained by their having any greater structural knowledge of food conservation techniques than the British.

The argument on dietary preferences of African slaves poses a similar problem. Many sources indicate that European slavers were well informed on the advantages of feeding their captives with African staple foods. Instructions to, and observations by, ships' captains of all nations advised to prepare food with some local ingredients, even if it was just a condiment such as palm-oil or melegueta pepper.[32] Traders believed that this reduced sickness and mortality, and that it helped to get Africans slowly used to European food. It cannot entirely be ruled out that British slavers were, on the whole, more sensitive to the dietary preferences of slaves than Dutch or French slavers, but the many documented cases of British slavers using force to feed slaves who refused their food makes this an unlikely interpretation (Rediker 2007, pp. 263–264 and 284–288).[33]

---

32 In their instructions to captains, the directors of the West India Company recommended that all beans be flavoured with "….een weinig sap" and "…wat oly de palm" (quoted in Balai 2011, p. 250). Likewise the Royal Africa Company stated that its ships were to purchase a proportion of corn, palm oil and malaguetta pepper (Donnan II, 164). Later ships of the Middelburgsche Commercie Compagnie regularly stocked up on palm oil and pepper, regardless of other provisions they bought. A recipe for soup served aboard French slaving vessels included locally bought corn, pepper and palm oil as well as beans or rice (Mandelblatt 2008, p. 412).

33 There is also evidence that African slave raiders used food as a strategy to dislocate their captives from their home environment, by feeding them staples they were not used to.

It is far more likely that the Dutch and French had other reasons to rely on European provisions. Were food price differentials sufficiently large to influence provisioning choices? And if so, were these consistent with the different strategies pursued? Figures 2.6a and 2.6b present the food price observations gathered from the RAC accounts for the years 1680–1730[34], complemented by yam prices in Biafra in the 1780s derived from Behrendt et al. (2010), and rice and yam prices from the MCC records.[35] Figure 2.7a compares West African rice prices with British domestic prices of rice and wheat flour. Figure 2.7b compares British barley and bean prices with West African corn and yam prices.[36] All prices have been standardized in pence per 2,000 kcal using the metrics listed in Appendix 2.3.

Figure 2.7a indicates that West African rice prices were considerably lower than European rice prices. Part of this difference may be explained by differences in quality, but with a price gap of three hundred percent the Windward coast obviously offered more value for money. That said, large price differences between Sherbo and Cape Coast Castle show that it also mattered where or when slavers bought foodstuffs in West Africa. It is possible that the price of rice sold to slavers at Cape Castle followed British market prices, and perhaps the rice was even first imported from Europe in order to supply British forts, before being partly resold to British slave ships.

Figure 2.7b indicates, though, that a West African rice diet was not necessarily cheaper than a diet of European barley and beans. The costs of corn from the Gold Coast were also in the same range. In fact, there seems to have been only one major bargain available in West Africa, namely yams from Biafra, which were much cheaper than any other staple sourced from either Britain or West Africa. Yams were harvested only once a year, which increased

---

Smallwood (2008) and Byrd (2010) argue that as soon as people were kidnapped, captured or sold a process began to separate them from the social context which had previously defined them as members of a community, and reduced them to commodities (Byrd 2010, 29). Smallwood (2008, pp. 43–44) argues that the food given to slaves was an important part of this process.

34 For the forts, the data comes from Sherbo (Sierra Leone) and Cape Coast Castle (Gold Coast) for 1686, 1687 and 1688. These primarily show purchases of African products in local currencies which are converted into pound sterling. For ships, information from ship accounts in the invoice books of the RAC are taken, which show both quantities and prices of European foodstuffs.

35 Information to derive prices for yams can be found in Behrendt et al. 2010, pp. 90–91, 102, 108, 135, 140, 170; Behrendt 2001, p. 182; Thomas 1999, p. 418.

36 The British annual price series are farm-gate prices from Clark (2006) to which were added a 30% mark-up to adjust for transportation and transaction costs incurred in getting foods from the countryside to the belly of slave vessels in the harbours of Bristol and Liverpool. This 30% mark-up closes the gap between the farm-gate prices and the unit prices reported in the slave ship trading accounts studied here.

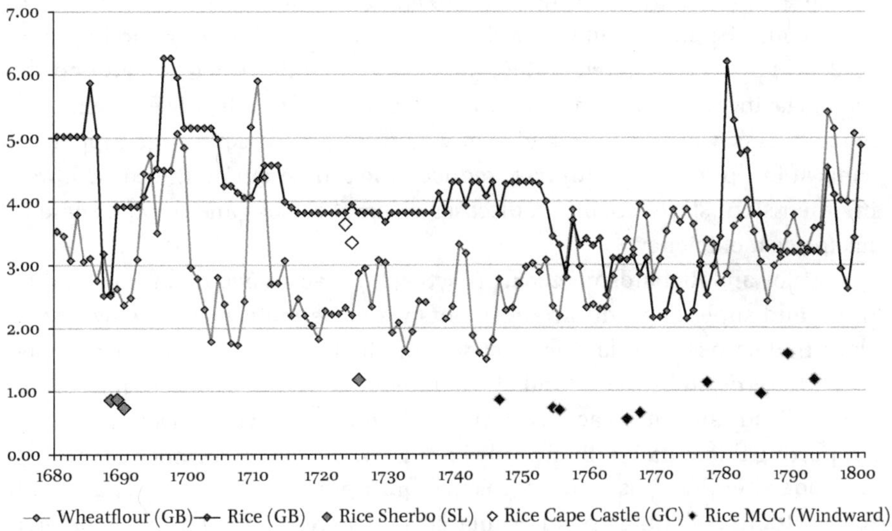

FIGURE 2.7a British prices of rice and wheat flour *versus* West African rice prices, pence per 2,000 kcal

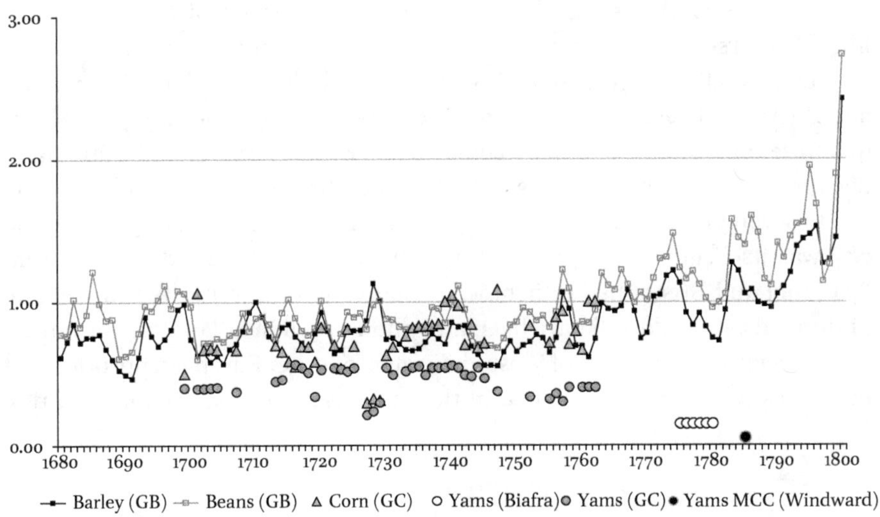

FIGURE 2.7b British prices of barley and beans *versus* West African prices of corn and yams, pence per 2,000 kcal
Sources: GB Data: Clark (2006), MCC Data: Zeeuws Archief, MCC Inventaris, Reizen 1730 – 1790, Yams Biafra: Behrendt et al. 2010, Yams, Palm Oil, Corn (Gold Coast): Ronnback 2014, Rice Sherbo (SL): TNA T70/880, Rice Cape Castle (GC): TNA T70/763; Notes: GB is Great Britain, GC is Gold Coast, SL is Sierra Leone, MCC is Middelburgse Commercie Compagnie

pressures on captains to time their voyages accurately, but once obtained, yams could be successfully stored for long periods of time (Behrendt 2001, p. 183). Moreover, as noted earlier, the densely-populated regions around the major slaving ports of Bonny and Old Calabar, with their highly efficient trading networks, were able to significantly increase production. Large supplies of yams at low prices may thus have reduced the time spent on the coast, lowering the risk of slave rebellions, diseases or naval attacks and, more generally, raising cost efficiency.

Lovejoy and Richardson (2004, pp. 378–380) have argued that faster loading times and superior credit arrangements were the main reasons why British slave traders began to favour what was originally considered a 'horrid hole', with its less desirable slaves and higher rates of mortality for both captives and crew.[37] Ready and cheap access to yams in Biafra may have been another factor supporting this shift. Yet, Biafra only became of central importance to the British trade after the 1750s which Nwokeji (2010, pp. 49–53) has argued had much to do with the opening up of new markets for slaves in the densely populated central region. Cheap yams may thus explain why British slave ships continued to rely on African provisions to a greater extent than the French or the Dutch – who traded much less in this area – but they cannot explain the already existing differences in provisioning strategies.

Behrendt (2001) has argued that "During peak periods of the slave trade, English food supplies could not meet the requirements of all Guineamen. Merchants thus relied on African provisions, particularly during late summer and fall…." (p. 181). There is no doubt that the slave trade at its peak required huge quantities of food. If one were to count the crew and slaves aboard ships out of Liverpool as additional mouths to be fed, then they would have added some five to seven percent to the total population of Lancashire in an era when the city was itself growing rapidly.[38] Yet, even if British slavers departing from Liverpool and Bristol had difficulties in sourcing food from their immediate hinterlands, it would still have been an option to call in at London, the largest commercial and naval hub of Western Europe, or other European ports for that matter, as was common practice in the purchase of exchange commodities,

37 Slaves from Biafra were lower valued by buyers in the New World as they were regarded as more disease prone. This is also borne out by analyses of mortality rates during the middle passage with slaves from the Biafra region dying at nearly twice the rate as those from other areas (Klein 2010, Thomas 1999).

38 Population estimates from Wrigley (2007).

such as textiles, guns, alcohol, tobacco, iron and copper rods.[39] French slavers leaving from the port of Nantes sometimes first sailed northwards to the Dutch port of Rotterdam to take in provisions.[40]

The most likely explanation for the differences in provisioning strategy, therefore, cannot be found in the availability of foodstuffs in Europe, but rather in the differential access to West African food markets over the long term. British ships had long relied on buying food at various fortified coastal stations in Sierra Leone and the Gold Coast, before taking a leap to the Bight of Benin, where food access was problematic. In the later eighteenth century English merchants, principally from Liverpool made considerable efforts to develop stable trading relations with African elites at Bonny and Biafra where they possessed no permanent forts. Merchants corresponded with local traders, and developed intimate relations with local elites.[41] This allowed them more dependable supplies to support a strategy of relying on local provisions. The Dutch had always had fewer forts along this part of the coast and with the critical exception of Elmina, these also played a less significant role in the slave trade itself. With less dependable supplies along the coast it made sense to stock up in Europe, even if this may not have given the best value for money. MCC ship logs reveal that there were very few places along the coast where they could obtain reliable supplies.[42] This is not to say that French, Danish or Dutch ships did not buy any West African commodities at all, but they did buy much less of the main staples.

French ships had even fewer permanent establishments along the coast for stopping over. Writing in 1764, the Nantais merchant Joseph Mosneron, stated that the captain of his ship decided to set sail for the Caribbean, despite not having his full complement of slaves because: "*Les provisions de France étaient*

39 Records from the accounts of forts along the coast of Africa show that they were importing trade goods from around the world, including Swedish iron, Indian textiles, Danish guns, Brazilian tobacco and Caribbean rum. TNA T70/928 – 930.

40 Based on personal correspondence with Gerhard de Kok. I thank him for sharing this insight. Mandelblatt (2008) notes that while the majority of provisions on French ships were bought in France, they also purchased rice in London and Salt Beef from Ireland (p. 417).

41 Behrendt et al. 2010 , pp. 73–78

42 The database of MCC ships provides 75 observations of specific locations used by ships to purchase provisions. Of these, 27 come from the short stretch of coast from Axim to Elmina on the western side of the Gold Coast, and 34 from the equally small area between Grande Mesurado and Sestra Kru on the Windward Coast. The prominence of the latter area may be due to the fact that it saw less competition from more established traders on other parts of the coast (Vos 2009, p. 32).

en grande partie consummées...." (Pétré-Grenouilleau 1995, p. 75). Other captains, like Van Alstein, had to sail to the islands of Fernando Po and São Tomé: "Il *n'en est pas de meme de la Cote d'Or ou de Juda; quand on manque de vivres, on peut aller relacher a l'Isle des Princes ou a celles de Saint-Thome et d'Annobon qui n 'en sont pas eloignees.*" (Rinchon 1964, p. 264). Since most French merchants were, unlike the British and Dutch, not specialised in the slave trade, but undertook it as a side activity to bilateral commodity trade with the Caribbean (Michon 2007), there were lower incentives for them to invest in reliable African coastal stations.[43]

The idea that Dutch and French slave traders may have had more diversified portfolios is also important in another respect. Recent research by Gerhard de Kok reveals that landowning elites in the Dutch province of Zealand invested heavily in the MCC trade.[44] They outfitted ships with supplies from local farms, some of which they owned themselves. Differences in European investor-supplier networks may thus offer an additional explanation as to why Dutch slavers piled up the bulk of their provisions in home ports, such as Middelburg. Future research will need to clarify whether such links were weaker in Bristol and Liverpool, and whether path-dependencies in the commercial organization of the slave trade can account for different logistic approaches.

But even the British, with the advantage of having a string of forts along the West African coast, faced considerable problems with West African supplies at a time when the trade was just a fraction of its eighteenth-century peak. Correspondence from and to RAC officials stationed in the forts along the Gold and Slave Coast in the 1680s and 1690s, reveals that, especially in the months of March to July, there were frequent mentions of food 'scarcity' causing trouble to traders (see Figure 2.8). In 1686, Captain Woodfine stated that he was unable to move on to Whydah until he had sufficient corn, and that there was none to be had except at inflated prices.[45] Likewise, Captain Jefferies, in 1692, mentioned he was unable to move on to the Bight of Benin for want of sufficient corn.[46] Local forts, which were often suppliers of slaves as well as provisions,

43 An analysis of the Chaurand papers in the Nantes archives from 1777 to 1787 (101 J 26, 27, 28) shows that they sent out 27 West India ships to only 11 slave ships. These slave voyages were all concentrated between 1783 and 1787, a period of rapid growth in West Africa and that after 1787 they withdrew from the slave trade to again concentrate on the bilateral trade with St Domingue. A further study of the comparative impacts of specialisation in the British as opposed to the French slave trade would merit further study.

44 Based on personal communication with Gerhard de Kok.

45 Law (1997a) Book 2, May 16 1686 Ref 904.

46 Law (1997a) Book 3, November 13 Ref 10.

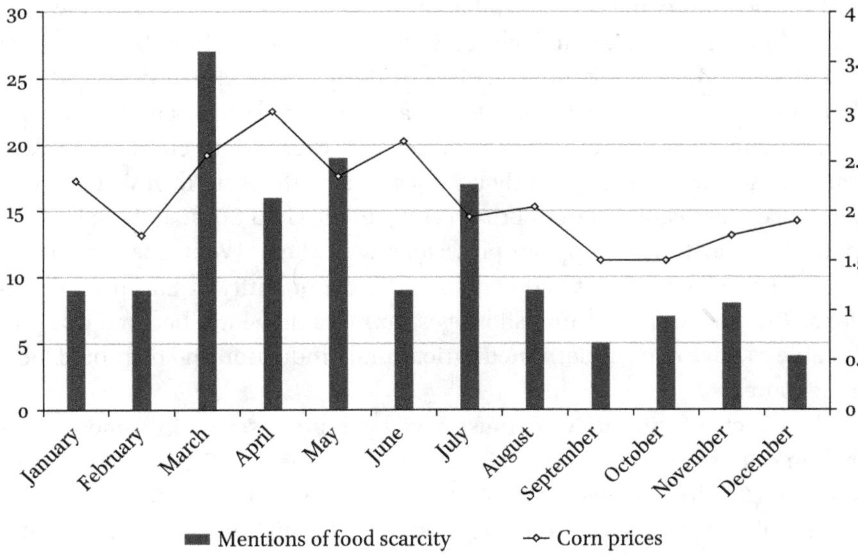

FIGURE 2.8 Monthly mentions of provisioning problems in RAC correspondence (left-hand axis) and monthly corn prices in gold ackies (right-hand axis), 1680–1699
Source: Calculations based on the letters between British forts and slave ships compiled by Law (1997a).
Note: Gold ackies were an African coastal currency unit worth c. 1 British shilling (12 pence)

were equally affected by insecure food supplies. In 1681 the factor at Accra stated that he was unable to buy more slaves as there was no corn to be had.[47] Figure 2.8 shows that the average monthly prices of corn coincided with numerous mentions of scarcity. The reasons for failing supplies were not only related to the seasonality of harvests. Local wars and disputes, as experienced by the Egya fort, near modern day Cape Coast in Ghana[48], could put a complete ban on food supplies reaching the coastal forts. Such problems were not confined to the Gold Coast or the Bight of Benin. In Senegambia food shortages caused by warfare or drought were also the 'biggest bottleneck' in the slave purchasing chain (Searing 2003, p. 81).

47 Law (1997a) Book 1, October 25 1681 Ref 417.
48 Law (1997) Book 2, March 8 1687 Ref 647.

If the possibility of speedier embarkation was the main reason for the British to shift their trade to the Bight of Biafra, this indicates that they, too, were sensitive to provisioning-induced risks of delay. There is tentative evidence that the demand for African foodstuffs was stretching supplies in the main regions of embarkation. For instance, during the severe contraction of the slave trade in the late 1770s to the early 1780s, caused by the American War of Independence, slave captains from Britain going to the Gold Coast and the Bight of Biafra took far fewer European provisions with them. When the slave trade resurged after the conflict had ended, so did the quantity of European provisions.[49] Apart from structural shortages, supplies may have become less predictable as slave raids undermined agricultural production and disrupted local trade routes.

The effects of internal wars must have been more severe in some regions than in others. In this respect, it is interesting to see that British slave vessels sailing off to the Windward Coast and the Gold Coast took about sixty two percent of total provisions from their home ports, while vessels sailing to Biafra brought about thirty four percent in the 1790s and 1800s. This issue will be discussed in greater detail in Chapter 6, but the difference seems consistent with Nwokeji (2010), who has argued that the demographic impact of slave raiding in Biafra was mild compared to the region around the Bight of Benin, which suffered a serious decline in population (Manning 1982, 30–34). In Biafra fewer slaves were obtained through violent slave raiding and instead far more through the use of judicial punishment (Nwokeji 2010, pp. 68, 76, 130, 179, Martin 1988, p. 27, Lovejoy 2011, p. 82). According to Nwokeji (2001, p. 626) a more balanced sex ratio and the willingness of people to accept and incorporate outsiders meant that "*....Igboland retained a high population density not because it escaped heavy slaving.....but in spite of it.*"

In summary, British access to African provisions was not only more secure because of a string of forts that could mediate the risk of local food shortages, but also because it shifted its trade to the region where local merchant networks were geared towards ensuring a quick, abundant and secure

49 During the period of the American civil war, ships belonging to the Liverpool merchant William Davenport were taking as little as 3% of their provisions from Liverpool. However, by the 1790s ships were taking on average of 30%. This figure did vary according to region and ship captain. The log of the slave ship Ranger (STD ID: 83272, LRO: 387 MD 55), one of the few to itemise the food given to slaves, shows that they were fed around 3700 kcals / day with European beans and rice and around 2000 kcals of corn from the Gold Coast. To put this into perspective, sailors on British ships who were far more physically active were fed around 4800 kcals / day in total (MacDonald 2004, p. 177).

supply of foodstuffs to slave traders eager to minimize their embarkation times.

This chapter asks to what extent the increasing demand for food provisions by European slave ships may have boosted commercial agriculture in the long eighteenth-century both across West Africa, but also in different regions along the coast. Exploring the provisioning strategies of British, French, Dutch and Danish slave ships has shown that a considerable share of the calories and proteins required to maintain African slaves were supplied from Europe. It has also revealed that the relative costs of European-sourced slave provisions remained relatively stable, while slave purchasing prices quintupled between 1755 and 1807. Hence, the Atlantic slave trade played a smaller role in the development of West African commercial agriculture than previous studies have suggested, and was definitely much smaller than the aggregate value of such West African commodity exports to Britain during the mid-nineteenth-century.

Apart from assessing orders of magnitude, the new analysis has revealed two interesting patterns of variation in slave ship provisioning strategies. Firstly, British slavers relied to a much larger extent on African food markets than continental slavers. It is hypothesized here that the main reason for this difference is that British slavers enjoyed more secure access to provisions, especially because their string of trading forts and stronger trading relations with local merchants on the West African coast reduced the risk of supply failure.

There were also notable differences in the size of food exports across various regions of slave embarkation. Expanding food exports in West Africa were confined to a few key regions. In the Bight of Biafra, the slave trade stimulated the development of coastal food markets and placed a stepping stone for the nineteenth-century commercial transition. In the Gold Coast, the provisioning trade was important but, as will be argued in later chapters, not influential in the commercial transition, which was initially based on other exports from the interior. In those areas where markets for food provisions remained underdeveloped, i.e. WCA and Benin, the commercial transition either failed to accelerate the non-slave sector or development occurred much later. The next chapter will examine the expansion of the trade in commodities that were destined for sale in Europe.

Appendices

APPENDIX 2.1 Eltis' estimates of the five-year average annual value of African-sourced provisions in the Atlantic slave trade, 1681–1807 (all estimates in GB£ 1700)

	Slaves purchased (fob Europe/ Americas)	African-sourced provisions (fob Europe/ Americas)	African-sourced provisions (cif Africa)	African-sourced provisions for slave ship crews	African-sourced provisions (total)
	1	2	3	4	5
1681–1685	1,07,587	26,897	53,794	1,614	55,407
1686–1690	86,610	21,653	43,305	1,299	44,604
1691–1695	1,10,731	27,683	55,366	1,661	57,026
1696–1700	2,02,723	50,681	1,01,362	3,041	1,04,402
1701–1705	1,96,478	49,120	98,239	2,947	1,01,186
1706–1710	1,96,241	49,060	98,121	2,944	1,01,064
1711–1715	2,48,689	62,172	1,24,345	3,730	1,28,075
1716–1720	3,61,423	90,356	1,80,712	5,421	1,86,133
1721–1725	5,12,750	1,28,188	2,56,375	7,691	2,64,066
1726–1730	3,92,838	98,210	1,96,419	5,893	2,02,312
1731–1735	2,62,800	65,700	1,31,400	3,942	1,35,342
1736–1740	3,85,436	96,359	1,92,718	5,782	1,98,500
1741–1745	4,05,049	1,01,262	2,02,525	6,076	2,08,600
1746–1750	4,49,280	1,12,320	2,24,640	6,739	2,31,379
1751–1755	5,37,147	1,34,287	2,68,574	8,057	2,76,631
1756–1760	3,96,019	99,005	1,98,010	5,940	2,03,950
1761–1765	7,96,786	1,99,197	3,98,393	11,952	4,10,345
1766–1770	12,46,728	3,11,682	6,23,364	18,701	6,42,065
1771–1775	15,03,464	3,75,866	7,51,732	22,552	7,74,284

	Slaves purchased (fob Europe/ Americas)	African-sourced provisions (fob Europe/ Americas)	African-sourced provisions (cif Africa)	African-sourced provisions for slave ship crews	African-sourced provisions (total)
	1	2	3	4	5
1776–1780	6,98,969	1,74,742	3,49,485	10,485	3,59,969
1781–1785	13,17,247	3,29,312	6,58,624	19,759	6,78,382
1786–1790	23,81,871	5,95,468	11,90,936	35,728	12,26,664
1791–1795	17,17,428	4,29,357	8,58,714	25,761	8,84,475
1796–1800	18,12,184	4,53,046	9,06,092	27,183	9,33,275
1801–1807	21,65,957	5,41,489	10,82,979	32,489	11,15,468
1681–1807	7,62,158	1,86,494	3,72,989	11,190	3,84,179

Source: Eltis (2013) Table 1.2, p. 39; Column 1 is taken from Table 1.1, p. 33

Note: By taking 25% of slave purchasing prices for 1681–1807 and multiplying these with slave export volumes (column 1) from the Trans-Atlantic Slave Trade Database (Eltis and Richardson 2010), Eltis expressed the average annual value of West African food exports in European exchange goods f.o.b. (column 2)*. These were then multiplied by two to account for the costs of freight and insurance (c.i.f.) in the transportation of European exchange commodities to the regions of slave purchase (column 3). Adding a share of 3% to account for African-sourced provisions for slave ship crews (column 4), his final estimates (column 5) indeed suggest a total annual average demand impulse of close to one million British Pounds

* Slave prices series for 1681–1699 were derived from Eltis (2000, p. 296) and for 1700–1807 from Richardson (1991, 52–56)

APPENDIX 2.2a Summary statistics of the sample of 187 voyages

No	Voyage no. TSTD	Name vessel	Year arrived	Nation	No. of slaves embarked	Main provisions	Total kcal taken on board in Europe (millions)	Main African provisions
0	1	2	3	4	5	6	7	8
1	35161	Cron Printz Christian	1755	DK	125	Beans, Stockfish	27.14	Millet, Palm Oil
2	35181	Fredensborg	1768	DK	265	Beans, Barley	76.29	Millet, Palm Oil
3	33330	Diligent	1732	FR	256	Beans	50.80	Corn, Cassava
4	30484	Reine de France	1744	FR	404	Beans, Rice	63.91	Corn, Yams, Cassava
5	30754	Thélémaque	1764	FR	365	Beans, Rice	76.67	Corn, Yams, Cassava
6	30911	Pompée	1770	FR	390	Beans, Rice	148.01	Corn, Palm Oil, Yams, Cassava
7	32283	Duc de Laval	1775	FR	393	Beans, Rice	152.42	N/D
8	31639	Pactole	1784	FR	428	Beans, Rice	63.91	Corn, Rice, Palm Oil, Yams, Cassava, Plantains
9	30808	Jeune Reine	1765	FR	169	Beans	40.64	N/D
10	30864	Saint François	1768	FR	534	Biscuits, Beans	140.56	N/D
11	30874	Saint Jacques	1769	FR	528	Beans	106.67	N/D
12	30875	Mars	1768	FR	373	Beans	45.64	N/D
13	30882	Saint Laurent	1769	FR	473	Biscuits, Beans, Rice	140.56	N/D
14	30893	Prince Grasse	1769	FR	415	Beans, Rice	115.41	N/D

Total kcal taken on board in Africa (millions)	Major region of slave embarkation	Average no. of days on board at African Coast (TAC)	Average no. of days on board during Middle Passage (MP) + 1 st. dev.	No. daily rations required	% share European provisions of total required (kcal)
9	10	11	12	13	14
7.72	Gold Coast	134	150	27.125	50.0
25.25	Gold Coast	130	117	48.23	79.1
5.25	Bight of Benin	113	128	47.232	53.8
23.37	Bight of Benin	152	154	92.92	34.4
7.23	West Central Africa North	163	83	60.043	63.8
61.63	West Central Africa North	163	83	64.155	115.4
N/D	West Central Africa North	163	83	64.649	117.9
75.29	Bight of Benin	130	96	68.908	46.4
N/D	Senegambia	90	53	16.562	122.7
N/D	West Central Africa North	328	109	145.782	48.2
N/D	Bight of Biafra	365	36	115.368	46.2
N/D	Other Africa	216	140	92.504	24.7
N/D	West Central Africa North	137	70	65.511	107.3
N/D	West Central Africa North	208	61	68.475	84.3

APPENDIX 2.2a Summary statistics of the sample of 187 voyages (*cont.*)

No	Voyage no. TSTD	Name vessel	Year arrived	Nation	No. of slaves embarked	Main provisions	Total kcal taken on board in Europe (millions)	Main African provisions
0	1	2	3	4	5	6	7	8
15	30926	Saint François	1770	FR	520	Biscuits, Beans	147.94	N/D
16	30927	Saint Jacques	1770	FR	582	Biscuits, Beans	174.81	N/D
17	30948	Saint Jean Baptiste	1772	FR	571	Beans, Rice	121.35	N/D
18	30967	Glaneuse	1772	FR	172	Beans, Rice	36.91	N/D
19	30970	Nymphe	1772	FR	336	Beans, Rice	50.70	N/D
20	31000	Saint Jean Baptiste	1774	FR	462	Beans, Rice	124.76	N/D
21	31009	Nymphe	1775	FR	460	Biscuits, Beans, Rice	154.05	N/D
22	31026	Saint Jean Baptiste	1776	FR	435	Beans, Rice	121.26	N/D
23	31180	Madame	1787	FR	643	Beans, Rice	210.03	N/D
24	31184	Fine	1787	FR	198	Beans, Rice	51.13	N/D
25	31188	Bailli de Suffren	1787	FR	569	Beans, Rice	107.72	N/D
26	31189	Passepartout	1787	FR	14	Beans, Rice	4.21	N/D

Total kcal taken on board in Africa (millions)	Major region of slave embarkation	Average no. of days on board at African Coast (TAC)	Average no. of days on board during Middle Passage (MP) + 1 st. dev.	No. daily rations required	% share European provisions of total required (kcal)
9	10	11	12	13	14
N/D	West Central Africa North	164	60	73.84	100.2
N/D	West Central Africa North	163	58	81.189	107.7
N/D	West Central Africa North	139	50	68.235	88.9
N/D	West Central Africa North	60	62	15.824	116.6
N/D	Bight of Biafra	137	56	41.832	60.6
N/D	West Central Africa North	93	47	43.197	144.4
N/D	West Central Africa North	267	57	87.63	87.9
N/D	West Central Africa North	87	59	44.588	136.0
N/D	Southeast Africa and Indian Ocean islands	134	102	108.667	96.6
N/D	West Central Africa North	207	59	32.175	79.5
N/D	West Central Africa North	174	53	79.66	67.6
N/D	West Central Africa North	139	58	1.785	117.8

APPENDIX 2.2a Summary statistics of the sample of 187 voyages (*cont.*)

No	Voyage no. TSTD	Name vessel	Year arrived	Nation	No. of slaves embarked	Main provisions	Total kcal taken on board in Europe (millions)	Main African provisions
0	1	2	3	4	5	6	7	8
27	31209	Jeanne Thérèse	1788	FR	258	Beans, Rice	80.25	N/D
28	31220	Aimable Aline	1787	FR	516	Biscuits, Beans, Rice	121.20	N/D
29	31224	Louis	1788	FR	274	Beans, Rice	107.49	N/D
30	31279	Bailli de Suffren	1790	FR	440	Beans, Rice	115.25	N/D
31	9917	Charles	1681	GB	288		N/D	Corn
32	9870	Merchant Bonadventure	1683	GB	448		N/D	Corn
33	15074	Mary	1683	GB	507	Beans	0.61	Corn
34	20112	Saint George	1683	GB	550		N/D	Corn
35	9669	Jefferie	1685	GB	310	Beans	0.33	Corn
36	9668	Good Hope	1685	GB	376	Beans	0.58	Corn
37	9684	Sarah Bonadventure	1686	GB	404		N/D	Corn
38	9702	Kendall	1694	GB	600		N/D	Corn
39	9714	Hannibal	1694	GB	700	Beans	2.90	Corn
40	9701	Katherine	1694	GB	600		N/D	Corn
41	9726	Fauconberg (a) Falconberg	1696	GB	605	Beans	2.54	Corn
42	75599	Hannibal	1721	GB	273		N/D	Rice

Total kcal taken on board in Africa (millions)	Major region of slave embarkation	Average no. of days on board at African Coast (TAC)	Average no. of days on board during Middle Passage (MP) + 1 st. dev.	No. daily rations required	% share European provisions of total required (kcal)
9	10	11	12	13	14
N/D	Bight of Benin	164	198	72.24	55.5
N/D	Bight of Biafra	97	57	54.438	111.3
N/D	Bight of Benin	126	88	41.374	129.9
N/D	West Central Africa North	199	56	68.42	84.2
113.08	Bight of Benin	73	117	44.208	N/D
160.83	Bight of Benin	73	117	68.768	N/D
179.49	Gold Coast	107	110	82.895	0.4
251.29	Bight of Benin	73	117	84.425	N/D
114.88	Gold Coast	107	110	50.685	0.3
118.47	West Central Africa North	78	119	59.408	0.5
179.85	Bight of Benin	73	117	62.014	N/D
187.39	Bight of Benin	73	117	92.1	N/D
200.32	Gold Coast	107	110	114.45	1.3
252.37	Bight of Benin	73	117	92.1	N/D
280.01	Bight of Benin	73	117	92.868	1.4
2.56	Gold Coast	117	112	46.547	N/D

APPENDIX 2.2a Summary statistics of the sample of 187 voyages (*cont.*)

No	Voyage no. TSTD	Name vessel	Year arrived	Nation	No. of slaves embarked	Main provisions	Total kcal taken on board in Europe (millions)	Main African provisions
0	1	2	3	4	5	6	7	8
43	76371	Sherborough Gally	1721	GB	231		N/D	Rice, Palm Oil
44	75956	Otter	1721	GB	209	Beans	0.73	Corn
45	75330	Dispatch	1721	GB	110		N/D	Corn, Palm Oil
46	76147	Sarah Gally	1721	GB	250	Beans	1.45	Corn, Rice, Palm Oil
47	76399	Henry	1722	GB	367	Beans	1.86	Corn, Rice, Palm Oil
48	76405	Judith	1722	GB	107	Beans	0.51	N/D
49	76960	King Solomon	1722	GB	300	Beans	2.18	Corn, Rice, Palm Oil
50	76435	Sarah Gally	1723	GB	273	Beans	0.91	Corn, Palm Oil, Yams
51	75181	Bladen Frigate	1723	GB	250	Beans	3.39	N/D
52	76192	Squirrell	1723	GB	121	Beans	3.81	N/D
53	76693	Lady Rachel	1723	GB	221	Beans	2.18	Corn, Rice
54	75286	Clarendon	1723	GB	69	Beans	0.63	Corn, Rice
55	76542	Diligence	1723	GB	200		N/D	Corn, Palm Oil
56	76176	Sloper	1723	GB	282	Beans	2.54	Corn, Palm Oil
57	75181	Bladen Frigate	1723	GB	250		N/D	Corn
58	76965	Dove	1723	GB	237	Beans	0.85	Corn, Rice
59	76348	Whidah Frigate	1724	GB	300	Beans	6.77	Corn
60	76695	Cape Coast Frigate	1724	GB	205	Beans	2.12	Corn

Total kcal taken on board in Africa (millions)	Major region of slave embarkation	Average no. of days on board at African Coast (TAC)	Average no. of days on board during Middle Passage (MP) + 1 st. dev.	No. daily rations required	% share European provisions of total required (kcal)
9	10	11	12	13	14
22.57	Sierra Leone	137	75	33.149	N/D
32.31	Senegambia	132	100	34.694	1.0
49.55	Gold Coast	117	112	18.755	N/D
85.09	Gold Coast	117	112	42.625	1.7
113.27	Bight of Benin	113	128	67.712	1.4
	Senegambia	132	100	17.762	1.4
N/D	Gold Coast	117	112	51.15	2.1
70.01	Gold Coast	117	112	46.547	1.0
N/D	Bight of Benin	113	128	46.125	3.7
N/D	Bight of Benin	113	128	22.325	8.5
24.92	Senegambia	132	100	36.686	3.0
33.56	West Central Africa North	139	83	10.523	3.0
58.37	Gold Coast	117	112	34.1	N/D
69.05	Gold Coast	117	112	48.081	2.6
179.49	Bight of Benin	113	128	46.125	N/D
43.96	Bight of Benin	113	128	43.727	1.0
35.90	Bight of Benin	113	128	55.35	6.1
42.36	Senegambia	132	100	34.03	3.1

APPENDIX 2.2a Summary statistics of the sample of 187 voyages (*cont.*)

No	Voyage no. TSTD	Name vessel	Year arrived	Nation	No. of slaves embarked	Main provisions	Total kcal taken on board in Europe (millions)	Main African provisions
0	1	2	3	4	5	6	7	8
61	75258	Chandos	1724	GB	556	Beans	3.63	Corn, Palm Oil
62	76095	Royal African Packet	1724	GB	645		N/D	Corn, Palm Oil
63	76617	Portugal	1729	GB	327	Beans	40.64	Corn, Rice, Palm Oil, Yams
64	90937	Plumper	1763	GB	304	Beans, Stockfish	8.70	N/D
65	91213	William	1765	GB	77	Beans, Rice	19.89	N/D
66	92315	Sisters	1766	GB	280	Beans, Pease	20.33	N/D
67	91219	Dalrymple	1767	GB	383	Beans, Rice	24.36	N/D
68	91427	Neptune	1768	GB	169	Beans, Rice	9.91	N/D
69	91577	Little Britain	1769	GB	148	Beans, Rice	14.54	N/D
70	91428	Plumper	1769	GB	326	Beans, Barley, Rice	33.50	N/D
71	91553	Fox	1769	GB	180		N/D	Yams
72	91594	Andromache	1770	GB	162	Rice, Beans, Stockfish	8.49	N/D

Total kcal taken on board in Africa (millions)	Major region of slave embarkation	Average no. of days on board at African Coast (TAC)	Average no. of days on board during Middle Passage (MP) + 1 st. dev.	No. daily rations required	% share European provisions of total required (kcal)
9	10	11	12	13	14
161.73	Bight of Benin	113	128	102.582	1.8
184.20	Gold Coast	117	112	109.973	N/D
103.72	Gold Coast	117	112	55.754	36.4
N/D	Windward Coast	232	103	66.576	6.5
N/D	Senegambia	90	94	10.703	92.9
N/D	Bight of Benin	155	103	50.54	20.1
N/D	Bight of Biafra	155	103	69.132	17.6
N/D	Bight of Biafra	155	103	30.505	16.2
N/D	Windward Coast	232	103	32.412	22.4
N/D	Bight of Benin	155	103	58.843	28.5
3669.87	Bight of Biafra	155	103	32.49	N/D
N/D	Bight of Biafra	155	103	29.241	14.5

APPENDIX 2.2a Summary statistics of the sample of 187 voyages (*cont.*)

No	Voyage no. TSTD	Name vessel	Year arrived	Nation	No. of slaves embarked	Main provisions	Total kcal taken on board in Europe (millions)	Main African provisions
0	1	2	3	4	5	6	7	8
73	91221	Dalrymple	1770	GB	342	Rice, Beans, Stockfish	33.60	N/D
74	91573	Hector	1770	GB	260	Rice, Beans, Stockfish	30.48	N/D
75	91409	King of Prussia	1770	GB	164	Rice, Peas, Beans, Stockfish	16.68	N/D
76	91653	Swift	1770	GB	167	Beans, Rice, Stockfish, Pease	22.02	N/D
77	91545	Dobson	1770	GB	355		N/D	Yams
78	91595	Andromache	1771	GB	190	Rice, Beans, Stockfish	11.98	N/D
79	91743	May	1771	GB	176	Rice	15.78	N/D
80	91430	Plumper	1771	GB	348	Beans, Barley, Stockfish	20.50	N/D
81	91643	True Blue	1771	GB	365	Beans, Barley, Rice	19.69	N/D
82	91752	Dalrymple	1772	GB	243	Rice, Beans, Stockfish	28.82	N/D

Total kcal taken on board in Africa (millions)	Major region of slave embarkation	Average no. of days on board at African Coast (TAC)	Average no. of days on board during Middle Passage (MP) + 1 st. dev.	No. daily rations required	% share European provisions of total required (kcal)
9	10	11	12	13	14
N/D	Bight of Biafra	155	103	61.731	27.2
N/D	Bight of Biafra	155	103	46.93	32.5
N/D	Bight of Biafra	155	103	29.602	28.2
N/D	Bight of Biafra	155	103	30.144	36.5
3669.87	Bight of Biafra	155	103	64.078	N/D
N/D	Bight of Biafra	155	103	34.295	17.5
N/D	Bight of Biafra	155	103	31.768	24.8
N/D	Bight of Biafra	155	103	62.814	16.3
N/D	Bight of Benin	155	103	65.883	14.9
N/D	Bight of Biafra	155	103	43.862	32.8

APPENDIX 2.2a Summary statistics of the sample of 187 voyages (*cont.*)

No	Voyage no. TSTD	Name vessel	Year arrived	Nation	No. of slaves embarked	Main provisions	Total kcal taken on board in Europe (millions)	Main African provisions
0	1	2	3	4	5	6	7	8
83	91574	Hector	1772	GB	250	Rice, Beans, Stockfish	26.78	N/D
84	91410	King of Prussia	1772	GB	239	Rice, Peas, Beans, Stockfish	18.49	N/D
85	91979	Andromache	1774	GB	210	Rice, Beans, Stockfish	16.05	N/D
86	91813	Badger	1774	GB	243	Rice, Peas	15.24	N/D
87	91814	Badger	1775	GB	238	Peas, Beans, Rice	19.14	N/D
88	91575	Hector	1775	GB	141	Rice, Beans, Stockfish	27.49	N/D
89	92536	Badger	1777	GB	421	Peas, Beans, Stockfish	25.69	N/D
90	91576	Hector	1777	GB	236	Rice, Stockfish, Peas	20.22	N/D
91	91794	Swift	1777	GB	211	Beans, Stockfish, Pease	7.01	N/D
92	83174	Preston	1780	GB	210	Stockfish, Pease	1.72	N/D

Total kcal taken on board in Africa (millions)	Major region of slave embarkation	Average no. of days on board at African Coast (TAC)	Average no. of days on board during Middle Passage (MP) + 1 st. dev.	No. daily rations required	% share European provisions of total required (kcal)
9	10	11	12	13	14
N/D	Bight of Biafra	155	103	45.125	29.7
N/D	Bight of Biafra	155	103	43.14	21.4
N/D	Bight of Biafra	155	103	37.905	21.2
N/D	Bight of Biafra	155	103	43.862	17.4
N/D	Bight of Biafra	155	103	42.959	22.3
N/D	Bight of Biafra	155	103	25.451	54.0
N/D	Bight of Biafra	155	103	75.991	16.9
N/D	Bight of Biafra	155	103	42.598	23.7
N/D	Bight of Biafra	155	103	38.086	9.2
N/D	Bight of Biafra	155	103	37.905	2.3

APPENDIX 2.2a Summary statistics of the sample of 187 voyages (*cont.*)

No	Voyage no. TSTD	Name vessel	Year arrived	Nation	No. of slaves embarked	Main provisions	Total kcal taken on board in Europe (millions)	Main African provisions
0	1	2	3	4	5	6	7	8
93	83175	Preston	1782	GB	221	Beans, Pease	0.81	N/D
94	83176	Preston	1784	GB	302	Barley, Rice, Pease	1.80	N/D
95	17983	Alert	1789	GB	276	Beans, Rice	12.28	N/D
96	80687	Brothers	1789	GB	455		N/D	Yams
97	18057	Thomas	1790	GB	359	Beans	10.16	N/D
98	18068	Eliza	1790	GB	291	Beans	16.93	N/D
99	18080	Prince	1790	GB	396	Beans, Rice	14.68	N/D
100	18088	Wasp	1790	GB	249	Beans, Rice	19.70	N/D
101	18071	Hector	1791	GB	764	Beans	33.86	N/D
102	18112	Pilgrim	1791	GB	381	Beans, Rice	25.74	N/D
103	18077	Mermaid	1791	GB	140	Beans, Rice	35.68	N/D
104	18082	Royal Charlotte	1791	GB	140	Beans	14.90	N/D
105	18060	Albion	1791	GB	262	Beans	2.12	N/D
106	18092	Brothers	1791	GB	279	Beans, Rice	78.76	N/D

Total kcal taken on board in Africa (millions)	Major region of slave embarkation	Average no. of days on board at African Coast (TAC)	Average no. of days on board during Middle Passage (MP) + 1 st. dev.	No. daily rations required	% share European provisions of total required (kcal)
9	10	11	12	13	14
N/D	Bight of Biafra	103	98	33.04	1.2
N/D	Bight of Biafra	103	98	45.149	2.0
N/D	Gold Coast	147	95	46.506	13.2
146.03	Bight of Biafra	103	98	68.023	N/D
N/D	Bight of Biafra	103	98	53.671	9.5
N/D	Bight of Biafra	103	98	43.505	19.5
N/D	Bight of Biafra	103	98	59.202	12.4
N/D	Bight of Biafra	103	98	37.226	26.5
N/D	Bight of Biafra	103	98	114.218	14.8
N/D	Bight of Biafra	103	98	56.96	22.6
N/D	Gold Coast	147	95	23.59	75.6
N/D	Bight of Biafra	103	98	20.93	35.6
N/D	Sierra Leone	192	57	40.086	2.6
N/D	Bight of Biafra	103	98	41.711	94.4

APPENDIX 2.2a Summary statistics of the sample of 187 voyages (*cont.*)

No	Voyage no. TSTD	Name vessel	Year arrived	Nation	No. of slaves embarked	Main provisions	Total kcal taken on board in Europe (millions)	Main African provisions
0	1	2	3	4	5	6	7	8
107	18083	Royal Charlotte	1791	GB	336	Rice	8.81	N/D
108	18062	Alfred	1791	GB	316	Beans, Rice	16.49	N/D
109	18103	James	1791	GB	176	Beans, Rice	25.57	N/D
110	18075	King George	1791	GB	369	Beans, Rice	10.93	N/D
111	18097	Eliza	1791	GB	291	Beans, Rice	57.47	N/D
112	18096	Daniel	1791	GB	146	Beans, Rice	8.47	N/D
113	18117	Rodney	1791	GB	371	Beans, Rice	34.51	N/D
114	18120	Sarah	1791	GB	231	Beans, Rice	24.96	N/D
115	18078	Pearl	1791	GB	372	Beans, Rice	N/D	N/D
116	18115	Recovery	1791	GB	304	Beans, Rice	49.10	N/D
117	18158	Pilgrim	1792	GB	412	Beans, Rice	19.70	N/D
118	18142	General Orde	1792	GB	240	Beans	135.46	N/D
119	18101	Hester	1792	GB	243	Beans, Rice	33.31	N/D
120	18104	Lion	1792	GB	328	Beans	1.27	N/D

Total kcal taken on board in Africa (millions)	Major region of slave embarkation	Average no. of days on board at African Coast (TAC)	Average no. of days on board during Middle Passage (MP) + 1 st. dev.	No. daily rations required	% share European provisions of total required (kcal)
9	10	11	12	13	14
N/D	Bight of Biafra	103	98	50.232	8.8
N/D	Bight of Biafra	103	98	47.242	17.5
N/D	Windward Coast	211	68	30.536	41.9
N/D	Bight of Biafra	103	98	55.166	9.9
N/D	Bight of Biafra	103	98	43.505	66.0
N/D	Bight of Biafra	103	98	21.827	19.4
N/D	Bight of Biafra	103	98	55.465	31.1
N/D	Bight of Biafra	103	98	34.535	36.1
N/D	Bight of Biafra	103	98	55.614	N/D
N/D	Bight of Biafra	103	98	45.448	54.0
N/D	Bight of Biafra	103	98	61.594	16.0
N/D	Bight of Biafra	103	98	35.88	188.8
N/D	Bight of Biafra	103	98	36.329	45.8
N/D	Bight of Biafra	103	98	49.036	1.3

APPENDIX 2.2a Summary statistics of the sample of 187 voyages (*cont.*)

No	Voyage no. TSTD	Name vessel	Year arrived	Nation	No. of slaves embarked	Main provisions	Total kcal taken on board in Europe (millions)	Main African provisions
0	1	2	3	4	5	6	7	8
121	18131	Alfred	1792	GB	326	Beans, Rice	23.95	N/D
122	18113	Prince	1792	GB	359	Rice	17.62	N/D
123	18152	Mermaid	1792	GB	159	Beans, Rice	10.08	N/D
124	18153	Morning Star	1792	GB	56	Beans, Rice	9.62	N/D
125	18122	Swift	1792	GB	380	Beans, Rice	1.06	N/D
126	18138	Fame	1792	GB	200	Beans, Rice	79.99	N/D
127	18124	Trelawney	1792	GB	333	Beans, Rice	6.60	N/D
128	18113	Prince	1792	GB	359	Beans, Rice	18.63	N/D
129	18126	Wasp	1792	GB	235	Beans, Rice	16.93	N/D
130	18144	Hector	1793	GB	596	Beans	50.80	N/D
131	18140	Favourite	1793	GB	156	Beans, Rice	26.48	N/D
132	18182	Langrishe	1793	GB	416	Beans, Rice	21.51	N/D
133	18186	Royal Charlotte	1793	GB	210		74.50	N/D
134	18130	Albion	1793	GB	239	Beans	1.18	N/D

Total kcal taken on board in Africa (millions)	Major region of slave embarkation	Average no. of days on board at African Coast (TAC)	Average no. of days on board during Middle Passage (MP) + 1 st. dev.	No. daily rations required	% share European provisions of total required (kcal)
9	10	11	12	13	14
N/D	Bight of Biafra	103	98	48.737	24.6
N/D	Bight of Biafra	103	98	53.671	16.4
N/D	Senegambia	79	71	17.57	28.7
N/D	Sierra Leone	192	57	8.568	56.1
N/D	Bight of Biafra	103	98	56.81	0.9
N/D	Bight of Biafra	103	98	29.9	133.8
N/D	Bight of Biafra	103	98	49.784	6.6
N/D	Bight of Biafra	103	98	53.671	17.4
N/D	Bight of Biafra	103	98	35.133	24.1
N/D	Bight of Biafra	103	98	89.102	28.5
N/D	Bight of Biafra	103	98	23.322	56.8
N/D	Bight of Biafra	103	98	62.192	17.3
N/D	Windward Coast	211	68	36.435	102.2
N/D	Sierra Leone	192	57	36.567	1.6

APPENDIX 2.2a Summary statistics of the sample of 187 voyages (*cont.*)

No	Voyage no. TSTD	Name vessel	Year arrived	Nation	No. of slaves embarked	Main provisions	Total kcal taken on board in Europe (millions)	Main African provisions
0	1	2	3	4	5	6	7	8
135	18177	Catherine	1793	GB	345	Beans, Rice	41.21	N/D
136	18156	Nassau	1793	GB	190	Beans, Rice	17.54	N/D
137	18163	Roman Emperor	1793	GB	382	Rice	34.51	N/D
138	18146	Jupiter	1793	GB	400	Beans, Rice	27.95	N/D
139	18157	Pearl	1793	GB	400	Beans, Rice	34.51	N/D
140	18159	Prince	1793	GB	311	Beans, Rice	37.32	N/D
141	18214	Pilgrim	1796	GB	404	Beans	16.93	N/D
142	18259	Swift	1803	GB	389	Beans	37.25	N/D
143	18267	Alert	1806	GB	277	Beans, Rice	27.72	N/D
144	82379	Lottery	1798	GB	460	Beans, Rice	48.40	N/D
145	82382	Lottery	1802	GB	305	Beans, Rice	32.39	N/D
146	81302	Enterprize	1804	GB	412	Beans, Rice	44.96	N/D
147	81497	Fortune	1805	GB	343	Beans, Rice	75.95	N/D
148	10212	Leusden	1721	NL	446	Beans, Barley	196.86	N/D

Total kcal taken on board in Africa (millions)	Major region of slave embarkation	Average no. of days on board at African Coast (TAC)	Average no. of days on board during Middle Passage (MP) + 1 st. dev.	No. daily rations required	% share European provisions of total required (kcal)
9	10	11	12	13	14
N/D	Bight of Biafra	103	98	51.578	39.9
N/D	Sierra Leone	192	57	29.07	30.2
N/D	Bight of Biafra	103	98	57.109	30.2
N/D	Bight of Biafra	103	98	59.8	23.4
N/D	Bight of Biafra	103	98	59.8	28.9
N/D	Bight of Biafra	103	98	46.495	40.1
N/D	Sierra Leone	192	57	61.812	13.7
N/D	Gold Coast	147	95	65.547	28.4
N/D	Sierra Leone	192	57	42.381	32.7
N/D	Bight of Biafra	103	157	95.91	25.2
N/D	Bight of Biafra	103	193	74.573	21.7
N/D	Bight of Biafra	103	173	92.494	24.3
N/D	West Central Africa North	139	240	106.159	35.8
N/D	West Central Africa North	139	83	68.015	144.7

APPENDIX 2.2a Summary statistics of the sample of 187 voyages (*cont.*)

No	Voyage no. TSTD	Name vessel	Year arrived	Nation	No. of slaves embarked	Main provisions	Total kcal taken on board in Europe (millions)	Main African provisions
0	1	2	3	4	5	6	7	8
149	10213	Leusden	1722	NL	461	Beans, Barley	150.90	N/D
150	?	Francis	1723	GB	200	Beans	2.54	Corn, Palm Oil
151	10976	Raadhuis van Middelburg	1742	NL	272	Beans, Barley	61.47	N/D
152	10626	Groot Prooijen	1748	NL	328	Beans, Barley	78.68	N/D
153	10620	Granadier	1749	NL	270	Beans, Barley	114.74	N/D
154	10957	Prins Willem de Vijfde	1754	NL	232	Beans, Barley	87.75	N/D
155	10869	Middelburgs Welvaren	1754	NL	270	Beans, Barley	90.95	Corn, Rice
156	10870	Middelburgs Welvaren	1755	NL	289	Beans, Barley	48.25	Corn, Rice, Palm Oil, Yam
157	10527	Drie Gezusters	1756	NL	234	Beans, Barley	91.95	N/D
158	10958	Prins Willem de Vijfde	1756	NL	348	Beans, Barley	123.76	N/D
159	11114	Vrouw Johanna Cores	1757	NL	282	Beans, Barley	89.95	Rice
160	11088	Vliegende Faam	1757	NL	281	Beans, Barley	67.37	Corn, Millet

Total kcal taken on board in Africa (millions)	Major region of slave embarkation	Average no. of days on board at African Coast (TAC)	Average no. of days on board during Middle Passage (MP) + 1 st. dev.	No. daily rations required	% share European provisions of total required (kcal)
9	10	11	12	13	14
N/D	Bight of Benin	113	128	85.055	88.7
83.71	Gold Coast	117	112	34.1	3.7
N/D	Windward + Ivory + Gold + **Benin**	152	154	62.56	49.1
N/D	West Central Africa North	179	65	50.676	77.6
N/D	West Central Africa North	179	65	41.715	137.5
N/D	Gold Coast	134	150	50.344	87.2
126.20	Windward + Ivory + Gold + **Benin**	152	154	62.1	73.2
337.61	Windward Coast	172	93	51.731	46.6
N/D	Gold Coast	134	150	50.778	90.5
N/D	West Central Africa North	179	65	53.766	115.1
5.07	Windward + Ivory + Gold + **Benin**	152	154	64.86	69.3
273.81	Windward + Ivory + Gold + **Benin**	152	154	64.63	52.1

APPENDIX 2.2a Summary statistics of the sample of 187 voyages (*cont.*)

No	Voyage no. TSTD	Name vessel	Year arrived	Nation	No. of slaves embarked	Main provisions	Total kcal taken on board in Europe (millions)	Main African provisions
0	1	2	3	4	5	6	7	8
161	10528	Drie Gezusters	1758	NL	405	Beans, Barley	97.12	N/D
162	10959	Prins Willem de Vijfde	1758	NL	465	Beans, Barley	98.35	N/D
163	10965	Prins Willem de Vijfde	1758	NL	377	Beans, Barley	123.76	N/D
164	11116	Vrouw Johanna Cores	1761	NL	381	Beans, Barley	81.96	N/D
165	10906	Nieuwe Hoop	1765	NL	351	Beans, Barley	115.56	N/D
166	10963	Prins Willem de Vijfde	1766	NL	238	Beans, Barley	84.78	Corn
167	10907	Nieuwe Hoop	1767	NL	329	Beans, Barley	100.70	Rice, Palm Oil
168	10544	Enigheid	1767	NL	315	Beans, Barley	111.47	N/D
169	11119	Vrouw Johanna Cores	1768	NL	249	Beans, Barley	102.50	N/D
170	11178	Zanggodin	1770	NL	67	Beans, Barley	36.31	N/D
171	11125	Watergeus	1774	NL	375	Beans, Barley	179.90	N/D
172	11134	Welmenende	1774	NL	203	Beans, Barley	59.27	N/D

Total kcal taken on board in Africa (millions)	Major region of slave embarkation	Average no. of days on board at African Coast (TAC)	Average no. of days on board during Middle Passage (MP) + 1 st. dev.	No. daily rations required	% share European provisions of total required (kcal)
9	10	11	12	13	14
N/D	West Central Africa North	179	65	62.573	77.6
N/D	West Central Africa North	179	65	71.843	68.4
N/D	West Central Africa North	179	65	58.247	106.2
N/D	West Central Africa North	168	83	63.627	64.4
N/D	West Central Africa North	168	83	58.617	98.6
3.59	Gold Coast	130	117	43.316	97.9
5.82	Gold Coast	130	117	59.878	84.1
N/D	West Central Africa North	168	83	52.605	105.9
N/D	Windward + Ivory + Gold + **Benin**	191	132	56.648	90.5
N/D	Bight of Biafra	155	103	12.094	150.1
N/D	West Central Africa North	168	83	62.625	143.6
N/D	Windward + Ivory + Gold + **Benin**	191	132	46.183	64.2

APPENDIX 2.2a Summary statistics of the sample of 187 voyages (*cont.*)

No	Voyage no. TSTD	Name vessel	Year arrived	Nation	No. of slaves embarked	Main provisions	Total kcal taken on board in Europe (millions)	Main African provisions
0	1	2	3	4	5	6	7	8
173	10787	Jonge Willem	1775	NL	163	Beans, Barley	71.66	N/D
174	11085	Vis	1775	NL	238	Beans, Barley	103.40	N/D
175	10590	Geertruida en Christina	1775	NL	335	Beans, Barley	109.10	Millet
176	11180	Zanggodin	1775	NL	127	Beans, Barley	58.61	N/D
177	10591	Geertruida en Christina	1777	NL	303	Beans, Barley	103.90	N/D
178	11126	Watergeus	1777	NL	325	Beans, Barley	179.90	N/D
179	11210	Zorg	1778	NL	246	Beans, Barley	76.86	Rice
180	10666	Haast U Langzaam	1780	NL	373	Beans, Barley	101.30	Corn, Rice, Palm Oil
181	10913	Nieuwe Hoop	1785	NL	215	Beans, Barley	101.30	N/D
182	11056	Vergenoegen	1787	NL	386	Beans, Barley	108.75	Corn, Rice
183	11182	Zeemercuur	1789	NL	270	Beans, Barley	118.54	Rice, Palm Oil, Yams
184	11057	Vergenoegen	1790	NL	266	Beans, Barley	131.14	N/D

Total kcal taken on board in Africa (millions)	Major region of slave embarkation	Average no. of days on board at African Coast (TAC)	Average no. of days on board during Middle Passage (MP) + 1 st. dev.	No. daily rations required	% share European provisions of total required (kcal)
9	10	11	12	13	14
N/D	Bight of Biafra	155	103	29.422	121.8
N/D	Windward + Ivory + Gold + Benin	191	132	54.145	95.5
40.04	Windward + Ivory + Gold + Benin	191	132	76.213	71.6
N/D	Bight of Biafra	155	103	22.924	127.8
N/D	Gold Coast	130	117	55.146	94.2
N/D	West Central Africa North	168	83	54.275	165.7
5.07	Gold Coast	130	117	44.772	85.8
31.71	Windward + Ivory + Gold + Benin	191	132	84.858	59.7
N/D	Gold Coast	147	95	36.228	139.8
18.64	Gold Coast	147	95	65.041	83.6
33.30	Gold Coast	147	95	45.495	130.3
N/D	West Central Africa North	168	83	44.422	147.6

APPENDIX 2.2a Summary statistics of the sample of 187 voyages (*cont.*)

No	Voyage no. TSTD	Name vessel	Year arrived	Nation	No. of slaves embarked	Main provisions	Total kcal taken on board in Europe (millions)	Main African provisions
0	1	2	3	4	5	6	7	8
185	10463	Brandenburg	1792	NL	226	Beans, Barley	110.34	N/D
186	11183	Zeemercuur	1793	NL	174	Beans, Barley	119.80	Corn, Rice, Palm oil, Yams
187	11058	Vergenoegen	1795	NL	367	Beans, Barley	131.14	N/D

Source: see pages 43–46

Total kcal taken on board in Africa (millions)	Major region of slave embarkation	Average no. of days on board at African Coast (TAC)	Average no. of days on board during Middle Passage (MP) + 1 st. dev.	No. daily rations required	% share European provisions of total required (kcal)
9	10	11	12	13	14
N/D	Windward + Ivory + Gold + **Benin**	130	96	36.386	151.6
17.80	Windward + Ivory + Gold + **Benin**	130	96	28.014	213.8
N/D	West Central Africa North	168	83	61.289	107.0

APPENDIX 2.2b Summary statistics of 36 'full data' voyages

No	Voyage no. TSTD	Name vessel	Year arrive	Nation	No. of slaves embarked	Main European provisions	Total kcal taken on boa[rd] in Europe (millions)
0	1	2	3	4	5	6	7
1	35161	Cron Printz Christian	1755	DK	125	Beans, Stockfish	27.14
2	35181	Fredensborg	1768	DK	265	Beans, Barley	76.29
3	33330	Diligent	1732	FR	256	Beans	50.8
4	30484	Reine de France	1744	FR	404	Beans, Rice	63.91
5	30754	Thélémaque	1764	FR	365	Beans, Rice	76.67
6	30911	Pompée	1770	FR	390	Beans, Rice	148.01
8	31639	Pactole	1784	FR	428	Beans, Rice	63.91
34	15074	Mary	1683	GB	507	Beans	0.61
36	9669	Jefferie	1685	GB	310	Beans	0.33
37	9668	Good Hope	1685	GB	376	Beans	0.58
40	9714	Hannibal	1694	GB	700	Beans	2.9
42	9726	Fauconberg (a) Falconberg	1696	GB	605	Beans	2.54
45	75956	Otter	1721	GB	209	Beans	0.73
47	76147	Sarah Gally	1721	GB	250	Beans	1.45
48	76399	Henry	1722	GB	367	Beans	1.86
51	76435	Sarah Gally	1723	GB	273	Beans	0.91
54	76693	Lady Rachel	1723	GB	221	Beans	2.18
55	75286	Clarendon	1723	GB	69	Beans	0.63

Main African provisions	Total kcal taken on board in Africa (millions)	Major region of Slave Embarkation	% total provisions from Europe	% total provisions from Africa
8	9	10	11	12
Millet, Palm Oil	7.72	Gold Coast	77.9	22.1
Millet, Palm Oil	25.25	Gold Coast	75.1	24.9
Corn, Cassava	5.25	Bight of Benin	90.6	9.4
Corn, Yams, Cassava	23.37	Bight of Benin	73.2	26.8
Corn, Yams, Cassava	7.23	West Central Africa North	91.4	8.6
Corn, Palm Oil, Yams, Cassava	61.63	West Central Africa North	70.6	29.4
Corn, Rice, Palm Oil, Yams, Cassava, Plantains	75.29	Bight of Benin	45.9	54.1
Corn	179.49	Gold Coast	0.3	99.7
Corn	114.88	Gold Coast	0.3	99.7
Corn	118.47	West Central Africa North	0.5	99.5
Corn	200.32	Gold Coast	1.4	98.6
Corn	280.01	Bight of Benin	0.9	99.1
Corn	32.31	Senegambia	2.2	97.8
Corn, Rice, Palm Oil	85.09	Gold Coast	1.7	98.3
Corn, Rice, Palm Oil	113.27	Bight of Benin	1.6	98.4
Corn, Palm Oil, Yams	70.01	Gold Coast	1.3	98.7
Corn, Rice	24.92	Senegambia	8.0	92.0
Corn, Rice	33.56	West Central Africa North	1.8	98.2

APPENDIX 2.2b Summary statistics of 36 'full data' voyages (*cont.*)

No	Voyage no. TSTD	Name vessel	Year arrive	Nation	No. of slaves embarked	Main European provisions	Total kcal taken on boa[rd] in Europe (millions)
0	1	2	3	4	5	6	7
57	76176	Sloper	1723	GB	282	Beans	2.54
59	76965	Dove	1723	GB	237	Beans	0.85
60	76348	Whidah Frigate	1724	GB	300	Beans	6.77
61	76695	Cape Coast Frigate	1724	GB	205	Beans	2.12
62	75258	Chandos	1724	GB	556	Beans	3.63
64	76617	Portugal	1729	GB	327	Beans	40.64
149	?	Francis	1723	GB	200	Beans	2.54
157	10869	Middelburgs Welvaren	1754	NL	270	Beans, Barley	90.95
158	10870	Middelburgs Welvaren	1755	NL	289	Beans, Barley	48.25
161	11114	Vrouw Johanna Cores	1757	NL	282	Beans, Barley	89.95
162	11088	Vliegende Faam	1757	NL	281	Beans, Barley	67.37
168	10963	Prins Willem de Vijfde	1766	NL	238	Beans, Barley	84.78
169	10907	Nieuwe Hoop	1767	NL	329	Beans, Barley	100.7
177	10590	Geertruida en Christina	1775	NL	335	Beans, Barley	109.1

Main African provisions	Total kcal taken on board in Africa (millions)	Major region of Slave Embarkation	% total provisions from Europe	% total provisions from Africa
8	9	10	11	12
Corn, Palm Oil	69.05	Gold Coast	3.5	96.5
Corn, Rice	43.96	Bight of Benin	1.9	98.1
Corn	35.9	Bight of Benin	15.9	84.1
Corn	42.36	Senegambia	4.8	95.2
Corn, Palm Oil	161.73	Bight of Benin	2.2	97.8
Corn, Rice, Palm Oil, Yams	103.72	Gold Coast	28.2	71.8
Corn, Palm Oil	83.71	Gold Coast	2.9	97.1
Corn, Rice	126.2	Windward + Ivory + Gold + Benin	41.9	58.1
Corn, Rice, Palm Oil, Yam	337.61	Windward Coast	12.5	87.5
Rice	5.07	Windward + Ivory + Gold + Benin	94.7	5.3
Corn, Millet	273.81	Windward + Ivory + Gold + Benin	19.7	80.3
Corn	3.59	Gold Coast	95.9	4.1
Rice, Palm Oil	5.82	Gold Coast	94.5	5.5
Millet	40.04	Windward + Ivory + Gold + Benin	73.2	26.8

APPENDIX 2.2b Summary statistics of 36 'full data' voyages (*cont.*)

No	Voyage no. TSTD	Name vessel	Year arrive	Nation	No. of slaves embarked	Main European provisions	Total kcal taken on boa in Europe (millions)
0	1	2	3	4	5	6	7
181	11210	Zorg	1778	NL	246	Beans, Barley	76.86
182	10666	Haast U Langzaam	1780	NL	373	Beans, Barley	101.3
184	11056	Vergenoegen	1787	NL	386	Beans, Barley	108.75
185	11182	Zeemercuur	1789	NL	270	Beans, Barley	118.54

Source: see page 47

Main African provisions	Total kcal taken on board in Africa (millions)	Major region of Slave Embarkation	% total provisions from Europe	% total provisions from Africa
8	9	10	11	12
Rice	5.07	Gold Coast	93.8	6.2
Corn, Rice, Palm Oil	31.71	Windward + Ivory + Gold + Benin	76.2	23.8
Corn, Rice	18.64	Gold Coast	85.4	14.6
Rice, Palm Oil, Yams	33.3	Gold Coast	78.1	21.9

APPENDIX 2.3 Weights, measures and nutritional contents

Food type	Quantity measure	Kg	Kcal / kg	Protein / kg
Barley	Lb (Br)	0.45	3500	82
Barly	Lb (Middleberg)	0.47	3500	82
Barley	Sack	60.00	3500	82
Barley	Litre	6.20	3500	82
Barley	Last (Muddle,Schepel)	2000.00	3500	82
Beef flesh	Hogshead (Hhd)	228.82	1150	220
Bread White	Hundred Weight (cwt)	50.85	3410	77
Cassava flour	Bushel	0.00	3440	16
Cassava flour	Alquiers	14.00	3440	16
Corn Ears/Cobs	Piece	0.00	2450	20
Fish, dried, salted	Lbs (Br)	0.45	2250	470
Kidney beans, dry	Quarter	12.71	3330	236
Kidney beans, dry	Bushel	0.00	3330	236
Kidney beans, dry	Ton	1016.96	3330	236
Kidney beans, dry	Sack	60.00	3330	236
Kidney beans, dry	Last (Muddle,Schepel)	2133.80	3330	236
Maize flour, whole	Lb (Br)	0.45	3530	93
Maize flour, whole	English Chest	101.70	3530	93
Maize flour, whole	Dutch Chest	104.83	3530	93
Maize flour, whole	Stekan	1.77	3530	93
Millet, bulrush	Stekan	1.77	3410	104
Millet, bulrush	Chest	104.83	3410	104
Palm oil	Litres	1.00	8840	0
Palm Oil	Gallon	3.50	8840	0
Palm Oil	Aume	0.00	8840	0
Palm Oil	Anker	0.00	8850	10
Pigeon peas, dry	Lb (Br)	0.45	3430	217
Rice Polished	Lb (Br)	0.45	3610	65

Food type	Quantity measure	Kg	Kcal / kg	Protein / kg
Rice polished	Lb (Middleberg)	0.47	3610	65
Rice polished	Alquiers	14.00	3610	65
Rice polished	Barrels	81.72	3620	75
Wheat, whole	Hundred weight (cwt)	50.85	3230	126
Wheat, whole	Hundred weight (cwt)	50.85	3230	126
Yam	Piece	7.50	1180	15
Plantain	Piece	0.30	1350	12

APPENDIX 2.4 Average time spent on board of a slave vessel per region of embarkation, 1681–1807, 20-year time intervals

	Senegambia TAC				Senegambia MP				Senegambia Total Mean
Decades	**Mean**	**Median**	**S.D**	**N**	**Mean**	**Median**	**S.D.**	**N**	**TAC + MP**
1680–1700	**91**	80	41	13	**42**	36	19	31	**133**
1701–1720	**60**	61	24	12	**47**	43	15	28	**106**
1721–1740	**132**	104	83	69	**52**	42	48	70	**184**
1741–1760	**116**	83	85	80	**47**	43	20	65	**163**
1761–1780	**90**	62	81	58	**53**	42	41	71	**143**
1781–1800	**79**	63	55	91	**45**	38	26	117	**124**

	Sierra Leone TAC				Sierra Leone MP				Sierra Leone Total Mean
Decades	**Mean**	**Median**	**S.D**	**N**	**Mean**	**Median**	**S.D.**	**N**	**TAC + MP**
1680–1799	**160**	155	65	4	**56**	48	21	10	**216**
1701–1720	**49**	49	33	2	**65**	56	26	4	**114**
1721–1740	**137**	117	30	3	**56**	56	19	5	**193**
1741–1760	**186**	141	133	17	**60**	52	24	15	**246**
1760–1780	**244**	227	168	15	**55**	54	18	25	**298**
1781–1800	**192**	168	116	54	**44**	43	13	76	**235**

APPENDIX 2.4 Average time spent on board a slave vessel per region of embarkation, 1681–1807, 20-year time intervals (*cont.*)

	Windward Coast TAC				Windward Coast MP				Windward Coast Total Mean
Decades	**Mean**	**Median**	**S.D**	**N**	**Mean**	**Median**	**S.D**	**N**	**TAC + MP**
1680–1700	**ND**	ND	ND	ND	**ND**	ND	ND	ND	**ND**
1701–1720	**29**	29	23	2	**60**	59	17	4	**88**
1721–1740	**55**	55	8	2	**80**	80	34	2	**135**
1741–1760	**172**	173	55	23	**70**	61	23	22	**242**
1761–1780	**232**	204	95	20	**74**	62	29	21	**306**
1781–1800	**211**	161	142	38	**52**	50	16	46	**263**

	Gold Coast TAC				Gold Coast MP				Gold Coast Total Mean
Decades	**Mean**	**Median**	**S.D**	**N**	**Mean**	**Median**	**S.D**	**N**	**TAC + MP**
1680–1700	**107**	95	76	8	**78**	73	22	15	**184**
1701–1720	**133**	87	154	63	**68**	63	20	119	**201**
1721–1740	**117**	105	85	110	**82**	75	30	90	**199**
1741–1760	**134**	120	91	86	**94**	85	56	104	**229**
1761–1780	**130**	111	76	156	**84**	77	33	151	**214**
1781–1800	**147**	124	109	204	**68**	63	27	240	**215**

	Bight of Benin TAC				Bight of Benin MP				Bight of Benin Total Mean
Decades	**Mean**	**Median**	**S.D**	**N**	**Mean**	**Median**	**S.D**	**N**	**TAC + MP**
1680–1700	**73**	53	61	41	**91**	87	26	70	**164**
1701–1720	**96**	85	85	137	**85**	76	39	175	**182**
1721–1740	**113**	99	58	184	**97**	94	31	196	**210**
1741–1760	**152**	137	74	120	**117**	112	37	126	**269**
1761–1780	**191**	177	88	168	**100**	99	32	149	**291**
1781–1800	**130**	117	72	96	**64**	52	32	244	**194**

	Bight of Biafra TAC				Bight of Biafra MP				Bight of Biafra Total Mean
Decades	Mean	Median	S.D	N	Mean	Median	S.D	N	TAC + MP
1680–1700	ND	ND	ND	ND	93	85	28	16	ND
1701–1720	ND	ND	ND	ND	91	83	32	23	ND
1721–1740	72	72	0	1	127	94	80	3	199
1741–1760	118	128	63	17	86	82	24	19	203
1761–1780	155	127	114	42	78	78	25	57	234
1781–1800	103	91	76	195	66	60	32	243	169

	West Central Africa TAC				West Central Africa MP				West Central Africa Total Mean
Decades	Mean	Median	S.D	N	Mean	Median	S.D	N	TAC + MP
1680–1700	78	56	58	5	84	83	35	6	162
1701–1720	115	137	55	17	58	59	17	17	174
1721–1740	139	131	82	103	58	51	25	81	197
1741–1760	179	152	109	240	49	49	16	85	228
1761–1780	163	156	90	401	58	56	25	259	222
1781–1800	139	133	71	361	53	50	17	488	192

Source: Slavevoyages.org

APPENDIX 2.5 Price index of staple food basket (barley, beans, rice) on English and Dutch markets, 1681–1800 (1701 = 100)

Year	Britain	NL	Year	Britain	NL	Year	Britain	NL
1681	103.9		1721	93.1		1761	81.2	
1682	111.5		1722	85.4	75.2	1762	76.6	
1683	104.2		1723	87.4		1763	96.1	
1684	106.6		1724	96.7		1764	93.6	
1685	119.5		1725	93.9		1765	92.4	
1686	108.2	86.4	1726	94.3		1766	96.1	
1687	73.0		1727	95.8		1767	96.1	
1688	70.1	86.2	1728	108.1	85.1	1768	91.9	
1689	81.1	94.9	1729	101.9		1769	73.7	
1690	79.8		1730	91.3		1770	74.7	
1691	79.1		1731	91.6	73.0	1771	87.6	
1692	86.5	112.0	1732	89.4		1772	95.8	
1693	101.7		1733	87.6		1773	98.6	
1694	99.6		1734	87.5		1774	96.7	
1695	99.2		1735	88.1		1775	92.3	
1696	122.9		1736	89.5		1776	91.5	112.4
1697	123.9		1737	97.4		1777	83.1	104.0
1698	127.2		1738	92.1	83.2	1778	91.0	111.6
1699	119.1		1739	95.4	82.9	1779	91.8	133.0
1700	108.2		1740	102.8		1780	120.9	129.6
1701	100.0	100.0	1741	98.5		1781	109.5	137.8
1702	101.9		1742	101.5		1782	112.5	124.8
1703	99.3		1743	93.8		1783	131.6	
1704	99.1		1744	88.4		1784	116.0	139.2
1705	87.9	103.5	1745	87.9		1785	109.0	119.5
1706	92.5		1746	81.8		1786	105.9	
1707	92.9		1747	87.2		1787	101.4	122.3

Year	Britain	NL	Year	Britain	NL	Year	Britain	NL
1708	96.9		1748	92.1		1788	96.5	116.3
1709	100.9		1749	96.1		1789	95.3	114.8
1710	108.0		1750	93.3		1790	102.1	
1711	107.0		1751	96.2		1791	103.1	
1712	100.8		1752	96.4		1792	108.5	
1713	97.3		1753	94.6		1793	117.0	
1714	97.3		1754	87.5		1794	119.1	
1715	98.0		1755	81.0		1795	140.3	
1716	92.2		1756	80.0		1796	134.6	
1717	89.5		1757	106.6		1797	104.7	
1718	87.2	100.2	1758	96.0		1798	103.4	
1719	92.4		1759	84.1		1799	125.7	
1720	100.3		1760	83.1	104.1	1800	191.3	

Source: see Clark (2006) and Posthumus (1946) and page 57

APPENDIX 2.6 Estimates of the five-year average annual value of African-sourced provisions in the Atlantic slave trade, 1681–1807 (all estimates in constant British Pound sterling of 1700, new world provisions at 20%)

	Slaves purchased (fob Europe/ Americas)	Slave provisions (fob Europe/ Americas)	African-sourced slave provisions (fob Europe/ Americas)	African-sourced provisions (cif) (our estimates)	African-sourced provisions (Eltis)
	1	2	3	4	5
1681–1685	1,07,587	21,517	16,000	32,480	55,407
1686–1690	86,610	17,322	12,043	24,447	44,604
1691–1695	1,10,731	22,146	15,097	30,647	57,026
1696–1700	2,02,723	40,545	31,710	64,371	1,04,402
1701–1705	1,96,478	41,986	32,789	66,562	1,01,186
1706–1710	1,96,241	37,383	28,665	58,191	1,01,064
1711–1715	2,48,689	59,579	45,936	93,250	1,28,075
1716–1720	3,61,423	78,978	62,297	1,26,464	1,86,133
1721–1725	5,12,750	87,627	67,742	1,37,516	2,64,066
1726–1730	3,92,838	68,864	54,658	1,10,955	2,02,312
1731–1735	2,62,800	60,350	47,170	95,754	1,35,342
1736–1740	3,85,436	87,318	67,764	1,37,561	1,98,500
1741–1745	4,05,049	78,565	49,726	1,00,943	2,08,600
1746–1750	4,49,280	67,117	47,714	96,859	2,31,379
1751–1755	5,37,147	84,801	54,153	1,09,930	2,76,631
1756–1760	3,96,019	61,509	44,798	90,940	2,03,950
1761–1765	7,96,786	84,934	57,943	1,17,624	4,10,345
1766–1770	12,46,728	96,768	59,459	1,20,702	6,42,065
1771–1775	15,03,464	1,05,134	64,839	1,31,622	7,74,284
1776–1780	6,98,969	56,824	31,983	64,926	3,59,969
1781–1785	13,17,247	1,13,308	68,133	1,38,310	6,78,382

	Slaves purchased (fob Europe/ Americas)	Slave provisions (fob Europe/ Americas)	African-sourced slave provisions (fob Europe/ Americas)	African-sourced provisions (cif) (our estimates)	African-sourced provisions (Eltis)
	1	2	3	4	5
1786–1790	23,81,871	1,46,573	73,085	1,48,363	12,26,664
1791–1795	17,17,428	1,26,445	78,975	1,60,319	8,84,475
1796–1800	18,12,184	1,07,428	74,118	1,50,459	9,33,275
1801–1807	21,65,957	1,08,298	75,091	1,52,435	11,15,468
1681–1807	7,62,158	76,318	51,832	1,05,220	4,21,430

Source: see pages 43–44

CHAPTER 3

The Transatlantic Slave and Commodity Trades in the Second Half of the Eighteenth Century

> ...Africa had two sorts of commodities to offer us – her natural productions – and her slaves...
>
> THOMAS CLARKSON, 1789, p. 26

In the decades prior to the abolition of the British slave trade in 1807, those campaigning for an end to the traffic in Africans to the Americas made regular mention of the potential for trade in commodities (Clarkson, 1789, pp. 10–26; Equiano, 1794, pp. 356–358). Their assumption was that the trade in slaves effectively crowded out other forms of commercial exchange but that if both British and African merchants could be persuaded to switch to trade in commodities then this would economically benefit both parties. The analysis of abolitionists does not consider the fact that, as argued earlier, commodities had been an integral part of trade with Africa since the fifteenth century. The earlier period of commercial exchange is generally viewed as having a positive impact on economic growth in West Africa. For example, gold paid for both coerced labour and European iron into the Gold Coast region (present day Ghana) which greatly accelerated the process of forest clearance in that region. When combined with the introduction of meso-American crops such as maize, this led to an expansion of both population and economic activity (Evans & Ryden 2018, Wilks 1993).

However, after the 1630s the near continuous rise in the demand for slaves led, according to the analysis of Joseph Inikori, to the retarding of market development through two main mechanisms. Firstly, cloth and firearms replaced currency items as the principal forms of exchange with the Atlantic world, effectively limiting the capacity for regional exchange. Secondly, a growing regional exchange in products such as salt, copper, kola and locally made cloth was replaced by a rise in the violent capture of people. This growth undermined the development of regional specialisation and production for the market from the late seventeenth to the mid nineteenth century (Inikori 2002,

 DOI:10.1163/9789004417120_005

2008, p. 83, 86; 2011, pp. 651, 652). Inikori's arguments build on the work of earlier Marxist scholars, in particular Walter Rodney (1972, pp. 92–103, 110–112) who had also argued that in certain areas of West Africa the slave trade led to the loss of large numbers of people who could otherwise have engaged in production, thus undermining regional trade.

Inokori's conclusions have been critiqued from various angles. For instance, his observations regarding the decline of imports of goods used in Africa as currency items might well have been a rational response to inflationary pressures. There is evidence, for example, that there was a reduction in the quantity of imports of cowry shells in regions such as Dahomey, which used them for many types of economic exchange from around the mid eighteenth century. However, this decline might just have reflected a sufficiency of cowry shells in circulation and any further imports would have devalued existing supplies (Austin 2013a, 255/256, Law 1992). Green (2016) has taken this as evidence that Africa's economic development, vis-à-vis the rest of the world, was retarded as its currencies were devalued at the same time as its productivity was unable to develop due to the expansion of the slave trade.

Particularly relevant to this discussion are the contributions to a recent volume on the development of commercial agriculture in West Africa, which also questions Inikori's conclusions regarding the crowding out of other forms of market activities (Law, Schwarz, & Strickrodt, 2013). Law et al. (2013, p. 9) suggest that the evidence presented by Inikori does not support his conclusions regarding the eighteenth century as the commodities trade itself – while always much smaller than the trade in captives – did grow until at least the 1760s, and that declines in the output of some commodities such as gold were offset by an increase in other products such as palm oil and dyewoods. Law et al.'s conclusions are based on the calculations by David Eltis (2013) who estimates that, while the value of the trade in non-slave goods as a proportion of the total trade fell from a high of forty percent at the beginning of the century, it nonetheless remained significant. Even at the end of the eighteenth century, non-slave products made up around ten percent of the total value of a much larger African trade, which meant that the nominal value of these commodities grew by nearly fifty percent. Eltis' figures are based on the assumed value of goods taken back from Africa each year on both slave and specialist bilateral traders who only bought commodities. These estimates rest on figures from the accounts of the British Royal Africa Company at the end of the seventeenth century and other archival sources but, ultimately, they are best guess assumptions of the value of the commodity trade. Furthermore, Eltis' data gives no indication of regional or temporal differences, relying only on data for the total value of West Africa's commodity trade.

Other than Eltis' estimates, the only data that exists are the statistics on British trade compiled by Johnson, Lindblad and Ross (1990) and based on the custom ledgers held at the National Archives in London. The customs records contain the total recorded imports, exports and re-exports at Britain's principal-port prices from 1699. As a source, they are the most complete record of imports from Africa for that nation which, as will be argued below, bought the most commodities. Unfortunately, the customs ledgers are not the ideal source as they cannot account for smuggling, clerical errors, tax evasion and the fact that many ships bought and sold goods in other European countries (Johnson et al. 1990, p. 8). They also do not provide any records of imports of West African gold, which is a significant omission; as until the late seventeenth century, gold was, by value, the most important commodity sold on the coast (Eltis 1994). Lastly, the customs records in the eighteenth century only give Britain's aggregate trade with Africa and do not show the regional origins of imported products.

Marion Johnson was the first to attempt to input the customs data relying on 1980s technology, which involved inputting individual data points on punch cards (1984, 1990). Johnson et al. (1990), in contrast to Eltis (2013), show that the official value of the overall commodity trade grew by almost two hundred percent between 1737 and 1807. While the collection of Johnson's dataset was undeniably an impressive achievement for the time, the availability of modern spreadsheets has meant that it has been possible to improve and extend upon the original customs dataset. In particular, the reliance of the Johnson dataset on the official value of traded goods provides, as is argued below, a biased picture of the actual aggregate patterns of trade due to weighting the quantity of goods with an unchanging official price. Thus, what is currently lacking in the literature is accurate, detailed data on non-slave imports from Africa, which can be applied to a regional analysis of trade patterns over the eighteenth century at a time when the transatlantic slave trade was at its height.

To test the extent to which the transatlantic slave trade crowded out or inhibited the growth of non-slave market activities, this chapter will examine African commodity trade over the latter part of the eighteenth century. Using a newly constructed dataset, which includes a weighted measure of the quantity of goods from the customs records and a newly constructed time series of current prices for commodities in both West Africa and Europe over the eighteenth century, the chapter provides a more accurate estimate of the true value of and trends in the overall commodity trade during this period. If the total imports into Great Britain are analysed, the results show some important differences to previous estimates. Firstly, and in contrast to David Eltis, the value of the commodity trade grew in proportion to the total value of trade but was relatively less valuable than his calculations suggest, particularly for earlier decades in the eighteenth century. From the late 1730s to 1808 there was a six-fold increase in the real value of goods traded, which is triple the change shown in the official figures in the Johnson et al. (1990) dataset. While there were significant fluctuations in the imported real value of West African commodities, there is no evidence for a negative correlation between the trade in commodities and the quantities of captives bought, which suggests that the slave trade was not crowding out other types of exchange.

However, at a regional level the results are more nuanced. The customs data and a range of other sources allow an examination of regional output from the three case study regions. This analysis shows that in the last decades of the eighteenth century, imports of commodities from different areas of the Bight of Biafra did increase substantially at the same time as the region was embarking record numbers of captives. In contrast, along the Gold Coast, the evidence suggests that the rising slave trade did indeed negatively impact on the production of goods for the market. Lastly, the new data confirms the patterns observed in the previous two chapters by showing that very little, besides captives, was ever exported from the Bight of Benin. The data therefore support the analysis of Inikori, especially in the case of the Gold Coast. On the other hand, such data also provides evidence that the slave trade could be seen to stimulate the expansion of the non-slave export trade, as shown by the trade patterns from the Bight of Biafra.

1 Measuring the Volume and Value of the Commodity Trade

To re-assess the value of commodity trade originating from West Africa over the eighteenth century we construct a new index of the real value of trade.[1] The index is labelled 'real' because it compensates for annual price changes in the flows of commodities between Europe and Africa, allowing a meaningful comparison of the change in the traded value of a range of commodities over time, taking out the effects of price inflation completely. The real value of trade is based on annual data on the quantity of commodities imported from West Africa – taken directly from the British Customs Records – as well as a representative set of prices for these commodities. Between 1737–1808 the prices are updated at fixed intervals to ensure they always continue to reflect the relative price differentials between the commodities in the sample.[2]

1 Note that throughout this paper imports refer to goods entering Britain, exports refer to goods entering Africa.

2 Note that the dataset begins in 1737, as before this date the official values in the customs records do not substantially deviate from the revised calculations in this chapter.

1.1 *Real Value of Trade*

The analysis of the overall quantities of goods is based on the British Customs Records. Despite certain caveats, this still provides a good indication of the major trends in Africa's non-slave trade as the commodity trade was dominated by British merchants. New data compiled by Eltis et al. (2013) on ships trading solely for African commodities between 1699 and 1807 shows that over seventy percent left from English ports. An examination of the trading accounts of both Dutch and French slave and specialist commodity merchants shows that merchants of both nations were buying far smaller quantities than is evidenced in the customs records.[3] The only exception was Senegambia whose external trade, other than briefly from 1750 to 1776, was largely in the hands of the French and already subjected to detailed analysis (Curtin, 1975, Webb 1985, Searing 2003).

To obtain a single indicator of the development of West African trade it was necessary to aggregate the quantity of these various commodities into a single index. As is common practice, the results rely on a set of prices to weight the different commodities according to their respective relative values. Using prices, it is thus possible to compare, for example, a ton of ivory to a 1,000 gallons of palm oil with a single measure of value. Since this is done for all years over a period of 80 years, starting in 1730, the choice of these relative prices is crucial.[4] The official value of commodity trade listed in the British Customs Records and used in the work of Johnson et al. (1990), relies on official prices that were set in the late seventeenth century. Thus, all goods traded over the eighteenth and early nineteenth century were assigned a single, official price by the customs, which was left unchanged for over a century-and-a-half.

Index-number theory shows that fixing the base-period prices to a single year can cause serious distortions, particularly if done over long periods of time. This so-called substitution bias is the result of consumers substituting away from goods when they increase in relative price and vice versa (Ehemann, 2007). Such an index that relies on weights from some past period will overweight the goods that have decreased in price and underweight those that have undergone price increases, biasing the quantum index in the process. Table 3.1 provides a summary of the average prices observed in the dataset per decade for four important West-African commodities and compares them to the official prices used to calculate the official value in the Johnson et al. dataset.

3 For the Dutch, see the trade accounts of the MCC which records the sales of African commodities (Zeeuws Archief, MCC 1733–1736, 1739, 1740). For the French there was nothing in the records of 31 ships in the archives in Nantes to show that the majority of slave ships bought anything apart from slaves (Loire Atlantique 8J 10, 11; 101; J26, 101, J27) or very small quantities of ivory (Archives Loire Atlantique, 16J 1).

4 The time series begins in 1730 as this is the first year for which there are reliable prices.

TABLE 3.1 Average import prices vs official prices, 1730s–1800s

Decade	Ivory (£/cwt)	Palm oil (£/cwt)	Beeswax (£/cwt)	Redwood (£/ton)
1730s	5.3	2.2	2.8	3.7
1740s	5.8	2.6	2.8	6.2
1750s	7.1	2.8	3.4	2.8
1760s	10.0	3.3	3.3	2.3
1770s	14.9	3.0	3.4	2.1
1780s	15.7	4.1	4.6	2.0
1790s	11.8	4.9	5.4	2.6
1800s	21.9	5.9	6.7	4.5
Official	*6.00*	*1.00*	*4.75*	*40.00*

Sources: Johnson et al. (1990), see Table 3.2 for sources on current prices

Clearly, the official prices, both in absolute and relative terms, differed substantially from the observed prices, particularly for the later decades. Most notably for redwood, the official prices do not correspond to the average prices observed. What served as the basis for the official prices is not exactly clear, even for the customs officers at the time.[5] This chapter revisits the English customs records and constructs a real-value index that takes the changing weights into account, thus eliminating, or at least limiting, the substitution bias plaguing Johnson et al. (1993). For the new index of the real value of goods traded from West Africa, the results rely on a set of nominal prices as weights that were observed throughout the eighteenth and early nineteenth centuries, rather than weighting the various commodities by the official prices of 1697. These weights are updated roughly every twenty years, linking the resulting separate indices using a procedure called chaining, thus avoiding the problem of out-of-date weights.[6] This method suffers the drawback of being substantially more

5 'The Estimates in this office by which the goods imported and exported are valued were made about the year 1697 probably by the first appointed officer ... upon what principle he formed his estimates it is difficult to ascertain at this day […]' The National Archives (TNA), London, CUST 17/12, 1790.

6 The full workings of the method can be found at: https://www.aehnetwork.org/working-papers/commodities-prices-and-risk-the-changing-market-for-non-slave-products-in-pre-abolition-in-west-africa/

TABLE 3.2 Observations of prices for African commodities, 1737–1810

Commodity	Coast	European market	Total	Percent of sample
Beeswax	50	75	125	4.2
Gum	3	8	11	0.4
Ivory	197	2,439	2636	88.2
Malaguetta pepper	24	8	32	1.1
Palm Oil	25	48	73	2.4
Redwood / Barwood	19	56	75	2.5
Camwood	1	14	15	0.5
Ebony	4	19	23	0.7
Total	*323*	*2,667*	*2,990*	*100*

Sources: Zeeuws Archief MCC, De Reizen 76 voyages, MCC Venduboeken 1738–1740, MCC Factuurboeken van verkochte retournen 1729–1736, LRO D/Dav Ivory Book, LRO D/Dav Waste Book, TNA T1/566, TNA T1/594 9–12, TNA T70/1583, TNA C107/6/11, Letter book, etc, of Robert Bostock 1779–1792 V1&2 lro 387 MD 54/55, PP 1788 Report on the slave trade, PP 1816 (506) Report from the Select Committee on Papers Relating to the African Forts, Bennet & Brooks (1965), Sheriff (1987), Webb (1985)

data intensive. Whereas the fixed-weight official index requires only a single set of prices, the new index requires a different set of prices every twenty years. Finally, the new price data for commodities imported from West Africa, includes 2,647 observations for the European market and 323 prices recorded at the African coast, from a variety of British and Dutch merchant and government sources (see Table 3.2).[7]

To get to a unit price for all the goods and commodities it was necessary to standardise the weights and measures given in the sources. All the observations were converted into either pounds or gallons, and currency to British pounds

7 In years where there are no observations, the price has been extrapolated based on price movements for proxies, based on data by G. Clark, 'England, prices and wages since the thirteenth century', *Global Price and Income History Group, University of California, Davis, http://gpih.ucdavis.edu/Datafilelist.htm* (2006). For palm oil, oil lamp and soap are used as they were the two products often manufactured from Palm Oil (see M. Lynn, *Commerce and economic change in West Africa: The palm oil trade in the nineteenth century* (Cambridge, 1997). For African dyewoods, the series Wood is used, for Beeswax: Candles and for Malaguetta Pepper: Pepper.

TABLE 3.3 Observations of prices for British trade goods, 1768–1808

Trade Goods	European market	Per cent of sample	Trade Goods	European market	Per cent of sample
Alcohol	85	6.1	Lead	25	1.8
Calico	29	2.1	Linen	106	7.7
Finished cotton	100	7.2	Military stores / Guns	116	8.4
Cowries	12	0.9	Pans / Rods	61	4.4
Gunpowder	70	5.1	Pewter	22	1.6
India fabric	461	35.3	Tobacco	91	6.6
Iron	62	4.5	Woolens	104	7.5
Wrought iron	39	2.8			

Sources: TNA T70/928/929/930/931/932; LRO D/Dav Ships Accounts: Andromache & Hector 1769–1776, Swift, Deadnaught & Dalrymple 1772–1777, Lord Cassiles & May 1771–1776, Essex and Christopher 1784–1788, King George, King of Prussia 1767–1779, Preston 1780–1784, Quiote 1783–1785, Mars and Rover 1768–1787; lro Thomas Leyland Records Account Books, La Convention 387 MD 40, Lottery 1798–1799 387 MD41, Lottery 1802–1811 387 MD 42, Enterprise 1803–1804 387 MD 43, Fortune 387 MD 44, TNA James Rogers Paper Morning Star C107/6

(Denzel, 2010). Data on British goods exported to Africa are based on the records of both crown-protected and private traders, supplemented by data on prices from secondary sources, providing 1,383 observations for the period (see Table 3.3). Lastly, the prices of slaves in the Americas come from Eltis et al. (2005); for the British Caribbean, and the yearly observations in the slave trade database of prices in Jamaica and for the African coast from data by Lovejoy and Richardson (1995a).

1.2 *Regional Origin of Different Products*

In order to ascertain from which region different products were bought a variety of sources are used. Firstly, the customs records provide some regional information in 1810/1811 and then from 1827.[8] Secondly, there are records of ships and their cargo of slaves and commodities from the ports of Liverpool and Bristol from 1780 to 1799 based on data from local newspapers (see Appendix 3.1 and 3.2)

8 1810/1811: TNA CUST 4/6, 4/7. From 1827 TNA CUST 4/22.

and similar data from the Dutch MCC from 1742–1803.[9] These vessels were cross-referenced with the slave trade database to ascertain within which regions of Africa they were trading in order to identify which types of products each area was exporting. Finally, the results were checked against a number of contemporary reports, letters and publications from the period.[10]

2 Real Value and Structure of West Africa's Commodity Trade

Figure 3.1 shows the development of the nominal market value, the real value and the prices of the African commodity trade. Particularly the nominal and real value indices show a substantial degree of variance over time, but the trend is unquestionably upwards over this period. The trend-line for the nominal value of commodities shows that the market value rose 20-fold between 1737 and 1807. During this time, prices roughly tripled. The trend in real value shows that the volume of trade rose by a factor of six between the late 1730s and 1807.

Figure 3.2 compares the new real-value index of African commodity imports to the Johnson series (dashed line) and the estimates by Eltis (grey line). Over the first 40 years, the Johnson series moves roughly in tandem with the new estimates. After 1780, the two indices diverge. As the data underlying the quantities of African commodity imports is identical for both series, the discrepancy originates entirely from the updated set of prices. The official prices used by Johnson et al. are not representative for African commodities, introducing a bias that gets larger over time. Notably, the rise in the real value of commodity trade was far more substantial than observed for the slave trade, which was largely static during this period.[11] Eltis' estimates of

9 The methodology for the analysis of newspaper reports in the Manchester Mercury follows that of Behrendt et al., (2010), Dutch data from Zeeuws Archief, MCC, 196, 201, 206, 216, 220224, 229, 287, 330, 340, 384, 418, 425, 431, 448, 478, 483, 500, 505, 514, 538, 543, 546, 674, 677, 745, 749, 754, 777, 783, 832, 859, 863, 893, 897, 898, 905, 944, 969, 974, 1005, 1045, 1049, 1052, 1072, 1078, 1093, 1098, 1106, 1126, 1136, 1149, 1155, 1162, 1168, 1174, 1181, 1190, 1210, 1212, 1213, 1218, 1235, 1239, 1247, 1313, 1371, 1379, 1387, 1393, 1399, 1406, 1413, 1427.

10 In particular, British Library, Add Mss 12131, 'Mr Parfitts information on Trade between Sierra Leone and Cape Lopez w. Islands St Thomas etc'. and 'Extract of a Diary Kept by E.L. Parfitt on the Board the Sierra Leone Company's Ship *Calypso*', Papers Relating to Sierra Leone, ff. 174–320. Parfitt had been hired by the Sierra Leone company to investigate the potential for commodity trade with Africa, see Schwarz 2007, p. 262 for biographical details. The correspondence of the Bristol merchant James Rogers (TNA CO107) and the merchant guides written by Robertson (1819), Adams (1822), and Bold (1822).

11 In 1770, British ships embarked 41,738 slaves from Africa, which is above the mean of 33,583 for the period until 1808 and not too far below the peak of 49,906 captives taken in 1799 (Eltis http://www.slavevoyages.org).

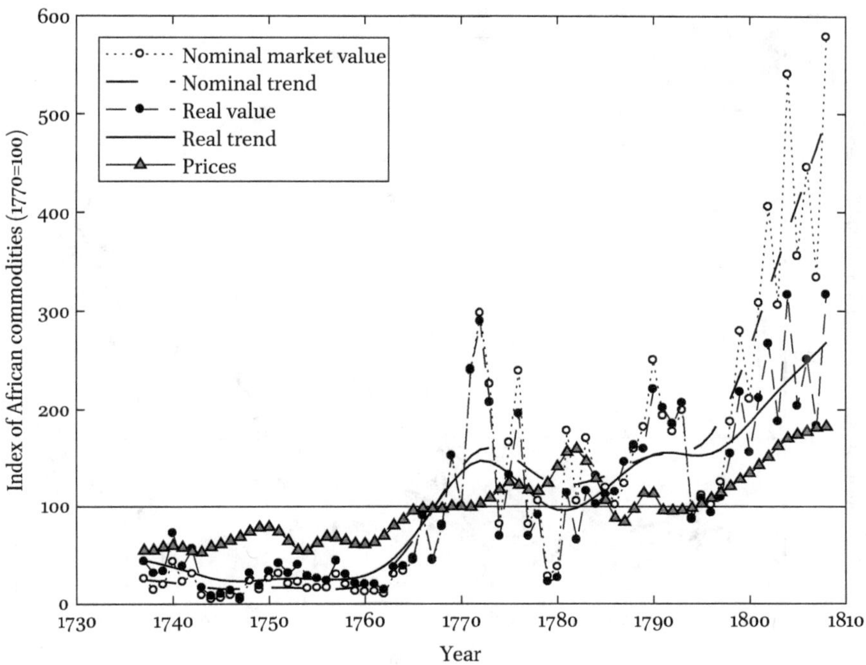

FIGURE 3.1 Nominal market value, real value and prices of African commodity trade, 1737–1807
Note: Trend derived using Hodrick-Prescott filter with a smoothing factor set to 100
Sources: see pages 119–123

the value of commodity trade are substantially higher than the new data, particularly for earlier years. However, according to his estimates the trend growth between 1737 and 1807 was quite modest. Eltis estimates the real value of commodities from West Africa to have risen by about thirty percent during this period, remarkably low compared to the new estimate of over six hundred percent.

Figure 3.3 illustrates the relative standing of commodities in the total trade coming from Africa. When compared to the value of the slave trade, the new estimates suggest commodities represented between two and eight percent of total trade, growing in importance after 1760. Eltis (2013) on the other hand shows a clear decline in the relative share of commodities, from about twenty in the 1740s to nine percent in 1807. Eltis – who based his figures on a dataset of produce and slave voyages combined with assumptions on the proportion of commodities in the total value of the cargo of slave vessels – clearly appears to overestimate the importance of commodities. Although the British Customs

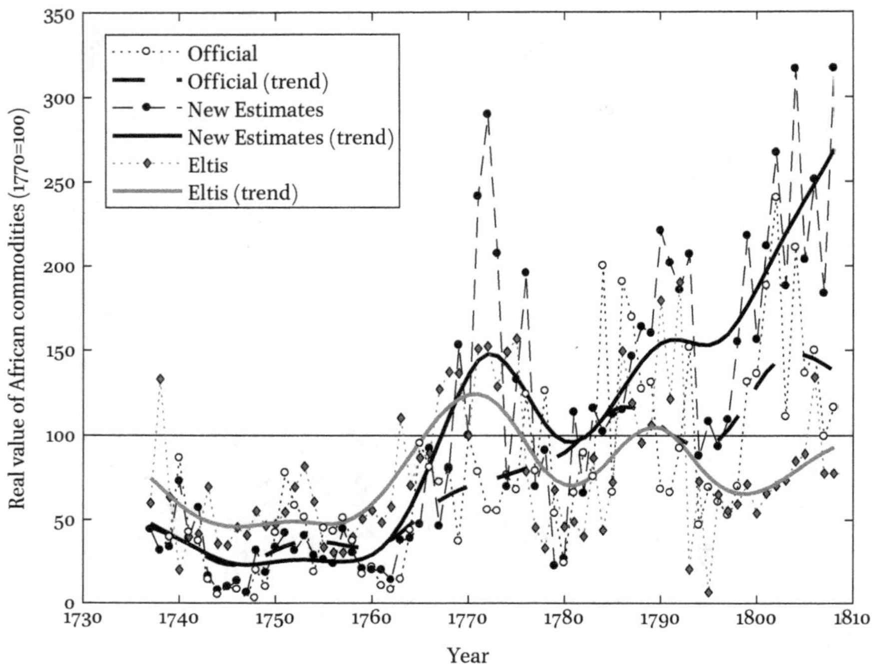

FIGURE 3.2 Real value of West African commodity imports, 1737–1807
Note: Trend derived using Hodrick-Prescott filter with a smoothing factor set to 100
Sources: see pages 119–123; Johnson et al. (1990); Eltis (2013)

Records do not account for all trade, as some commodity trade from West Africa might not have been reported to the authorities or was shipped by French and Dutch captains, it is unlikely that in reality the share of commodities in total trade was as high as suggested by Eltis.

Figures 3.1 and 3.2 already demonstrate significant fluctuations in the prices and value of West African commodities. For total West African trade, these booms and busts do appear to coincide with similar fluctuations in the slave trade, particularly during the American Wars of Independence (1776–1784) and after the outbreak of the French revolutionary wars and the slave revolt on Haiti after 1792. Crucially, there is no evidence for a negative correlation between the trade in commodities and the quantities of captives bought, which suggests that the slave trade was not inhibiting other types of commercial exchange. The long-run averages of the number of slaves embarked and the real value of commodities imported from West Africa show a limited but positive correlation of 0.58. Annual fluctuations correlate positively but are very weakly related (0.13).

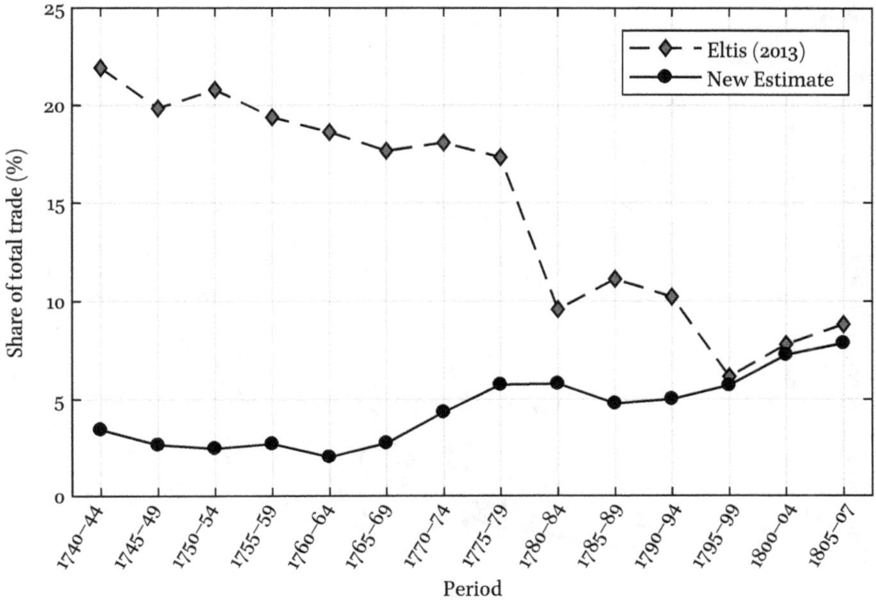

FIGURE 3.3 Share of commodities in total trade, 1737–1807
Sources: see pages 119–123 Eltis (2013)

2.1 *European Demand*

The rise in commodity exports, especially in the final decades of the eighteenth century, seems to have been driven by demand from slave traders. There were typically two types of vessel that went to Africa to trade. Firstly, ships that often bought some non-slave articles and secondly, specialist commodity traders. A new dataset compiled by Stephen Behrendt, David Eltis and Jelmer Vos has identified 1600 of what they believe to be the latter kind of voyages from 1672 to 1808 (Eltis 2013, p. 31). Their data, confirmed by the observations from Liverpool shipping data, show that the number of these voyages declined from a high in the 1770s to accounting for only around four percent of ships trading in Africa from 1780 to 1807 when commodity exports increased.[12] Those involved in this specialist branch of African commerce seem to have been pushed out of the trade by a combination of low profit

12 The veracity of these figures was checked by analysing information found in *The Manchester Mercury*. There were details on the arrivals of ships with African cargo between 1781 and 1799 which were not in the TSTD and therefore likely to have been bilateral traders. Only 51 such ships could be identified which would represent around 3.3% of Liverpudlian vessels bound for Africa.

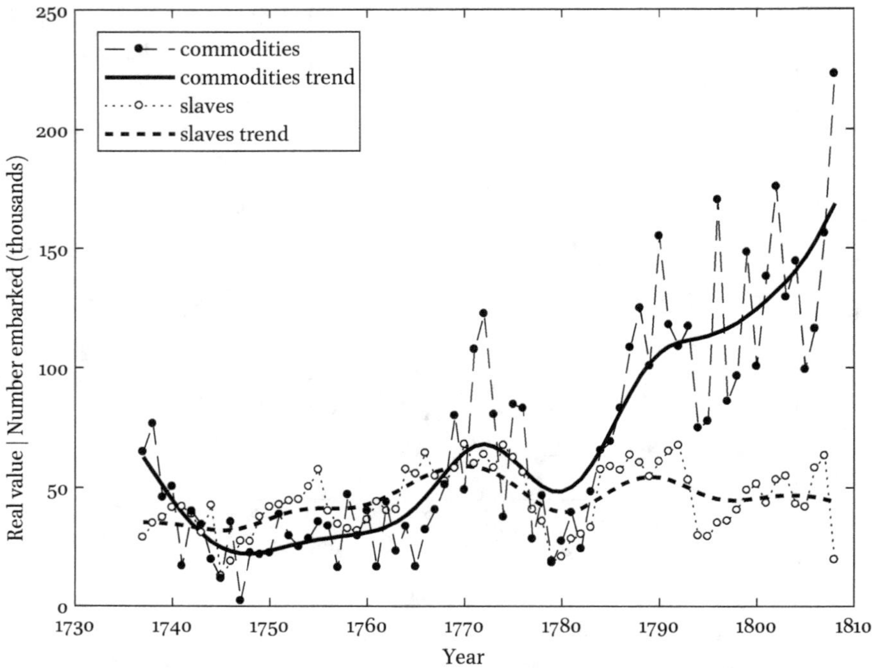

FIGURE 3.4 Real value of commodities and slaves embarked, 1737–1807
Note: Trend derived using Hodrick-Prescott filter with a smoothing factor set to 100
Sources: see pages 119–123 Eltis, *Voyages: The Trans-Atlantic Slave Trade Database*, http://www.slavevoyages.org

margins and competition from slave ships who were buying greater quantities of commodities.[13] The trading accounts of the Liverpool merchant William

13 Syndenham Teaste, Bristol's most important commodities trader, told parliament in 1788 that '[...] his House is in the Trade, and therefore goes on with it; but if his Capital was out of it, he would not now go in to it [...]' due to the low profits he made; Parliamentary Papers, London: Report of The Lords of the Committee of Council appointed for the Consideration of all Matters relating to Trade and Foreign Plantations (1788), 78. In the same report another commodities trader, Captain Dean, related how his business was '[...] much hurt from the Slave Ships purchasing the said Articles, which the Persons in his Branch of the African Trade go solely to bring home'. Writing home in 1792, the captain of a commodities ship from Bristol, complained of having to compete with slave ships in Gabon '[...] we find great opposition here, there are no less than 12 sail and 4 of them are for Red Wood [...]' (The National Archives C107/6).

Davenport suggest that captains of slaving vessels were actively incentivised to buy commodities with rates of commission similar to those paid for captives.[14]

There was clearly a demand for Africa's raw materials in a Britain that was seeing rising wages and a desire by an increasing section of the population to acquire status goods which had become markers of success and respectability (De Vries, 1994; Allen, 2009). For example, the elephants of the Cameroons provided the raw materials for piano keys and billiard balls (Johnson et al., 1990), beeswax was needed to meet the growing demand for higher quality candles, and pepper to satisfy people's desire for a more varied diet (Pomeranz 2000, p. 94). Liverpool's growing soap industry as well as the Lancashire wool manufacturing sector provided a growing market for palm oil (Lynn 1997), and redwood was in demand both as a dye in the textile industry and for the manufacture of violin bows, and furniture (Inikori, 2002).

In addition, commodities realised a relatively generous rate of return. The indices of prices for African products in European markets show that their value was growing more rapidly and with less volatility than that of slaves while the cost of trade goods taken to the coast was falling or stable (Fig. 3.5). However, the relatively generous mark-ups between Africa and Europe probably do not reflect anything more than a premium to compensate for the higher risks associated with Atlantic trade during the period, and do not on their own explain why slave merchants were actively engaging in other forms of trade.

One important incentive may have been that commodities also allowed slave captains and owners to minimise the considerable risks associated with this branch of commerce (McDade, 2011). Mortality rates on slave vessels were declining towards the end of the eighteenth century, but captains could still face considerable losses due to disease and the terrible conditions suffered by the people chained in their holds (Klein & Engerman, 1997). Behrendt et al. (2010, p. 87) note that commodities such as ivory could offer a more secure investment than slaves. Commodities also helped mitigate the financial risks

14 Davenport's captains were paid 4% commission on the value of slaves in addition to 2% 'privilege' (the latter giving them the right to sell a certain number of slaves). For commodities, captains were paid between 4% and 5% commission. Liverpool Record Office D/DAV, voyages of the Essex & Christopher 1784–1788, Dobson & Fox 1766–1771, Hawke 1779–1782.

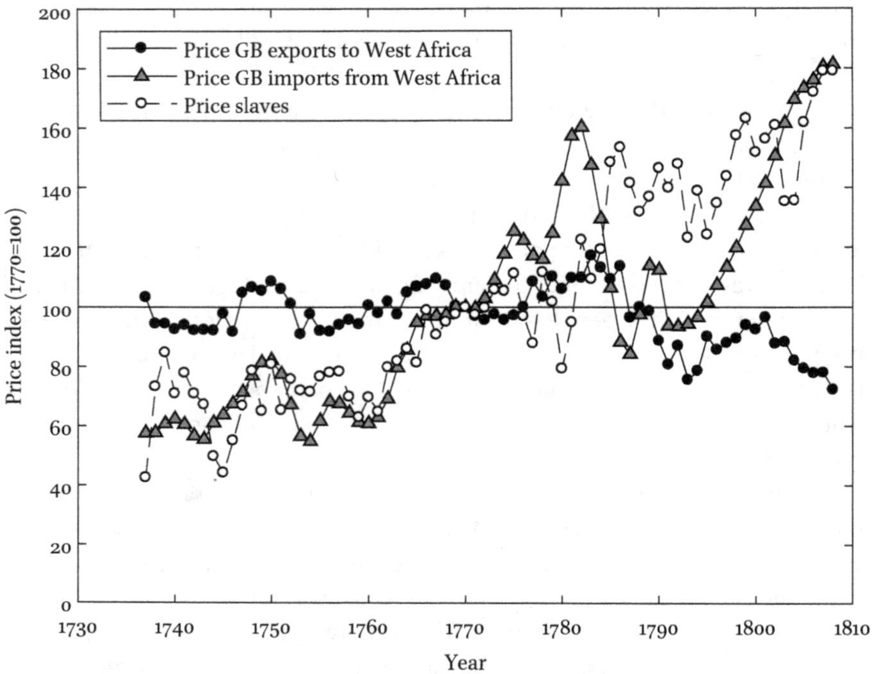

FIGURE 3.5 Price indices British trade with West Africa, 1737–1807
Note: Trend derived using Hodrick-Prescott filter with a smoothing factor set to 100
Sources: see pages 119–123

of the voyages. A recent paper by Radburn (2015) has quantified changes in the credit system that underwrote the slave trade. Merchants exchanged slaves for promissory notes called bills of exchange which could be redeemed in England. These bills of exchange allowed planters in the West Indies time to recoup their investment before having to pay for slaves and gave slave traders a more efficient system of payment, which was crucial in the expansion of the trade in the second half of the eighteenth-century (Pearson & Richardson, 2008). However, uncertainty across the Atlantic market, caused by warfare and planter indebtedness, led to increasing volatility and longer dated bills. Merchants responded with a variety of strategies. One such strategy was to pass on their bills of exchange to other traders in exchange for goods they needed for their next voyages. Such an exchange involved a discount and meant lower profit margins but nonetheless ensured liquidity. One Liverpool slave merchant, William Davenport, did this with around 90 of his bills and it was a common practice for the traders of the (MCC) (Morgan, 2005, p. 746, De Kok, 2016).

An alternative strategy was to invest in other types of business that realised cash or shorter dated bills of exchange. Many traders bought West Indian products on short dated bills from planters, which could then be sold on quickly in Great Britain, thus realising some capital while they waited for their slave bills to mature.[15] However, African commodities could be sold directly without having to rely on any credit mechanisms. In the surviving accounts of the Liverpool merchant William Davenport are the records of commodity sales. These goods were sold in 'Lots' at auctions in Great Britain and the sales were realised either in cash or often transferred directly to the accounts of other merchants to repay outstanding debts.[16] While the proceeds from ivory and other goods were far less significant than slaves, this practice ensured that Davenport's business had a ready source of liquidity. Diversification was also common in the Netherlands where the MCC auctioned commodities to cash buyers.[17] Correspondence between the captains of slaving vessels and their employers in Liverpool certainly suggest that the purchase of commodities was considered an important component of a successful voyage. For example, one slave captain was instructed to 'get all the Ivory you possible can, to secure the Voyage'.[18] Another Liverpool merchant, Thomas Staniforth, wrote '[pick] up what Ivory you can [...] as we think it will be most probable means of securing the voyage...'[19] Richard Rogers, a Bristolian slave captain, reassured his employer that 'I seem to have a thought of keeping the Juba when arrives until can put 275 good slaves on her with what Ivory Redwood and 20 puncheons palm oil if she can carry it and the remittance of her cargo [will] secure the voyage [...]'[20]

Thus, the broader macro evidence of rising imports of West African commodities, driven by a strong demand from transatlantic slave traders, would

15 For example, in 1793 the Bristolian merchants James Rogers was given bills of exchange for the sales of slaves at 12, 18 and 24 months (TNA, CO107/53, 2 February 1793, White to Rogers). He bought sugar the same year and this was sold in Bristol for bills of 45 days (TNA, CO107/53, 9 September 1793, Anderson to Dennisforth).

16 See Radburn (2009) for a thorough investigation of Davenport's use of commodities to offset credit risk. Examples I have found of the cash sales of ivory, gold dust, palm oil and wood can be found in the archives of the Merseyside Maritime Museum, D/DAV/2, Waste Book 1766–1780. In October 1764 Davenport settled a debt of £1281 with ivory sales, and again in December 1769 he paid off £549 to a creditor with ivory. Merseyside Maritime Museum, D/DAV/1, Ivory Book 1763–1779.

17 Zeeus Archief MCC 1749 Vendue book van retouren 1721–1762.

18 Davenport Papers, 'Henry' 1765.

19 Davenport Papers, 'King of Prussia', 1767.

20 The National Archives, C107/12. I would like to thank Nick Radburn for drawing my attention to these sources.

support the conclusions of Eltis (2013, p. 46) that the slave trade did not 'inhibit the emergence of non-slave activities'. However, when the evidence is examined at a regional level it shows that this argument only holds for some areas of the West African coast.

3 Regional Trade

The three case study areas, the Bight of Biafra, the Gold Coast, and the Bight of Benin show very different trends with regard to non-slave exports. Table 3.4 sets out the share of goods imported into Great Britain from West Africa using the new regionalised data.

3.1 *The Bight of Biafra*

During the second half of the eighteenth century this region was the principal destination for a third of all known slave trading voyages and, while subject to major fluctuations, embarkations of captives increased significantly as the Aro slave network expanded into south and central areas of Igboland from the 1730s (Lovejoy & Richardson 1999, pp. 382–3, Nwokeji 2010, p. 20).[21] At the same time, exports of commodities from across the region were also increasing. Redwood had been an important product from Africa since the beginning of the eighteenth century (Behrendt et al. 2010) and a very large percentage was likely bought either in the Bight of Biafra or further down along the Loango coast. In the customs' records from 1827–1830 as well as in the ships' records from Bristol and Liverpool, almost all the redwood was coming from the Bight of Biafra or West Central Africa. Within the Bight of Biafra some contemporary sources indicate that much of the redwood was bought around Old Calabar, but other records suggest that many ships were sailing to Gabon or even further south to stock up before leaving for the Americas.[22]

21 An estimated 15,349 captives were embarked between 1726 and 1750, while 261, 137 were embarked in the last quarter of the century. http://www.slavevoyages.org/assessment/estimates, accessed 17/10/18.

22 See Bold (1823), p. 80 and Robertson (1819), p. 313 for Old Calabar. For Gabon, see the records of the ship 'Triton' in the James Rogers papers. Having bought slaves, palm oil and some wood from Old Calabar, the Captain sailed down to Gabon for redwood which was much more plentiful there (TNA CO107/6 Cod to Rogers January 19th 1792, Cod to Rogers March 11th 1792, Prosser to Rogers April 10th 1792). Both Adams (*Sketches*), p. 115 and Robertson, 1819, p. 364 notes that Gabon and Mjumba further south were the most important sources for barwood/redwood.

TABLE 3.4 Composition of commodity imports from Africa per new estimates, 1737–1808 (percent share nominal value)

Period	Dyestuffs Red-wood	 Cam-wood	 Other	Ivory	Gum	Palm oil	Bees-wax	Pepper	Total West Africa	Other Africa[a]	Re-exports
1730s	3	0	4	8	0	0	4	0	*20*	79	1
1740s	6	1	3	16	2	0	9	0	*35*	62	3
1750s	7	0	1	18	2	0	8	1	*36*	62	2
1760s	3	0	0	23	21	0	4	1	*53*	41	6
1770s	2	0	0	18	47	1	4	0	*72*	25	3
1780s	3	0	0	38	6	7	3	0	*57*	39	4
1790s	1	0	2	21	8	10	4	4	*50*	42	8
1800s	3	0	0	21	15	16	3	2	*59*	38	3

Sources: see pages 119–123
Gum imports from West Africa refer to gum Senegal and exclude gum Arabic. Other imports from West Africa include cattle hides, malaguetta pepper, other wood, rice and sea shells.

a A proportion of Britain's trade did not originate in West Africa and has been aggregated into the category 'Other Africa'. Most of the commodities in this category were primarily sourced from Morocco and north Africa (almonds, calf & goat skins, ostrich feathers and gum Arabic) and Cape of Good Hope (aloes, hides and ostrich feathers). See Johnson et al. (1990, p. 11)

Palm Oil was the fastest growing African import in the last decades of the eighteenth century and the sources show that almost all of this was coming from the Bight of Biafra, and that Old Calabar was the centre of this trade, although some quantities of palm oil were also being bought in Bonny (Lynn 1997, Behrendt et al., 2010).[23] While the latter port did not begin exporting large quantities of palm oil as a commodity export until the nineteenth century, Chapter 2

23 Parfitt, 1796, p. 52 Robertson, 1819, pp. 313–314; Bold, 1823, pp. 75, 83; Adams, 1822, pp. 171–172. The Liverpool merchant Thomas Leyland instructed the captain of his ship 'Lottery' to buy '*a quantity of palm oil*' from Bonny in 1802, but for the ship's previous voyage in 1798

has shown that merchants at Bonny were nonetheless selling a lot of oil in order to provision slave ships. Furthermore, as argued in the previous chapter, British vessels trading in this region bought far greater quantities of provisions at Bonny and Old Calabar than in other slave trading regions.

Beeswax, ivory and pepper were bought in all parts of the coast, although how much came from any specific region is difficult to estimate. With regards to wax, the later customs records indicate that this product came almost entirely from Sierra Leone and Gambia, but this may not accurately reflect the situation in the pre-abolition era. In 1810 and 1811 the customs records differentiate between the coast from Morocco to the River Gambia, Sierra Leone and the rest of West Africa, and here well over half the beeswax was coming from outside the first two regions. In the 1790s Bristol ships were buying the vast majority of their beeswax from the Bight of Biafra, most likely from Gabon, which fits with analysis of the British merchant Parfitt, who noted that this area "is said by some people to be the first place in Africa for procuring the largest quantity of wax…"[24] However, Liverpool vessels were taking most of their wax from Gambia, so there was clearly a regional preference depending on your port of origin. This was also the case with regards to pepper or 'Guinea Grains', with Liverpool merchants taking on board this commodity mainly in the Bight of Biafra, while Bristolians favoured Sierra Leone or the Gold Coast.

Concerning ivory, the evidence indicates that merchants around the Bight of Biafra probably exported this in greater quantities than did other regions, although this was probably due to more British vessels trading in the region in the decades before abolition. Thus, while Bristol ships going to the Gold Coast in the 1790s took on average a greater quantity of ivory per vessel, more ivory overall came in from the Bight of Biafra because far more Bristolian ships traded there. Behrendt et al.'s (2010, p. 82) study of shipping data published in the Manchester Mercury between 1752 and 1808 estimates that twenty percent of the total ivory imported into Great Britain came from the Bight of Biafra. Our own figures from the same source for the period from 1780 to 1799 give a figure of thirty four percent suggesting that this trade could very well have been increasing in the last decades of the eighteenth century. Rising imports of this product were likely due to new trading routes were opening up in the Cameroon grasslands which held more abundant herds of elephants. This development was noted by traders at the time who either bought at source, or

the captain was told to only buy slaves (LRO 387/MD/42, 21 May 1802, Leyland to Kneale, LRO 387/MD/41, 2 July 1798, Leyland to Whittle).

24 Parfitt, 1796, p. 67.

firstly exported and then resold profitably via Efik traders in Old Calabar.[25] Lastly, the Bristol and Liverpool sources also show that vessels trading in the Bight of Biafra purchased a wider range of products than ships trading in other regions. Ships belonging to the Bristol merchant James Rogers bought ivory in the Gold Coast and around Sierra Leone, but it was only in the Bight of Biafra that other commodities in addition to ivory were purchased alongside slaves.[26]

There are at least two possible explanations for why the commodities trade was expanding in different areas within the Bight of Biafra. It has long been acknowledged that the slave trade helped stimulate the growth of palm oil production for exports and that the two trades were largely compatible (Northrup 1976). The growth, especially from Old Calabar, in non-slave exports was of particular importance as a way of luring slave traders away from the far more successful port of Bonny (Behrendt et al. 2010, p. 81, Lovejoy & Richardson 2004). Furthermore, once ships had purchased their cargoes from Bonny and Calabar they needed to sail south to the equator in order to catch the north Atlantic gyre that would take them over to the Americas, thus taking them past the new expanding markets in the Cameroons and Gabon where they picked up ivory, wax and dyewoods. Based on this evidence, the slave trade did not prevent the development of other forms of commerce in the Bight of Biafra and may very well have stimulated the growth of the non-slave sector, especially in the final decades of the eighteenth century.

3.2 *The Gold Coast*

By contrast, from around the middle of the eighteenth century; the transatlantic slave trade seems to have actively retarded the Gold Coast's production of commodities for the market. While ships from Bristol and Liverpool were buying other products in addition to slaves, fewer vessels visited this part of the coast which meant that the overall quantities bought were far lower than in the Bight of Biafra. More importantly, the evidence is that there was a significant reduction in the output of gold, the region's most important commodity, in the second half of the eighteenth century.

---

25 Robertson (1819), p. 322, writes that 'the trade here for elephants' teeth [in Cameroon] is more extensive than on any other part of the coasts of south west or north west africa'. This view is echoed by Parfitt (1796), p. 54. For more details of the trade see Behrendt, Latham, & Northrup, 2010, pp. 92–93,

26 TNA CO107/11 March 10 1791, Anamabo, Smith to Rogers, TNA CO107/14, January 23 1791, Benue Island, Williams to Rogers. For Calabar see for example correspondence from the Triton in which the Captain discusses buying palm oil, ivory and redwood in addition to slaves (TNA CO 107/11 7 February 1791, Old Calabar, Blake to Rogers).

Gerrard (1980, pp. 145–170) has estimated gold output from the Akan territories north of the Gold Coast which had the highest concentration of gold mines in West Africa (Dickson 1969, p. 180). Gerrard's estimations are based on a review of the figures and estimates in contemporary sources which, although not providing an indication of yearly changes, do show a broad pattern in which gold output declines during the eighteenth century and then rises again in the nineteenth after abolition when the region almost immediately ceased exporting captives (Fig. 3.6). To check these trends, we looked at the average quantity of gold dust bought along the Gold Coast using the records from ships that actually recorded this information.[27] The data shows that ships trading in the region were buying significantly less gold between 1750 and 1800 (Table 3.5).

Johnson (1966, p. 204) noted this trend some time ago but believed that supplies were largely constrained due to conflict between the Asante and the Fante in the 1760s and 1770s. However, sources from the 1780s and 1790s show that slave traders needed gold as part of the bundle of goods required to enable the purchase of slaves, making the region an importer of a product which it had previously exported.[28] Specialist commodity traders found themselves unable to purchase any gold as it was in such high demand as a means of acquiring captives.[29] Metcalf (1987, pp. 34, 35) argues against the interpretation by Rodney (1969) that this decline in output was due to labour being diverted from mining into slave exports, instead supporting La Torre's argument that transactions in the region were increasingly reliant on gold which encouraged hoarding. However, as will be argued in Chapter 4, exports of both gold and kola nuts for the Atlantic and Saharan markets increased substantially after abolition and, following Austin (2005, p. 155–171), this required substantial inputs of coerced labour providing indirect support for Rodney's line of reasoning.

---

27 The data on British voyages does not include information about gold until the nineteenth century.

28 Mr Norris, a witness to the 1788 parliamentary commission on the slave trade stated that "Gold is purchased so dear on the coast that it is not worth buying, but as a medium for the purchase of slaves," p. 67. In 1791 a Captain Smith wrote to his employer James Rogers informing him that he had to sell ivory to the governor at Cape Coast Castle in exchange for Gold in order to sell slaves. TNA CO107/11.

29 See the testimony of Captain Dean, a commodity trader to the 1788 parliamentary report on the slave trade: '…slave ships being obliged to have a quantity of it for carrying on their trade on the leeward coast, give a higher price for it than those employed in his branch of the trade can afford, for which reason the latter get very little of it'.

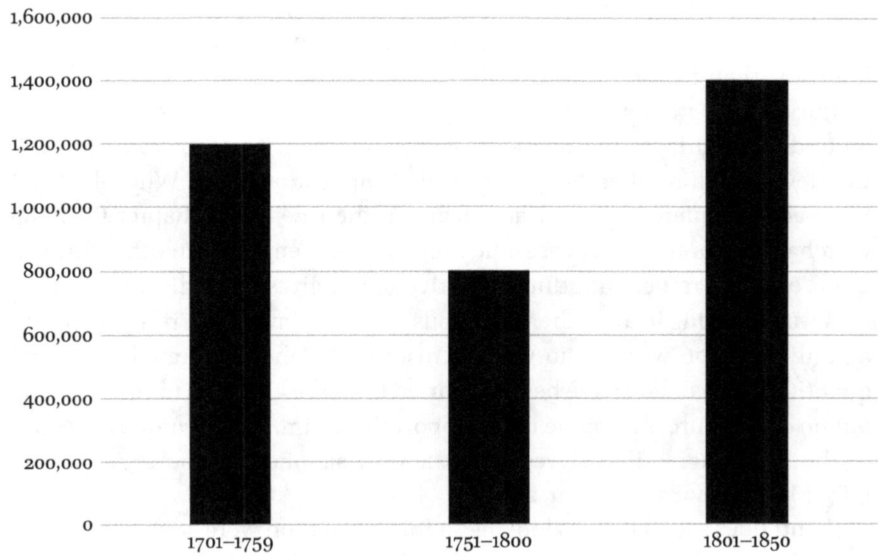

FIGURE 3.6 Exports gold Akan territories
Source: Gerrard 1980

TABLE 3.5 Sample ships gold exports

	Years	Ships	Ounces gold	Avg/ Ship	Grams
Dutch West India Company 'retourschepen'	1674–1749	334	503.024	1.506	42.697
Middleburgsche Commercie Companie *'retourschepen'* or specialist commodity vessels	1755–1803	11	1.443	131	3.72
Middleburgsche Commercie Companie slave vessels	1754–1789	9	748	83	2.356
British vessels trading on the Gold Coast	1822–1826	30	37.641	1.255	39.025

Sources: WIC data from Den Heijer (1997), pp. 96, 129. MCC data from Zeeus Archief, MCC 340, 431, 546, 674, 754, 777, 863, 1049, 1078, 1149, 1162, 1168, 1174, 1181, 1186, 1371, 1387, 1406, 1427. British data from TNA CO267/93 Appendix pp. 21–23. An ounce of gold in the Netherlands was equivalent to 28.35 gr. while in Britain it was 31.103 gr. (Den Heijer (1997), p. 425

3.3 *The Bight of Benin*

Slave exports from this region began to expand earlier, and with far greater intensity, than in the other two regions. Over the course of the eighteenth century over a million captives were embarked from its ports compared to around 700,000 from the Bight of Biafra and about 630,000 from the Gold Coast. Over a third of embarkations were from just one port, Whydah, which had been conquered by the Dahomeans in the 1720s (see Chapter 6). While merchants from the other case study regions were engaging in other forms of trade, only one rather doubtful qualitative source gives any indication that this area was engaging in any other major business but slavery. Norris (1789, p. 147), an anti-abolition writer who wrote a history of Dahomey, stated that "large quantities" of palm oil were being exported from the kingdom to Great Britain, but no other sources from the time support this claim. Furthermore, all studies of the region agree that slaves were the only significant export (Akinjogbin 1967, Manning 1982, Law 1991, 2004).

Parfitt does say that ships looking to trade in Gabon were advised to stop at either Lagos or Whydah to buy what he refers to as "Jebboe Cloths," which presumably means cloth from the Ijebu region of southern Yorubaland near Lagos (Adams 1823, p. 96). Apparently, these cloths made useful articles of trade when bartering for ivory, beeswax, redwood or ebony around the Cameroon River and Gabon. Further, Adams (1823, p. 97) suggests there was some demand for this cloth in Brazil where it was "*...held in much estimation by the black population;....not only on account of its durability, but because it is manufactured in a country which gave many of them, or their parents, birth.*" Bold (1823) notes that "*...vessels intending to trade to the Southward* (i.e. South of Bight of Benin) *should here lay a stock of Jaboo cloths, which are there greatly esteemed.*" However, he was referring to cloth from the kingdom of Benin, not Dahomey. In addition, this was clearly not a key item of trade as when Bold provides a list of trade goods suitable for the Cameroon market, he does not mention cloth from the Bight of Benin (p. 84). Norris (1789) and Dalzell (1794) both wrote extensive histories and descriptions of Dahomey which included numerous references to its production of cloth, yet neither ever mention that it was important as an item of export.[30] It is probably then safe to assume that while some quantities of local cloth were bought by European traders, this product did not constitute a major item of trade.

30 Dalzel (1793) gives descriptions of local cloth (ppvliv,122) and also mentions how it was sometimes distributed as a reward (pp. 137,147,190). Norris (1789) likewise provides descriptions of the cloth worn by Dahomeans (pp. 87,146) but again makes no mention of it being exported.

In terms of the ship data, no vessels from MCC or Bristolian ships bought any commodities from ports in the Bight of Benin. Ships from Liverpool did buy relatively significant quantities of ivory although the majority of these are recorded as having first traded along the Gold Coast or bought their slaves from the Popo or Porto Novo on the western and eastern sides of the bight. Very little ivory was bought on ships trading at Whydah in Dahomean-controlled territory.

4 Market Exchange and the Slave Trade

This chapter has examined whether the growth of the transatlantic slave trade in West Africa undermined or retarded the export of non-slave commodities over the second half of the eighteenth century. The newly constructed dataset on the quantities and value of goods imported from the region into Great Britain together with a range of archival and secondary sources provide new and more accurate estimates of both the overall value of the commodity trade and the output trends of the case study regions. While the macro data differs significantly from existing estimates, it nonetheless confirms Eltis' (2013) broad conclusions that commodity exports continued to rise despite the growth in slave embarkations, and that the transatlantic slave trade did not crowd out other forms of market exchange. However, at a regional level the picture is more nuanced. In the Bight of the Biafra demand from slave ships seems to have stimulated regional exports of commodities. In contrast, along the Gold Coast the evidence strongly suggests that the region exported fewer commodities and that exports of gold fell over the course of the second half of the eighteenth century. The reasons for this decline will be discussed in Chapter 4 but this result shows, at the very least, that the slave trade did not stimulate production for export market. Finally, in the Bight of Benin there is again no evidence that merchants or elites in this region ever exported anything other than slaves in *significant* quantities. Thus, the latter two case studies could be used in support of Inikori's argument that the slave trade hindered or retarded the development of commercial exchange.

Importantly, the results presented in this chapter further confirm that the main slave exporting regions of West Africa developed very different and specific patterns of external trade over the eighteenth century. The next chapters will take a case study approach to each region and argue why, and how, the patterns of trade that developed before abolition determined both the timing and nature of the commercial transition in each area.

Appendices

APPENDIX 3.1 Average quantity of commodities on Bristol slave ships 1790–1799

	Number of ships	Ivory (lbs)	Palm oil (gallon)	Beeswax (lbs)	Redwood (lbs)	Camwood (lbs)	Guinea grains (lbs)
Bight of Benin	3	0	0	0	0	0	0
Bight of Biafra	69	759	341	10208	8955	622	160
Gold Coast	17	2415	0	0	0	1581	3538
Senegambia	1	0	0	2688	0	0	0
Sierra Leone	24	5117	70	20	0	1657	2304
West Central Africa	6	181	0	0	0	0	0
Windward Coast	4	194	0	0	0	0	1381

Source: Bristol Presentments, Bristol Library

APPENDIX 3.2 Average quantity of commodities on Liverpool slave ships 1780–1799

	Number of ships	Ivory (lbs)	Palm oil (gallon)	Beeswax (lbs)	Redwood/ Barwood (lbs)	Camwood (lbs)	Guinea grains (lbs)	Gum (lbs)	Ebony (lbs)
Bight of Benin	29	4793	0	53	154	0	596	278	0
Bight of Biafra	151	2983	926	86	6419	638	2314	21	163
Gold Coast	31	6462	263	65	29119	0	30	0	0
Senegambia	7	5598	0	26152	0	8320	193	0	0
Sierra Leone	22	14746	2	59	0	2803	123	142	0
West Central Africa	100	1595	42	11	14591	101	324	27	165

Source: Manchester Mercury, 300 voyages

Notes: The figures on Redwood/Barwood for the Gold Coast do not give a true reflection of trade patterns. Only two ships visiting this region took on redwood and one of them, Brilliant (1783, VoyID80632) took 400 tons in a single trip. If this is one ship is removed then eighty percent of imports of Redwood/Barwood come from the Bight of Biafra

PART 2

The Long-term Roots of the Commercial Transitions: Case Studies

CHAPTER 4

The Gold Coast: Gold, Wealth and Power Amongst the Akans

> "Sika ne ɔhene" Gold is King (Asanti proverb)
>
> WILKS, 1993, p. 127

In the Introduction, it was argued that the abolition efforts of the British navy were not sufficiently effective, before the 1830s, to deter Atlantic traders from buying and transporting West African slaves. However, the literature on the subject has generally taken the view that the British naval patrols and their castles made embarking captives from the Gold Coast particularly difficult, and were therefore the reasons why this region moved so quickly away from the transatlantic slave trade. Eltis (2009) argues that; "*The Gold Coast castles were too exposed and too much a part of a European government presence to be well suited to clandestine slave trading...*" (p. 728). This view is supported by Lovejoy (2011) "*...the system of trade centred on European trade castles at Cape Coast, Elmina...made it difficult to smuggle slaves. Some slaves were taken farther west, but Asante was forced to abandon the slave export business.*" (p. 164). Johnson (1986a, p. 100) writes that "*...on the Gold Coast, abolition of the slave trade was largely effective...*" before the 1820s. Studies of the Asante kingdom by Wilks (1975, pp. 680–681) and McCaskie (2003, p. 26) assume that the abolition of the slave trade cut the region off from the transatlantic slave trade, thereby forcing the state to look for alternative markets for its products. It will instead be argued that, by engaging in a more long-term analysis of the patterns of trade in the region, it would be more appropriate to apply the demand side hypothesis modelled on Senegambia, which has been suggested by Austin (2013a). While the withdrawal of the British from the slave trade in 1808 was a significant shock, its effect acted more as a catalyst to an already established trend. Essentially, the change from a slave to a commodity export economy was because the application of coerced labour to production had already become more valuable to the region's elites and households than exporting captives to the Atlantic market.

Furthermore, the chapter will show how the presence of gold was crucial in shaping the region's states and societies from the fifteenth century, strongly

 | DOI:10.1163/9789004417120_006

influencing the area's long-term trade patterns, internal politics and institutional developments. Unlike that of the states in the Bight of Benin, gold ensured that the Akan states were never dependent on the transatlantic *slave* trade as a source of wealth, or as a means of asserting and maintaining the power of elites. External commercial relations were important as Asante (and other states before them) relied on imports of firearms to maintain their military effectiveness (Thornton 1999, pp. 57–64). However, they could obtain foreign manufactures through sales of gold or ivory, thereby releasing themselves from dependency on exports of captives. As will be argued in Chapter 5, palm oil had a similar impact around the Bight of Biafra. Many recent studies of the region have focused on the changes wrought by either the Atlantic slave trade in the eighteenth century (Shumway 2014, Sparks 2014, Ronnback 2014, Ipsen 2015) or the very significant developments in the nineteenth century (Wilks 1993, Dummet 1998, McCaskie 2003, Austin 2005). There are few examinations which link the earlier seventeenth-century history of the region studied by Kea (1982) with the events and developments in the following centuries. This study seeks to demonstrate that initial trade contacts and political developments are crucial for understanding later patterns of trade. In this region, the transatlantic slave trade should be seen more as a relatively brief interruption of very different longer term export patterns.

The structure of the chapter is as follows. Initially, it shows how, over the *longue durée,* the region's trade output had generally been based on the application of coerced labour to the production of export commodities. Next, the withdrawal of the British from the slave trade was a significant shock, especially given their dominance of the trade along the Gold Coast. However, the presence of British held forts, and the military campaign waged by the British navy against slaving vessels from other nations, cannot explain the sudden, and near complete stoppage of slave embarkations from the region. Warfare on the coast may have played a role, but continuing demand for coerced labour in the Americas, and the fact that exporting people remained hypothetically more than possible, suggest that other; endogenous factors were of greater importance.

Three factors were particularly crucial. Firstly, the value of the new trade in commodities was at least equal to, and probably exceeded that of the slave trade. Secondly, and in contrast to the Dahomeans (Chapter 7), the Asante faced no significant external enemies or economic competitors from the 1740s until their confrontations with the British in the later 1820s. As a result, there was less need for labour for the military, meaning households were freer to pursue their own economic agendas. Thirdly, political developments meant that most slaves originated in areas to the north of Asante. Their status as outsiders afforded them less opportunity to incorporate themselves into households/lineage groups, giving them fewer of the rights and protections enjoyed by free people or even enslaved Akans (see below for a definition of this term). Consequently, their labour could be more intensively exploited, making them better suited to production than export.

Next, the chapter will show that the presence of gold, and later kola, within the territories of Asante had to a range of major impacts on institutional development and labour decisions. The Asante state, unlike those in the Bight of Benin, developed within a context where the control and monopoly of gold was the defining characteristic of power and wealth. This provided a strong incentive to increase the production of households, whose members could in turn use greater numbers of coerced labourers to help increase their own wealth. The growth of markets for kola on the savannah provided additional opportunities for both elites and commoners to enrich themselves, and in doing so gain greater social prestige. Both the state and aristocratic elites were motivated to support this productive activity, as it did not threaten their power, while increasing their wealth.

1 Area of study

This study will mainly be limited to the Akan speaking territories which lie roughly within the forest, coastal and southern savannah zones stretching from the Volta river in eastern Ghana to south eastern CÔte d'Ivoire. The peoples of this region, speak related languages and have several broad cultural and agricultural practises in common as a result of shared historical experience (Chouin & De Corse 2010, p. 123). However, at a more local level the area also possesses a great diversity of ethnicities, cultures and polities, making it beyond the scope of this wider comparative study to investigate them all. The focus will be on the kingdom of the Asante, which at its greatest extent covered the territory of modern day Ghana until the towns of Yendi and Wa in the north. It is however important to note that the state only exercised more direct control in the core metropolitan region around Kumasi.[1]

Outside this zone, it could broadcast power through its military or diplomatic corps and enforce tribute, but those in the outer provinces enjoyed greater autonomy than those closer to the capital. These areas, which contained both the Asante kingdom and the Fante states of the coast, are the focus

1 The Asante themselves measured this area in terms of the time taken for a messenger from the capital at Kumasi to leave and return from the frontier which was given at one month. At distances further from this, direct control was considered impractical (Herbst 2000, p. 49).

of this study as they were responsible for trading the vast majority of the region's America-bound slaves, and therefore were most affected by the shift from export slavery to 'legitimate commerce'. As in the other case study regions, the slave trade was concentrated in just a few ports which possessed the required commercial infrastructure and connections to inland networks to handle the complex credit arrangements required to facilitate exchange between Atlantic and African merchants (Eltis et al. 1999). In this area, the Fante port towns of Anomabo, Cape Coast Castle and Elmina handled around eighty seven percent of all embarkations from the sixteenth to the nineteenth centuries.

In terms of ecology, the coastal regions occupied by the Fante were characterised by a combination of mangrove, coastal scrub and grassland. Further inland the core areas of the Asante empire consisted mainly of dense forest, except in areas where clearances created regions where agriculture was possible. Further north, the forest gave way to drier savannah areas (Taylor 1952). Crucially for this study, the empire also contained the many of West Africa's most productive gold fields as well as areas rich in kola trees (Dummet 1998, pp. 29–31, 153, 180; Abaka 2005, p. 13).

2 Long-term Trade Contacts

The impact and importance of the early trade between Europeans and the Gold Coast is disputed. In a series of articles Wilks (1978, 1985, 1993), supported by Austin (2008a, p. 611) and Yarak (1996), developed what has become known as the 'big bang' theory of Akan state development, namely the rapid change in the forest areas from a largely hunter/gatherer economy to one based on food crop production. Gold had been imported from West Africa to the Mediterranean since around the twelfth century via a Muslim community of traders known as the Wangara. This trans-Saharan trade had probably been the source of most of Europe's gold during the middle ages. It was gold that first drew Portuguese traders to this region in the 1480s (Thornton 1998, p. 32), and by the early sixteenth-century sources suggest that they were buying between 24,000 and 26,000 oz/year (Wilks 1993, p. 4). Wilks argues that this was facilitated by a highly sophisticated inland trading system, suggesting that the gold fields in the Akan territories were already being exploited before the arrival of European traders. The Portuguese found themselves in direct competition with Malian merchants able to supply almost all the products demanded by local consumers, such as manufactured cloth and metals. The Portuguese, however, had the capacity to use their ships to supply slaves, principally from the Kingdom of Benin, which greatly encouraged exports of gold (Law 1991, p. 116).

Between 1500 and 1530 Wilks estimates that over 12,000 slaves were imported into the region via their fort at Elmina. These additional labour inputs allowed for large scale clearances, which in turn made agriculture possible within the forest environment.

However, recent archaeological investigations, summarised by Chouin & Decorse (2010), have shown convincing evidence that the forest region had been settled by more complex, agricultural polities since around the ninth century, although many of these settlements were abandoned in the thirteenth and fourteenth centuries, possibly due to the impacts of the bubonic plague. These findings demonstrate that the expansion of agriculture in the region was not dependent on European intervention. However, the authors do acknowledge that at the time the Portuguese arrived on the Gold Coast, this was an area undergoing a recovery. As such, intensive labour would have been required to at least cut back forest regrowth and begin planting for agriculture, would have benefited from imports of slaves.[2] Alternatively, captives could have been put to work in mining to expand the region's output of gold. In the sixteenth century, North Europeans did not have American empires and therefore had few demands for slaves, while the Portuguese and Spanish were able to acquire most of their captives from West Central Africa (Van den Boogaart 1992). This meant that trade, at least in the Gold Coast, was focused on commodities, which is most clearly and physically demonstrated in the most expensive European investments in the region (until the railways of the twentieth century), the trading forts. The purpose of these forts was to protect the gold and ivory traded on the coast from attacks by pirates from the sea, and other European rivals, and only later were they primarily used to hold captives before embarkation on the middle passage (Lawrence 1963).

Thus, the region's early trade contacts with the Atlantic world were based on the *importation* of unfree labour and its application to the production of food, gold and other commodities. As a result, slaves within the region were highly valued for their productive capacities, as well as their potential as commodities for the Atlantic market. This is very like the situation at the beginning of the nineteenth century in the Bight of Biafra (Chapter 6), but in stark contrast to the Bight of Benin where Atlantic trade was entirely based on the *export* of people. Long trading contacts also led to the development of the most urbanised coastal environment in West Africa, which was not a product of transatlantic slave trade, and therefore not dependent on it (Kea 1982, p. 26, Shumway 2014, pp. 51, 52). Finally, it should also be noted that, while the

2 To give some idea of the scale of the labour required, Wilks (1993, pp. 56–59) estimates that clearing one hectare of virgin forest would have required moving 1,250 tons of moist vegetation, needing 500 days' labour, given the available technology.

Atlantic trade became increasingly important to the region, the gold trade continued to the savannah and trans-Saharan markets.[3] As a result, the export economy was never wholly beholden to Europe and the Americas.

It was only towards the end of the seventeenth century that slaves became a more important item of export, especially for the British (Eltis 1994, p. 249, Shumway 2014, p. 25). However, even then gold was still the main attraction for many traders. Den Heijer's (1997) research into Dutch West India Company (WIC) accounts shows that between 1674 and 1740, sixty four percent of the goods dispatched to Africa for trade were intended for non-slave commodities, and of these around eighty seven percent were intended for gold.[4] However, in terms of value, slaves were already generating slightly more income for the WIC in the last decades of the eighteenth century, and were far more valuable than gold and ivory in the period between 1701 and 1730 (Den Heijer 1997, pp. 129, 136, 159). From around the 1730s, slaves became the region's principal export, but this did not last long as slave exports began to decline in the 1780s (Austin 2013a). Chapter 7 will argue that declining numbers of captive exports from the Bight of Benin can be largely explained by exogenous shocks, especially the Haitian revolution and the withdrawal of the French, who were then the most important trading nation in that region. However, in the Gold Coast, no such external explanation has been identified in the literature.

The trade with the northern savannah remained an extremely important part of the Asante economy in the eighteenth century. Garrard (1980) estimates that between a third and a half of all gold was flowing to northern markets (Table 4.1). Wilks (1975, p. 257) suggests that trade in other commodities was also increasing from the 1730s and there are well documented cases of considerable fortunes made by Asante elites involved in the northern trade (McCaskie 2003, pp. 59, 60). By at least 1806 Muslim Hausa merchants were established in Kumasi under the protection of the state. They maintained links with a diaspora linking the forests of Asante with major urban centres in the interior, such as Kano. From 1800, the government in Kumasi began a policy of channelling all its northern trade through the market town of Salaga, which made it far easier for Asante producers to market their kola and gold to foreign traders (see below).[5] The reasons behind this policy were twofold. On the one hand,

3 Garrard (1980) estimates that in the sixteenth century northern markets probably took more gold than that of the Atlantic. In the seventeenth century, this changed with around 25% going north to the Savannah kingdoms of the interior and 75% to Europeans.

4 During this period, the TSTD indicates that Dutch vessels were responsible for around 20% of slaves exported. The WIC was responsible for over 90% of these.

5 Salaga was located north east of the capital near crucial fording points of the Volta river and on the caravan routes to the markets of Hausaland (Lovejoy 1982, p. 254).

the state needed a new trade centre after the destruction of the town of Gbuipe by Asante forces, which had previously been an important merchant hub (Wilks 1975, p. 262). On the other hand, declining revenues from slave outputs and/or a desire to diversify the economy away from dependence on the Atlantic might also have played a role (Wilks 1975, p. 262, Lovejoy 1982, p. 254). However, crucially, the decision was taken before the British withdrew from the slave trade, indicating that abolition was not a key driver of economic change. Unlike the Dahomeans and the merchants in Biafra, the Asante already had well established trade networks with alternative markets in Africa. The existing growth in these markets prior to 1808, made it easier for them to rapidly re-orientate themselves away from an Atlantic, slave export economy.

In the nineteenth century, the region's exports were once again dominated by export commodities. The broad story of economic change in the Asante kingdom during this period is fairly uncontested (Wilks 1975, Austin 1995, McKaskie 2003). Central to this change was the rise of the Sokoto caliphate in the first decade of nineteenth-century under the leadership of Usman den Fodio. He was an ethnic Fulani who had been a scholar at the Hausa court of Gobir, but had become disenchanted with what he considered as the decadence of the region's rulers, and had launched a jihad aimed at restoring Islamic purity (Last 1969, Lovejoy 1978). He and his followers were to eventually conquer a vast swathe of territory roughly analogous to the northern regions of today's Nigeria. For the Asante, this created a new, rich economic zone that could effectively compete with Atlantic markets as both a market for, and supplier of, goods. It was the kola nut, or rather a specific variety *cola nitidia*, that was probably the most important commodity in the trade with the north. This nut is a powerful stimulant[6] and is not specifically mentioned in the koran as being *haram*. As a result, its consumption was generally tolerated in Muslim regions (Sharrett 1995, p. 21). In an atmosphere of Islamic revival, demand for kola nuts soared, which was to greatly benefit the economy of Asante. Their empire encompassed almost all the region's *cola nitidia* trees, giving them a near monopoly on regional output (Abaka 2005, Lovejoy 1980). In exchange they received slaves, leather goods, shea butter and livestock, as well as Hausa cloth which was becoming increasingly sophisticated both in quality and design (Austin 2013b).

With regard to the Atlantic trade, the main export was gold and these exports increased significantly after abolition (Table 4.1). This was almost

6 Containing both caffeine and theobromine, stimulants found in coffee and cocoa (Lovejoy 1995, p. 98).

TABLE 4.1 Akan gold exports, 1651–1850 (ounces)

	Northern trade	European trade	Total
1651–1700	500	1,500,000	2,000,000
1701–1750	400	1,200,000	1,600,000
1751–1800	400	800	1,200,000
1801–1850	200	1,400,000	1,600,000

Source: Garrard (1980, p. 163)

certainly to ensure that enough European and American trade goods, in particular weapons, ammunition and cloth that were seen as vital to the Asante state and society, continued to be imported (see Section 4.3 for an estimate of the volume and value of these trades). The Gold Coast also had a far more diverse export economy in the nineteenth century than it had during the era of slave exports. In the eighteenth century, there is no evidence that anything other than gold or ivory was exported in any quantity.[7] The CUST records indicate that from the 1820s the region was exporting increasing quantities of ivory, hardwoods (teak and ebony), dyewoods (camwood and barwood) as well as pepper and palm oil.[8] Furthermore, the provisioning trade seems to have continued, at least along the eastern side of the coast.[9]

7 For example, the region did not export either hardwoods or dyewoods, which were both in demand. Richard Miles, a former governor of Cape Coast Castle who worked for the Company of Merchant Venturers from 1765 to 1784 in his evidence to a parliamentary committee in 1789 stated that: "*I never knew a single stick* (of woods) *of any kind produced on the Gold Coast.*" PP, Minutes of Evidence taken before a committee of the whole house to whom it was referred to consider the circumstances of the slave trade (1789), p. 115.

8 From 1828 to 1840 British ships visiting the Gold Coast imported the following quantities: Hardwoods/Dyewoods: 2535 tons, Foodstuffs (coffee, rice, pepper, maize, coconuts): 423 tons, Palm oil 12, 504 tons, Ivory 7317 cwt, Beeswax 281 cwt, gums (animi/copal) 425 cwt (TNA CUST 4/23–4/35).

9 Meredith (1811, pp. 179, 180) mentions that maize and other agricultural products are sold east of Winnebah. Bold (1822), discussing the area around Accra notes that the "*...whole of the neighboring country (which is extremely fertile) has recently been cultivated to a very considerable extent, and is now become celebrated for the produce of maize, or Indian* wheat..." (p. 59). In 1817, the governor of the fort at Commenda noted that agricultural production had increased due to "*....vessels having come to this part of the coast for the cargoes of corn...*" TNA T70/1603 State and Condition of Commenda Fort.

Examined over the *longue durée*, the Akan region's export economy was only ever briefly focused on the export of people. For at least the first two centuries of external trade contact, and then again from 1808, output from the Gold Coast was dominated by commodities, not slaves. Thus, the early and complete withdrawal of the area from the transatlantic slave trade should be viewed as a reversion to the norm, not an aberration. However, a number of questions remain, in particular regarding the actual impact of British abolition. This will be subject of the next section.

3 A New Interpretation of the Impact of Abolition

The British, for almost all of the eighteenth century, embarked the greatest numbers of captives and had the most substantial physical presence on the Gold Coast. The sudden withdrawal of British ships from the trade in 1808 can explain the *timing* of the ending of slave exports from the region. However, in the eyes of some officials, the presence of the British meant that the Akans were *incapable* of continuing the export of people, thus forcing them to switch to commodity exports. This was argued, for example, in an 1827 report: "*That the number* (of slaves) *exported from the Gold Coast is small, can be attributed only to the obstacles which the European settlements oppose……Should this part of the coast be abandoned, all efforts to suppress the slave trade will be vain.*"[10] Yet there is evidence to suggest that had there been sufficient slaves to buy, then traders from the Americas would have stepped in, at least initially. Local merchants such as Samuel Brew were known to have retained contacts with Spanish traders and were accused of continuing to sell slaves (Bowdich 1819 p. 339). Reynolds (1974, pp. 39, 40) quotes a number of primary sources suggesting that Spanish and Portuguese ships continued to visit the coast, especially around the Dutch fort of Accra.

American vessels were also active during this period and, even though their government had officially outlawed the trade, hostility to the English meant that they were unwilling to enforce their treaties or aid in the abolition campaign. As a result, many US merchants carried on trading with impunity (Brooks 1970). An analysis of vessels reported arriving at or passing by the main British fort at Cape Coast Castle shows that in the immediate wake of abolition there was an increase in the number of Portuguese and American ships (Figure 4.1). Thereafter this decreased, but sufficient numbers were passing by

10 CO267/93 1827 Report of the Commissioners of Inquiry in the State of the Colony of Sierra Leone, Second Part, p. 25.

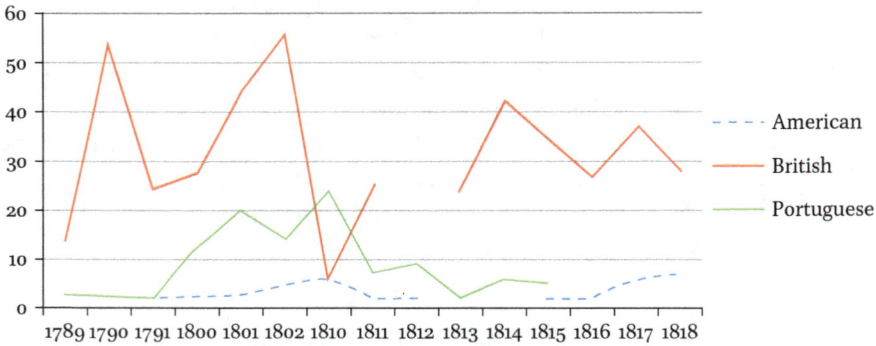

FIGURE 4.1 Number of ships reported arriving or passing Cape Coast Castle 1789–1791/1800–1802/1810–1818 by nationality
Source: TNA: T70/1561–1604

to pick up slaves, had any been available. For example, in 1812, 8 ships from Portugal/Brazil and 2 from the US passed by Cape Coast. For the period from 1808 to 1820 Portuguese ships to West Africa carried an average of 280 captives, and those from the US 122. Had the ships in 1812 decided to embark slaves somewhere on the Gold Coast region, they could have loaded around 2,480 slaves.

The next question is whether these forts could act as an effective military deterrent to determined slave traders, which the evidence suggests they did not. For a start, the British government pursued a policy during this period of reducing both the number of settlements and personnel stationed permanently on the coast, and relinquishing ultimate authority to the governor in Sierra Leone.[11] Even before this policy was enacted, the British forts were far from being an effective military deterrent to slave ships. Crews on slaving voyages tended to be fairly substantial, given the need to control large numbers of unwilling prisoners, and were for this reason also very well armed (Thomas 1999, Rediker 2007, Harms 2008). While slightly smaller than during the apogee of the trade, crews in the era of abolition averaged 25 men per ship.[12] With the exception of the major forts at Cape Coast Castle and Anomabo, the British forts were not particularly well manned or armed, and had long been the

11 An 1817 report recommended that "*….the number of those forts and settlements should be diminished by the disposal or abandonment of such as may, upon strict inquiry, appear not be of service in a sufficient degree fully to compensate for their expense*" Parliamentary Papers, Report from the Committee on African Forts (431).

12 Source: TSTD, crew size 1808–1860.

subject of parliamentary criticism for their generally poor defences and lack of proper maintenance.[13] In 1811, Henry Meredith, an employee of the British company of merchants, published an account of the Gold Coast. He had been present at Cape Coast Castle during the Asante invasion and recounted how the small garrison was only barely able to keep out an assault by Asante forces. Perhaps as a result of his experiences, one of his key aims was to try and convince the British government to invest more money and provide more soldiers for the forts (Meredith 1811, p. 128). As can be seen from Table 4.2, his concerns were justified as, apart from Cape Coast Castle and Anomabo, the British forts were neither well manned nor sufficiently equipped. At Winnebah, where he was governor, Meredith wrote that "*…garrison of this fort amounts to no more than seven soldiers; a number not capable of defending itself against the natives…*", and noted further that the fort was not even able to employ its guns against the landing area due to the number of houses built between it and the beach.

Even at Cape Coast, he noted that the governor was never able to enforce his authority over the Fante (Meredith 1811, pp. 99, 172, 174). Another weakness of the forts was that, at that time, they seemed to have relied entirely on European soldiers.[14] It has long been known that the West Coast of Africa hosted a range of tropical maladies that, more often than not, proved fatal, or at the very least debilitating, to Europeans, severely limiting their military effectiveness (Curtin 1972, p. 9, Shumway 2014, p. 63, Rönnback & Öberg 2016). Sparks' (2014) history of Anomabo has demonstrated that power rested securely in the hands of local elites, and attempts by overbearing British officials to force events usually led to their humiliation or removal. This fact was acknowledged in an 1816 report which noted that "*…as a means of checking the slave trade, our forts on the Gold Coast do not appear to be of any further use than merely to prevent its being carried on within their own walls. Outside of that small range, they either have not, or do not exercise any jurisdiction.*"[15]

13 One report noted that forts were "*….in bad condition and some of them so ruinous as to be in no degree tenable…*" and that local officials were abusing their positions to make money at the expense of other merchants. T70/177 Return from the commissioners for the Trade and Plantations to the honourable House of Commons, relating to the General State of the trade with Africa the Condition of the forts and settlements there belonging to the African Company January 1777, p. 7.

14 Rönnback (2014) finds no record of Africans being employed in a military capacity. Likewise, in an 1816 report on the Gold Coast forts, which lists both African workers and slaves, there is no mention of non-European solders; PP: (506) Report from the Select Committee on Papers Relating to the African Forts 1816, pp. 182–191.

15 PP: (506) Report from the Select Committee on Papers Relating to the African Forts 1816, p. 137.

TABLE 4.2 British personnel and ordnance at Gold Coast forts 1811 and 1816 (excluding Cape Coast Castle and Anomabo)

Fort	No. European staff (soldiers)		No. cannon (remarks)		No. muskets (remarks)	
	1811	1816	1811	1816	1811	1816
Sekondi	4	5 (3)	0	N/A	7	N/A
Commenda	8	10 (8)	28	34	6	6
Dixcove	10	10 (8)	29	31 ('Gun carriages rotten')	6 (old)	8 ('In bad order')
Appollonia	7	8 (7)	0	N/A	5	N/A
Accra	14	12 (9)	29	29 ('the cannon indifferent except a few')	12	12
Tantumquerry	9	9 (8)	17	N/A	10	N/A
Winneba	8	9 (7)	13	13 ('The Guns are very old')	12	12
Prampram	2	Closed	0	Closed	0	Closed

Source: TNA T70/1593, PP: (506) Report from the Select Committee on Papers Relating to the African Forts 1816, pp. 181–192

A further complication is that by 1816 the Asante kingdom had acquired direct control over routes to the coast, allowing them to easily bypass the small and rather ineffectual forts. One of the key features of the Asante state was its system of roads which headed away from Kumasi like spokes on wheel to the north and south of its territories (Wilks 1975, p. 8). This allowed it to more effectively project power from the centre, and to better receive tribute from its more distant vassals (McCaskie 2003). In the 1740s it had extended road V to the coast as far as Accra, but access to the Atlantic along roads VI and VII were blocked by the Fante coastal coalition. This coalition was a loose alliance of states along the coast, from the Pra River to Accra, based on the kinds of cross-cutting horizontal lines of authority described by McIntosh (1999). These were strengthened by the development of a shared culture, centred on the religious shrine of Nananom Mpow, and language (Shumway 2014, p. 131). Nonetheless, this union was not entirely stable, and individual states and towns within it were often at war with each other. However, it was able to lessen the negative impacts of the slave trade for the Fante people by providing some measure of protection against enslavement, and was also strong enough to protect the region from Asante and other regional powers throughout the eighteenth century (McCarthy 1983, p. 7).

While Elmina had always been closely aligned to the Asante due to the longstanding Dutch alliance with Kumasi[16] (Yarak 1990), road VII still needed to pass through Fante territory. As will be argued below, control of the slave trade was probably not a key foreign policy objective of the Asante state, and warfare in the south was expensive as the Fante controlled walled towns and possessed firearms which required a heavy military commitment to overcome (Klein 2001). It was not until 1806 that Asante was either provoked or had a sufficient pretext to commit to a large-scale campaign against the Fante. Whatever the ultimate reasons, the proximate cause for war, outlined in a letter by Asantehene to the British envoy Bowdich (1819),[17] was a succession dispute in Assin, a tribute kingdom of Asante on the borders of the coastal coalition. According to sources, one of the claimants to the throne sought and gained the support of the Fantes, who also murdered Asante messengers/diplomats sent to the coast. A series of invasions followed in 1807, 1811 and 1816 which saw the total defeat of the Fantes and which were marked by an unusually high level of brutality and slaughter.[18]

This war may have been an important contributing factor to why the slave trade was to end so abruptly after abolition. Commercial activity, which required that Europeans could entrust large quantities of trade goods to local merchants in the expectation that slaves would be delivered at an agreed future date, would have been severely curtailed with the presence of Asante forces blockading the trade roads. Correspondence from the British forts along the coast make it clear that the conflict was extremely damaging to trade. In 1807 officials mention that Asante raids threatened the British fort and that

16 Yarak (1990) argues that Dutch activity on the coast diminished considerably during the nineteenth-century, which was itself closely linked to the decline of the WIC and the rising power of the English. This meant they were always more reliant on the support and goodwill of Asante.

17 Also confirmed by an earlier account by Meredith (1812), the governor of the British fort of Winneba, who witnessed the conflict at first hand.

18 Dupuis (1824), a British diplomat sent to Kumasi to renegotiate a peace settlement with Asante notes "….the utter extermination of the Fantes was contemplated, and orders were issued to spare neither the aged nor young children; but both sexes, and all ages were for a time doomed to expire by the sword and the musket, or in the flames of their houses." p. 255.

there was little that they could do to prevent them or protect their Fante allies. The governor of Tantumquerry fort noted that "…*they* (the Fante) *consider themselves no better situated in regard to the protection of the British than a flock sheep which is dispersed in every direction would have the right to expect from a lamb*…."[19] In 1811, the fighting meant it was impossible to continue any kind of trading, with one official telling his superiors in London that "…*in mentioning trade I may at once declare that it is nearly annihilated at all your forts except Accra and Appollonia*…."[20] Trade was still badly affected in 1814 when the Governors at Sekondi, Accra and Dixcove forts all noted that trade between the interior and the coast continued to suffer due to the instability and mistrust caused by the conflict.[21]

However, while no doubt disruptive in the short term, the result was that the entire Fante coast was then in theory part of the empire of Asante "…*with the reservation of a judicial authority to the company over such towns as stood in the vicinity of any of the castles*…" (Dupuis 1824, p. 263). Thus, by around 1816, Asante had the potential to control both the supply and sale of slaves along a 200 km stretch of coast that had supplied the Americas with around 15% of its coerced labour in the previous century. As noted in Chapter 1, the demand for such labour had not diminished in the nineteenth century. It is also important to note that this window of opportunity was not long open. Despite some losses, a British coalition with various southern powers was able to defeat an Asante army at the battle of Katomonso in 1825. In subsequent peace negotiations, Asante agreed to give up their right of tribute from the coastal towns and to ensure that lawful, or non-slave, trade would continue, which essentially saw the exchange of Asante to British power over the coast (Wilks 1975, pp. 182–192). However, in the 18 years before this, had the Asante kings wanted to export substantial numbers of slaves, it would have been possible.

As will be argued in Chapter 6, the Dahomeans were able to devise new ways of exporting slaves from different parts of the Bight of Benin during the 1840s, when the slave patrol was a far more effective operation. They did have an advantage that slaves could be more rapidly transported along the inland lagoons which paralleled the coast (Law 2004, pp. 192, 193). However, the Dahomeans also had more limited routes upon which to march slaves from the interior to the coast. Asante slave dealers could simply have taken slaves down

19 TNA T70/1586 Hamilton to Torrance 12th July 1808 , see also Torrance to Committee 12th June 1807.

20 T70/1593 White to committee 1st July 1811. See also correspondence on January 1811, 26 March 1811, 26 May 1811 and when he notes that *"In mentioning trade may at once declare that it is nearly annihilated at all your forts except Accra and Appollonia…."*.

21 T70/1598 19, 22, 27 April 1814.

road v to western ports such as Pram Pram which had no European presence by 1816. Alternatively, slaves might even have been carried to the Bight of Benin for sale. One obvious place, would have been Little Popo, located in modern day Togo near the Volta river. Asante had long maintained trade relations with the town and exerted at least some political influence there (Wilks 1975, p. 57). In addition, the river had long taken goods, for instance salt, to northern markets such as Salaga (Reynolds 1974, p. 27) and was to serve as an artery of commerce for palm oil from the Krobo region from the 1820s (Lynn 1997, p. 39). The town of Salaga was already an established slave market in the early nineteenth-century (see below for further discussion) and was situated within a few days journey from the mouth of the Volta. Law (2004, p. 40) shows that Gold Coast merchants had been taking the sea route to Benin since the mid-seventeenth-century to trade for cloth and other goods. Strickrodt (2015, p. 195) notes that there is some evidence to suggest that small numbers of slaves were being taken by canoe from Accra for sale in Popo. However, there is no evidence to suggest that there was any concerted effort to develop an alternative outlet for coerced labour by either the Asante state or its traders.

To conclude this section, the gold coast region displayed a long-term preference for commodity exports and neither the British withdrawal, nor the disruptions caused by the Asante-Fante wars, provide a fully satisfactory explanation for why Asante did not re-engage with transatlantic slave trading after 1808. It seems that to understand *why* the Gold Coast region withdrew so abruptly from the slave trade, as well as explain *when* it happened, it is necessary to examine factors internal to the wider Gold Coast region. The next section will investigate what factors might have been influencing the Asante at the turn of the nineteenth century.

4 Economic and Political Considerations in 1808

4.1 *The Financial Cost of Abolition*

The first factor considered is whether Asante suffered financially by moving away from slave trade. To calculate this an estimation of the combined value, in GB£, of the exports of gold and kola from 1808 to 1850 is calculated. Secondly, to construct another hypothetical estimate of how much the Asante state and its traders would have gained had they continued trading in gold and slaves, and not diverted labour towards kola production and mining. Comparing these two totals gives at least a rough approximation of whether or not Asante paid any kind of financial price for giving up the export of captives. These calculations are also based on the assumption that the increase in production could be met with the labour available within the kingdom. To test this, it is necessary to estimate how many extra people would be required to mine gold and grow kola, and compare the findings with what is known about labour capacity. This method is far from ideal and is almost certainly a very pale reflection of reality for a number of reasons.

Firstly, given the limited data, it isn't possible to show changes over time. The final calculation only shows the overall value of trade for the period as a whole. Secondly, all of these goods were bartered for commodities and manufactures of the Americas, Europe or the Savannah. The sterling price of these goods cannot fully reflect their social, political or economic value to the elites and households in Africa (although later sections will deal with these issues in more detail). However, this was a monetised region and goods were assigned monetary values that can be at least roughly compared to sterling as evidenced by Austin (2015, pp. 128–34) and Lovejoy and Richardson's (1995) work on slave prices in the African interior. Additionally, there are no equivalent records to the British customs ledgers which itemise the volumes of kola which were produced and sold, as it was only marketed to northern savannah markets. As a result, all of the figures used come from estimates and assumptions based on scattered references in primary sources. To account for this low, high and median estimates of kola output from Asante territories are calculated to add to the slightly more reliable figures for gold provided by Garrard (1980).

Finally, the calculation for commodity exports is a rather conservative figure. It does not include the output of other commodities such as palm oil and woods which, as stated in earlier, had become relatively substantial by the 1840s. However, as already mentioned, it is likely that the majority of these goods, and especially palm oil, were coming from the eastern side of the Gold Coast and therefore outside Akan areas. Furthermore, the calculation does not account for the internal trade in slaves. Following abolition, the falling prices of slaves led to a rise in slave ownership along the coast (Adu-Boahen 2010, Manning 1990, 144). These slaves were largely supplied by Asante traders who were, by the 1840s, according to contemporary sources, exporting large numbers of captives taken from areas to the north (Cruikshank 1853, Vol 2 p. 244, McSheffrey, 1983, p. 353). However, there is currently no study on the numbers of those exported and, until the 1820s, the coastal areas (at least in Fante territories) were still devastated by the conflict with Asante and were not in the position to take advantage of opportunities for slave ownership (Sanders 1982, p. 53).[22] For these reasons this trade is excluded from the calculations.

22 The governors of the various forts along the Gold Coast made regular mention of how the war had disrupted trade. See for example tna, T70/1601 1816 State and Condition of

The output of gold from the Asante kingdom is based on the estimates found in Garrard (1980).[23] Gold prices on the coast are taken at £3 12sh/ounce (Wilks, 1975, p. 418, Garrard 1980, pp. 258, 259) and are assumed to reflect international gold prices by remaining extremely stable during the period under study (Officer & Williamson 2016). There are no accurate figures on the output and production of kola until the colonial era but it is possible to calculate a rough estimate. For full details of the workings and sources see Appendix 4.1. The basis for the calculations comes from sources quoted in Lovejoy (1980). One such source suggests that in around 1820 roughly 1,000 donkeys per year were leaving from the Salaga market laden with kola nuts, and another that, in the 1850s, this figure had increased to 6,000 (Lovejoy 1980, p. 116). These have been taken as base measurements for the low and high estimates of output. Kola nuts were measured in headloads, or *apakan,* each weighing around 80 lbs, and, according to one source, each donkey could carry around 100 lbs or 1.2 headloads (Lovejoy 1980, p. 116). Prices were measured in headloads and sources quote figures which range from around £0.375 (Wilks 1975, p. 268) to £2.5 (Bowdich 1819, p. 333) per load. These have been taken as low and high estimates. If the low estimate for the number of donkeys is multiplied by 1.2 by the low-price estimate, it gives a very conservative estimate of value. The high estimate uses the figure of 6,000 donkeys quoted by sources in Lovejoy and headload price of £2.5 from Bowdich.

For the hypothetical value of the slave trade, had the region continued exporting captives after 1808, the average slaves exported per year from the Gold Coast between 1770 and 1808 have been taken and compared this to the average slaves embarked in the Bights of Benin and Biafra between 1809 and 1850. These all average around 4,800 per year, so this figure is taken as an estimate of output. Slave prices are from the price data on the coastal value of slaves in Lovejoy and Richardson (1995). It is also the case that the region would have continued to export gold, but that the quantity would probably have been less. As will be argued in later, increases in production required additional inputs of coerced labour, which would have been scarcer if slaves were still being exported. Gold output figures have therefore been taken from the second half of the eighteenth century, as they were somewhat lower than those of the next century when more labour was available.

Commenda Fort, 1816 State and Condition of Annamabo Fort, T70/1603 1817 State and Condition of Apollonia Fort, 1818 State and Condition of Accra Fort, 1818 State and Condition of Tantumquerry Fort.

23 These are also used by Austin (2005).

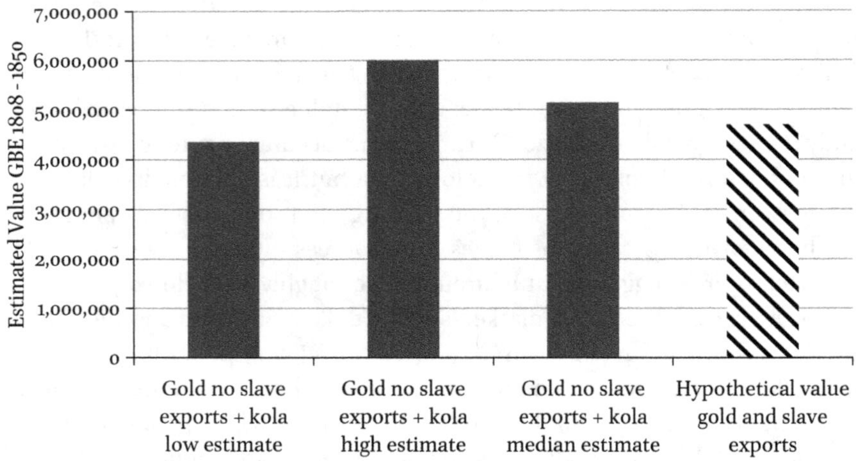

FIGURE 4.2 Estimated value (GB£) of the trade in kola, gold + hypothetical slave exports and gold with a slave trade 1808–1850
Sources: see pages 156–158

The combined value of the hypothetical nineteenth-century gold and slave trade from 1808 to 1850 is £4,670,771. The value of the commodity trades is higher on every estimate except when taking the low value for kola (£4,353,750) and even then the difference is not substantial. Furthermore, as will be shown in Chapters 5 and 6, the transatlantic slave trade in West Africa in the nineteenth century was extremely volatile with output impacted by changing prices, the growing effectiveness of the slave trade patrol and regional political events. By contrast, both gold and kola seem to have enjoyed both stable prices and steadily rising demand over the entire period.[24]

The state also benefited directly from the commodity trade. For example, it took steps to ensure that its own kola merchants enjoyed greater advantages than private traders. The government would not allow Asante farmers or traders into the market until its own officials had arrived, and they were also exempted from a toll paid on each load of kola (Lovejoy 1982, p. 251). These measures, along with the fact that the king owned more slaves and land, probably ensured that the state had a substantial minority share of the trade, and of course also benefitted from the taxes levied on foreign merchants and its own citizens who paid tolls to use the roads to Salaga (Austin 1996, p. 26).

24 Lovejoy's (1980, p. 120) data on the retail price of kola nuts in Savannah markets over the nineteenth-century suggests that prices, once one has accounted for inflation, were remarkably stable until the 1890s.

Furthermore, individuals were required by law to send each nugget of gold they found to the capital, where it would be turned into gold dust. A proportion of this was claimed by the state, some by the chief or stool holder of the land, and the rest was given back to the household who originally mined or panned the gold. Furthermore, gold was also liable as a duty on the death of a household head (Wilks 1993 pp. 148, 149, McCaskie 2003, p. 48). Therefore, increased production led to more wealth flowing upwards to the king, thus increasing his ability to reward elite supporters and maintain his position as the kingdom's economic top dog.

This increase in production, with the land-extensive or Niebeor/Domar conditions of the region, required a more intensive use of coerced labour (Austin 2005 pp. 166, 167, Perbi 2004, pp. 70–86, Wilks 1993, p. 96). It must be assumed that if this had meant that elite groups faced shortages of labour to support them and their retinues, or the kingdom did not produce sufficient food for its major urban centres, then the use of slaves in the production of gold and kola would have been opposed (Arhin 1990, pp. 525, 526). However, there is no indication that this was the case in the first half of the nineteenth century. Austin (1995 p. 164) estimates that one man could mine around 1/62 of an ounce of gold per day. Garrard (1980, p. 163) suggests that output increased from around 27,000 ounces per year in the later eighteenth-century to 35,000 ounces/year in the first half of the nineteenth century. To produce 8,000 extra ounces per year would therefore require between 320,000 to 496,000 extra days worked per dry season.[25] Given an average dry season of around three months from late November to February (Wilks 1993, p. 56), this meant that an additional 3,500 to 5,500 labourers were required during the ninety-day period.

Kola also needed considerable labour inputs. It was most intensively grown in the clay loam soil and ochrosal forest zone of the central region of the Asante kingdom. Kola trees were typically planted alongside yams, cocoyams and cassava in between the 'hills' or mounds built from soil and vegetation which served as beds for their propagation. These mounds offered shade and protection for kola seeds which, when fully grown trees themselves, provided shade and helped prevent soil erosion. Harvesting took place in the dry season, which meant that labour did not need to be diverted from the production of subsistence crops except when previously fallow land needed to be cleared.[26] Abaka

25 During the rainy seasons artisanal mining in Asante was impossible and labour was required in food production (Dummett 1998, p. 51). In the dry season, existing household labour was still necessary for a wide range of agricultural and household tasks (Wilks 1993, pp. 56–63).

26 Wilks (1993, pp. 59–61) suggests that forest clearance was necessary around once every three years.

(2005) shows that this dry season labour was fairly intensive. The nuts needed to be picked, processed[27] and stored in specially made huts called *apata* which kept out the sunlight. Tree management was a year-round job and involved cutting away the roots and branches of other trees that could act as transmitters of pests or pathogens, and cutting down and removing trees which became sick or infected.

To give some idea of the scale of the new trade we can take the estimates of the number of headloads taken to Salaga. Wilks (1975, p. 268) quotes sources which say that each headload contained around 2,000 nuts. If we multiply this by the low, high and median estimates we have rough figures for the number of nuts produced. Abaka (2005, p. 33) quotes colonial reports from the early 20th century as giving an average annual yield of 765 nuts per kola tree. Dividing this figure by the total production figures means that in the first half of the nineteenth century Asante households were tending between 3,137 and 39,216 trees with a median figure of 21,176 trees (full workings see Appendix 4.1), representing a significant investment in time and labour.

However, these labour demands could almost certainly have been met by existing labour capacity. The population had probably been growing from the fifteenth century for a number of reasons. Firstly, the 'Columbian exchange' with the Americas had introduced a range of new crops such as maize and cassava, which allowed for longer growing seasons and improved the calorific quality of diets (Kiple 1984, pp. 24, 25). Secondly, the early exchange of gold for slaves for purposes of forest clearance expanded the agricultural potential of the forest zone (Austin 2005, p. 56). Thirdly, the conquests and expansion of the Asante empire in the eighteenth century led to many captives being sold, but also many were retained within the kingdom which swelled the population and increased its productive potential (Bowdich 1819, p. 323). Finally, the security brought by Asante military conquests (see below), and the law that forbade the selling of free Asantes into slavery (Maier 1990, p. 122), meant that the transatlantic slave trade did not have the destructive demographic impact that it had in other regions such as the Bight of Benin. The evidence suggests that in the earlier nineteenth-century the population of Asante grew and did not contract until the 1860s (see Appendix 4.2b). Furthermore, over the last twenty years of the slave trade the region was exporting an average of 7,325 captives (TSTD). If these were diverted from the Atlantic, into the domestic, economy there would have been more than enough additional workers to meet the new labour demands for use in kola and gold production.

---

27 This involved soaking the nuts, washing and draining them, removing bad nuts and then 'curing' them in baskets wrapped in banana leaves (Abaka 2005, pp. 32, 33).

This evidence suggests that over the first half of the nineteenth century, the region as a whole did not lose out financially by the ending of the transatlantic slave trade. Furthermore, there was sufficient labour to substantially increase production.[28] The next question is why the Asante elites, like those in the Bight of Biafra, were prepared to support the development of an economy based on commodity production. Hopkins' (1973) analysis of the impact of abolition was that it led to the rise of small scale units of production whose growing wealth came at the expense of elite groups who had previously grown rich from the slave trade. As will be argued in Chapter 6, this analysis can, to an extent, be applied to the Dahomean state, which maintained a slave export model for as long as it was able largely due to the huge economic, military and political benefits enjoyed by its elites as a result of capture and sale of captives. However, in the case of Asante and, for different reasons the Bight of Biafra, elite groups were prepared to not only tolerate, but actively support, household producers using coerced labour to produce exports instead of selling the slaves to external markets. For the Asante state, an important reason was that, unlike Dahomey, it did not face any significant external threats either to its borders or regional economic power from the 1740s. As such, it needed to devote far fewer resources to military activities and the result was a very different attitude towards trade.

4.2 *Asante and Regional Hegemony*

The forest clearances and population boom in the sixteenth century were instrumental in the development of a number of states that began to compete for control of the region's gold and people. The second half of the seventeenth century saw a military revolution among the various emerging Akan states. The introduction of firearms, paid for with gold and slaves, led to a change in both battlefield tactics and the mass mobilisation of populations (Kea 1982, pp. 154–164, McCaskie 2007, p. 10). The new methods in war allowed the Denkyira and the Akwamu to become the region's dominant powers from the 1660s, especially after the former captured most of the region's gold-producing land in around 1690. However, the military revolution soon spread to other areas and the Denkyira were in turn defeated by a Kumasi based coalition in 1701 led by Osei Tutu, and the priest Anokye, seen as the founding figures of the Asante state. By 1742 the Asante coalition had defeated its last serious rivals for power, Akyem (in the region around Accra) and incorporated the kingdom of Akwamu (Wilks 2001 pp. 118–125). Thereafter, they continued a period of

28 Although some groups may have suffered, such as the *caboceers* in the Fante region who had previously controlled the marketing of slaves to Europeans (Sparks 2014).

expansion, which both consolidated their power over the region and produced a large flow of captives to be sold to growing numbers of European traders at the coast (Maier 1990).

After its defeat of the Akwamu in the 1740s the Asante state did not face any serious military threat to its integrity. Campaigns from this period were about the enforcement of its authority or to exact tribute payments, not to protect their borders from equal or greater powers. This security was perhaps due to the fact that unlike the Dahomeans its territory did not border on more the powerful militarised states and empires of the savannah (see Chapter 6). In addition, the Asante controlled trade routes to the interior, so they were able to restrict the sales of guns to the states and societies on their northern borders, therefore maintaining an insurmountable advantage in warfare (Wilks 1975, p. 20).[29] In their southern territories the various kingdoms did possess guns, but lacked centralised political authority. This ensured that, while effective defensively, they lacked the political unity to organise offensive warfare, although they did regularly rebel against central authority.[30]

The result was twofold. Firstly, there was less of a need to maintain such a highly-militarised state like that of Dahomey, which also meant there were lighter labour demands on their population. There was, for example, no standing army (Maier 1990 p. 125, McCaskie 2003, p. 85), meaning that there were fewer non-productive elements in society who required the labour inputs of producers to feed and support them. Furthermore, this relative security meant fewer costly wars which reduced both the treasury and manpower.[31] In the 80 years from 1740 to 1820, the Asante army is recorded as campaigning for 35 years, but also enjoyed 46 years without going to war (Maier 1990, p. 130, Table 4.3). Of course, simply because there is no official record of conflict this does not mean there was no military activity. However, as will be argued in Chapter 7, official Dahomean ideology *required* that the king campaign annually. The absence of wars in official Asante chronology indicates at the very

29 One possible exception might have been the rebellion in 1798, led by the mainly Muslim states of Gyaman and Kong in support of a deposed king. They had access to cavalry which posed a severe threat to the infantry armies of the Asante, but never able to threaten the core area of the state (Wilks 1975, p. 254, Dupuis 1821, pp. 245, 246).

30 See for example, Dupuis (1821, p. 244) for the 1781 revolt by Assin, Akim and Aquapin.

31 Wilks (1975) notes that the disastrous campaign against the British and Fante forces in 1826 involved 40,000 men and cost the treasury around 29,000 oz gold dust and 20,000 oz gold nuggets which was equivalent to around 1 year's national income (p. 439). Austin (2005) suggests that losing campaigns against the Ewes, the Fante and the British from 1869–1873 led to such heavy losses from casualties and disease that it contributed to a decline in the kingdom's population (p. 58).

least that it was less concerned with warfare from an ideological standpoint. As a result, the state had less pressure to directly manage and control the labour forces of the kingdom, which would be crucial to household labour decisions.

The absence of pressing threats to the kingdom's territorial integrity in the eighteenth century; also allowed for the development of elite coalitions favouring the promotion of trade and wealth above war. Wilks (1975, p. 481) suggested that in the nineteenth century two very broad 'parties' dominated nineteenth-century Asante state policy:

> ...those subscribing to mercantilist policies and reading the state as essentially organised for the promotion of trade – the adherents of the peace party – and those subscribing to imperialist policies and regarding the state as essentially organised for the control of territory and the exaction of tribute – the adherents of the war party.

While this interpretation of Asante history has been subject to some criticism as being overly simplistic (Aidoo 1977), others have used the framework as means of analysing the broad coalitions impacting Asante state policy (Austin 1996, p. 4). Wilks (1975, p. 678) suggests that the 'peace party' only became more influential after abolition when slave raiding became less profitable. However, as noted in earlier, the Asante state and its traders had already begun investing in the northern trade before 1808. State policy was already being influenced by those advocating investments in trade as well as war. In Chapter 7 we will see that no such faction ever emerged among the ruling coalition in Dahomey, and that this was probably largely owing to threats faced by the state from other states such as Oyo, or hostile competitors such as the Popos or Porto Novo along the coast.[32] The security enjoyed by Asante elites encouraged the development of alternative policy options to warfare. The politics of the region also had an impact on the origin of the slaves acquired by the Akans and this in turn played a role in determining how they were used.

4.3 *Outsiders as Slaves*

During the period of Asante expansion, the southern area of modern day Ghana provided the rich pool of slaves for capture. However, the associated

32 There has been at least one interpretation of Dahomean history which suggests that there were, as in Asante, 'Peace and War' parties favouring either commodities or slave trades. Yoder (1974) labelled these the 'Fly and Elephant' parties which, according to his analysis, developed in the 1840s. However, this hypothesis has not been taken up by other scholars.

violence and insecurity also motivated people to organise better means of defence. One example comes from the Krobo people of eastern Ghana, who moved into the defensible mountain areas north of Accra, which kept them safer from raiders (Wilson 1991). The coastal peoples themselves engaged in slave trading, which provided them with guns. They also built walled towns and created self-defence militias, known as *Asafo,* companies which provided a substantial military deterrent (Shumway 2014). As a result, slave raiding and buying by the Asante came to increasingly focus on the territories to their north (Lovejoy 2011, p. 175, Austin 2005, p. 116), although many captives were also bought in the market at Salaga.

The "*...stateless or near-stateless peoples on both sides of what is now Ghana/Burkina Faso border.*" (Johnson 1986c. p. 346) were much easier targets as the Asante were able to prevent the people of the region acquiring firearms, thus ensuring they possessed an overwhelming military advantage (Wilks 1975, p. 67). Furthermore, the open savannah terrain made it more difficult to evade capture. Archaeological work in the area suggests that people were being forced to adopt the kinds of offensive measures suggested by the predatory state theory in the nineteenth century (Swanepoel 2009). Maier (1990, p. 128) estimates that in the late eighteenth-century, Asante's five northern provinces all gave tribute in slaves, estimated at around 1,000 each/year. This figure is to be contrasted with a total of just 500 from all of its five southern provinces.

The 'foreign' origins of these slaves is important, as these captives were non-Akans and this made them significantly more valuable as workers. Free Akans were organised around matrilineal clans, the *abusua,* which traced their roots to a common ancestress. Those outside the abusua were essentially non-people who could be treated as such until granted some rights of kinship (McCaskie 2003, p. 96). The authority to grant such rights was in the hands of the state or its local representatives, giving them a powerful tool of coercion to control the large numbers of slaves living amongst free people (McCaskie 2003 p. 97). Incorporation depended on many factors but was considerably easier for those who already spoke an Akan language and were accustomed to the local culture.

Those from northern regions were handicapped by their lack of a common language, and were often physically different from their owners with distinctive facial scars that marked them clearly as outsiders (Lovejoy 2011, p. 169). Within Akan society they were referred to as *ndonko* so as to separate them from Akan slaves and were subject to a good deal of discrimination (Lovejoy 1982, p. 271). Cruikshank (1852, p. 244) describes the "*Donko*" as characterised by "*...an extraordinary degree of stolidity and brutishness and exhibit a very low type of intellect and breeding.*" He goes on to note that, along the coast, northern slaves who arrived as children had a far better chance of quickly assimilating, but an adult was destined to remain as "*…a dull, stolid beast of burden all the days of his life…*" (p. 245). In a telling remark, he notes that adult slaves were far more valuable than children, suggesting that their value was a reflection of their immediate labour potential.

As the Akans were absorbing large numbers of people from outside their territories, there were means by which the non-free might eventually gain more rights. This might be through military service as in the case of the *Asafo* companies in the Fante areas, or by slow integration over several generations (Shumway 2014, p. 150, Perbi 2004, p. 113) However, it was probably the case that slaves from outside of Akan territories could not generally be expected to quickly assimilate and gain at least some of the rights enjoyed by their owners, which might have made them doubly appealing to those who wished to increase their wealth through production by exploiting unfree labour.

To summarise these sections, the Asante state was orientating its economy away from slave to gold and kola exports in the late eighteenth-century. The lack of external threats created sufficient stability to encourage certain elites to begin investing in trade instead of war, and the commodity trade was at least as, if not more, valuable than the export of captives. Furthermore, the slaves that were being captured or imported into Akan territories were more suited to production than to export. The next section will examine the impact of gold on the development of Asante state and society, and argue that its centrality in the culture meant that it would always be prioritised over slave exports.

5 Gold and the Asante State

The aim of the Asante state, or more specifically the palace organisation based around the Asantehene or king, was the preservation of its own power and wealth. However, it faced a number of challenges common to many West African ruling groups. Firstly, projecting power in land extensive conditions was costly and difficult (Herbst 2000). Secondly, the state's power was always checked by elites who controlled the lineage groups to whom most of their free subjects owed their primary loyalty. Finally, as already mentioned, the Asante kingdom never maintained a permanent standing army (see below for a wider discussion on this point), instead relying on levies of troops from the very lineage groups it sought to control, which meant that it could rarely rely on violence to enforce its rule within the kingdom (Wilks 2003 pp. 85–88). However, while there were a number of coups or 'destoolments' during the 1780s and 1790s, none of these seriously threatened the cohesion or stability of the ruling coalition over the eighteenth or early nineteenth centuries (Aidoo 1977, Wilks 1975, p. 372, McCaskie 2003, p. 49). This success was predicated on the maintenance of a hierarchal system of patronage and reward which ultimately depended on control over the production and distribution of gold.

Working with the framework developed by North et al. (2009, p. 43) the Asante kingdom can be characterised as a basic natural state which had developed a "*...durable and stable organisational structure...*" To remain in control the ruling coalition headed by the Asantehene had to reward the powerful elites for their support and ensure that their privileges, goals and organisations were closely aligned with the state. The system that developed was what Arhin (1990, p. 525) characterised as a patrimonial state based on a 'regulated ranking system'. This is perhaps best illustrated by a schema developed by Wilks (1993, p. 145) in Figure 4.3. The power of the Asantehene was represented by two symbolic artefacts: the *Sika Dwa* or Golden Stool representing his political/judicial supremacy and the *Sika Mena* or Golden Elephant's tail, which again only an Asantehene could carry, symbolising his position at the top of the economic food chain.[33] All wealth within the kingdom flowed upwards towards the king, who could then distribute favours down to the elites. The hierarchy was actively maintained through sumptuary laws and regulations designed to restrict

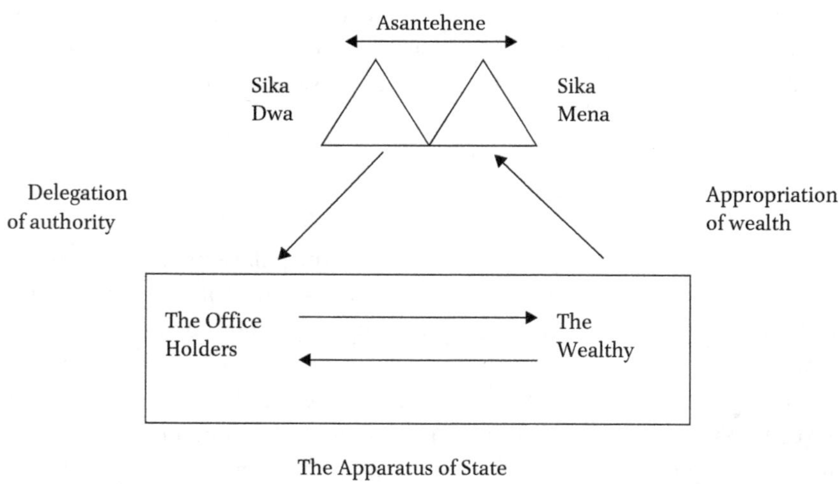

FIGURE 4.3 Wealth and authority in Asante: a schema
Source: Wilks (1993), p. 145

33 Wilks (1993, p. 147) notes that Asante went to war against the neighbouring kingdom of Gyaman, because the king there had created his own golden stool, thus symbolically placing himself as equal to the Asantehene.

the wealth of other elites through various forms of appropriation (Arhin 1990, p. 530, McCaskie 2003, p. 48).

However, wealth creation itself was actively encouraged, as long as it did not challenge the authority of the state. There was in Asante the principle of 'accumulation': a system in which all strata of society attempted to enrich themselves in order to separate themselves socially and politically from both those of lower social classes and from competitors within their own class through the conspicuous (but regulated) displays of wealth (Wilks 1975, p xlviii, Ahrin 1990, McCaskie 2003 p. 37, Lovejoy 2011, p. 167). This was officially called *Poatwa* – the exhibition of wealth according to rules set out by the state which ensured that you could not put yourselves too far above your station or rank. Should you do so, this was *ahomaso,* which implied a threat to the social order (Arhin 1990, p. 532). When a man reached a certain level of wealth he could apply to the Asantehene to wear a certain kind of woven cloth called *nyawɔho* or "you have become rich." A richer man could apply for the honour of carrying a horse tail switch and the very wealthiest would be allowed to carry an elephant tail switch. In essence this system does not differ substantially from that which existed in Dahomey (see Chapter 6) where the king's authority and the social position of the elites also rested to a large degree on the conspicuous consumption of luxury goods and ostentatious displays of wealth. What set Asante apart was that all wealth was measured by, and usually based on, gold.

The only recognised currency within the Asante kingdom, was gold dust, which had originally been based on Islamic gold coins known as the *mithqal* and *uqiya* (Johnson 1968).[34] The literature agrees that at all levels of Asante society, the most important (although not the only) marker of wealth was the possession of gold, either in the form of currency or ornamentation (Wilks 1975 p. xlviii, Garrard 1980 p. 66, Wilks 1993, p. 127, Austin 1996, p. 9, Arhin 1990 pp. 532, 533, McCaskie 2003, p. 38). A key part of official state policy, and one of the means by which an Asantehene maintained his legitimacy, was to ensure that the *Adaka Kese,* or Great Chest, kept at the treasury in Kumasi remained full. This alone required 400,000 oz of gold dust valued at around £1.5 million in the early nineteenth-century (Wilks 1975, p. 418, 445). Men seeking to advance themselves were given loans in gold dust by more senior elites and were expected to increase this wealth (Arhin 1990, p. 529, Wilks 1993, p. 133). Even

34 There were two exceptions; in the northern regions and along the coast, cowry shells and barter were also accepted for the purposes of trade, but this was always forbidden in other areas of the empire as it was seen to be a threat to the collection of gold (Cruikshank (1853, Vol 2 pp. 41–44, Arhin 1990, p. 527).

commoners needed to acquire gold dust in order to buy more basic but necessary goods from markets such as salt, farm tools and household implements (Arhin 1990, p. 527).

While the export of captives was extremely important, control of the region's gold was always the core focus of Asante policy over the eighteenth century (McCaskie 2007, p. 9, Garrard 1980, p. 63, Dummet 1998, pp. 41, 44) as a means of financing warfare, providing an organising principle and justification for further expansion, and later allowing Asante to receive tribute in slaves from conquered territories.[35] An analysis of the location of major Asante military campaigns from 1740 to 1816 (Table 4.3) shows that there was far more activity in regions with gold deposits. Other political factors played a role but it wasn't until 1806 that they engaged in warfare directly against the Fante states, which marketed the majority of the region's exported slaves (Wilks 1975, pp. 26, 27, 145). As suggested earlier this war was probably motivated by political considerations, rather than from a desire to control the marketing of the slave trade.

A hesitancy to engage in warfare against southern states or coalitions was likely due to the fact that they were generally well armed and, in the case of the Fante, possessed fortified towns (Shumway 2014, pp. 144, 145). However, these factors did not discourage Asante from launching repeated attacks against the region of Wassa from 1765 to 1785 in order to gain control of its gold supplies. By contrast, the Dahomean kings, who were far more dependent on the slave trade for their wealth and power, conquered the key slave 'port' of Whydah in the 1720s and expended considerable effort holding it against repeated attacks from other hostile powers until the 1780s (see Chapter 6). This suggests that control of the slave trade, while important, was not a key objective of the Asante state, unlike the gold trade.

This had profound implications for the market in slaves within the kingdom. After sufficient land had been cleared in the seventeenth century, a dual market developed that allowed the option to either sell slaves to Atlantic or Saharan traders, or to retain them as producers who could additionally augment the prestige of their owners (McCaskie 2003, p. 38). There was therefore always an internal demand that competed strongly with an external one. For most of the eighteenth century it seems that the kingdom was able to benefit

35 For example, during their 1772 invasion of Dagomba captives who would otherwise have faced slavery were ransomed for gold or greater numbers of slaves. After the Fante wars in 1816 entire villages were founded in under developed regions by captives taken into slavery by victorious generals who thereby increased both their wealth, productive capacity and prestige (Maier 1990 pp. 122, 123).

TABLE 4.3 Location of major Asante military campaigns 1740–1816

Year	Area	Area(s) of gold supplies	Trade route to the savannah	Trade route to the Atlantic
1740–1741	Gyaman	✓		
1742	Akyem, Accra	✓		✓
1744	Akwamu			
1745–48	Bassa, Kete Krakye, Dagomba		✓	
1749	Krepi Akyem	✓		
1751–1752	Eastern and Central Gonja, Kpembe		✓	
1753	Wassa, Twifo, Denkyira, Akyem, Abuakwa	✓		
1759	Gyaman	✓		
1763	Bron, Kwawum, Akyem		✓	
1764	Dahomey			✓
1764–1765	Wassa, Twifo, Denkyira, Akyem, Abuakwa	✓		
1766–1767	Gyaman	✓		
1767	Akyem Abuakwa	✓		
1772	Dagomba	✓		
1772	Akuapem			✓
1773	Akyam Abuakwa	✓		
1773–1774	Banda	✓		
1798–1799	Gyaman	✓		
1800–1801	Gbuipe		✓	
1806–1807	Assin; Fante			✓
1809–1810	Elmina, Accra			✓
1811–1816	Akuapem, Krobo, Ada			✓

Sources: Campaign list from Maier (1990) p. 130, areas of gold supplies from Dickson (1969), p. 180, trade routes from Wilks (1975) p. 8

from both the sale of slaves, and from using their labour to produce gold (Maier 1990, Shumway 2014, p. 57). However, the centrality of gold in the social and economic fabric of society meant that slave labour was ultimately more important than their value as commodities, and in the late eighteenth and early nineteenth centuries the rising value of gold discouraged the export of slaves.

McCaskie (2003, p. 39) argues that gold only started to become scarce, and therefore more valuable, after abolition, when the kingdom was required to begin relying solely on the export of gold to purchase crucial European goods such as guns and gunpowder. This situation exacerbated other factors identified by Wilks (1993, p. 129), including the melting down of gold dust for ornaments, and hoarding. McCaskie is supported by Lovejoy (2011, p. 167) and to a lesser extent by Austin (1995, p. 101), who note that the glut of slaves in the kingdom post 1808 helped the development of commodity production. However, the evidence indicates that gold was already becoming scarcer in the late eighteenth-century. As it did so, demand rose, which encouraged output and diverted slaves from export to production.

From the 1750s the domestic price of gold began to rise and from the 1770s exports contracted (Johnson 1966, Metcalf 1987). Barters were always converted into a trading currency called the ounce, which contained 16 ackies. This was a means by which complex assortments of goods from different points of origin could be valued in relation to the price of slaves. In the first half of the eighteenth century, the price of an actual ounce of gold to a trade ounce had doubled from 1:1 to 1:2. Johnson (1966) quotes a British trader in 1777 complaining that it was necessary to buy gold in other parts of Africa at more than the prime cost of his goods in order to trade at Anomabo. In his analysis of the accounts of one British trader, Metcalf (1987) notes that by 1776 ninety three point six percent of his barters for slaves included gold, and that this constituted around ¼ the total cost. Both Metcalf and Johnson argue that gold was becoming more valuable and the Asante were therefore starting to hoard their supplies instead of exporting them. The rise in the value of gold, can also explain why fewer slaves were exported in the 1790s and the first 8 years of the nineteenth century, even though the prices for slaves on the coast were higher than they had ever been (Lovejoy and Richardson 1995a). As will be argued later, the increasing value of gold to all sections of society encouraged production, which required greater numbers of slaves.

To conclude, the presence of gold was crucial to the development of both the institutions and trade patterns of the Gold Coast region. It was the basis of wealth and legitimacy for the elites, and the principal form of currency in a monetized economy, and therefore central to the lives of commoners. As it grew scarcer in the eighteenth century, the productive value of slaves would have increased relative to their value as commodities, especially given the rise in demand for kola nuts from the newly zealous Islamic states of the savannah. The next section will examine how this impacted on the labour decisions of both households and elites.

6 Household Labour Decisions

It has already argued that there were various reasons why elite groups within Asante were willing to actively support the growing commodity trade.[36] However, why were households, who were the main unit of production for both gold and kola (Dummet 1998, 2010, Lovejoy 1980, Abaka 2005), prepared to commit their (free and unfree) labour to the expansion of gold and kola production? This section will argue that, in common with households in the Bight of Biafra, the commodity trade allowed commoners far greater access to the Atlantic and savannah markets. This allowed them the opportunity to purchase goods that enhanced both their wealth and social status.

The Asante state held the right to tax both a portion of every item of gold mined and also take a share of each person's gold in the form of death duties. Such appropriations, while probably not onerous (Austin 1996, p. 20), naturally led to tax evasion and attempts to conceal individuals' true worth (Wilks 1993, p. 150). However, there were other ways of keeping the states' fingers off your family's wealth. Slaves, unlike gold, were not subject to death duties and therefore once purchased became the perpetual property of the household/lineage (Lovejoy 2011 p. 167).[37] During the eighteenth century, most slaves were captured in wars or received as tribute, so their distribution was largely in the hands of the court at Kumasi (Maier 1990). Nevertheless, by engaging in the kola trade, commoners could directly purchase slaves from traders at Salaga. Sources from the time note that while kola could be exchanged directly for savannah products such as shea butter or manufactured goods like Kano cloth (Lovejoy 1980, p. 13), Asante traders were usually only interested in slaves

36 For example, there were investments in the market town of Salaga, which effectively connected Asante producers with their distant customers in the Sokoto caliphate. The state also maintained roads, and ensured that local producers did not have to suffer competitors by forbidding non-Asante, and especially Muslims, from engaging in either the transportation or production of nuts (Austin 2005).

37 Bowdich (1819), p. 254 noted that; "The king is heir to the gold of every subject, from the highest to the lower; the fetish gold and the cloths are generally presented by him to the successor to the stool, *from which the slaves and other property of the deceased are inseparable.*" (my italics)

(Lovejoy 1982, p. 268, Johnson 1986c, p. 346). A further factor was that the Asante followed a matrilineal system which meant that property and titles were inherited, not by a man's own children but by those of his sister or nearest female relative. Furthermore, a man's children always had significant responsibilities towards their maternal relatives that often superseded those of their father's. For men with sufficient wealth, the acquisition of slaves, either as wives or workers, provided dependants loyal to them, who could be fully exploited both for their reproductive and productive potential.

Thus, another way of estimating the value to the economy of the kola trade is to convert the figures on the estimated output of kola into their value in slaves. Bowdich (1819) states that at the time he was in Asante a basket of kola was sufficient to purchase a slave from "the markets of the interior." If this was the case (and of course supposing that they only bought people) then the kola trade would have been worth between 1,200 and 15,000 slaves a year. To put this into perspective, during the last three decades of the slave trade Gold Coast merchants (whose main supplier of slaves was Asante) bartered a high of 12,200 and a low of 3,300 people in exchange for European goods.

With regard to gold there were a number of other compelling reasons for households to direct their labour towards production. For a start, gold continued to increase in value during the nineteenth century, not least because the culture of conspicuous consumption at all levels of society led to gold dust being melted down and used as ornamentation (Garrard 1980, p. 112). This, and the practise of hoarding or burying gold to avoid taxes, meant that there was never sufficient gold in circulation to meet the needs of the entire population. Money was therefore very expensive, with loans in the early nineteenth-century given thirty three percent interest over 42 days (McCaskie 2003, p. 39, Wilks 1993, p. 129). However, this was of course also an incentive to acquire as much gold as possible.

Furthermore, gold could also purchase greater social prestige in the form of luxury foreign products, and particularly cloth, that continued to flow into the country from the Atlantic (McCaskie 2003, p. 50). Some very rough estimates of per capita consumption of British products imported into the region from 1827 to 1849 have been made (See Appendix 4.2a which includes sources and method).[38] Cotton manufactures and cloth were imported in the greatest quantities, although customers were also demanding glass, earthenware, and both manufactured and unmanufactured metals. These easily exceed the number of guns and gunpowder barrels essential for military campaigning,

38 The first year that the British customs records differentiate between regions.

which suggests that the trade was geared towards luxury consumption and not to provide essential goods for the state.

Wilks (1993, pp. 155–156) describes how these goods were distributed to the many smaller villages and towns of greater Asante. There were firstly the *adwadifo,* or small private traders, who bought goods in bulk and sold them through salesmen, called *mpaafo,* who went from village to village hawking their wares. They could only trade with permission from the state and were required to pay tolls on the main roads through Asante. Then there were the *Akwantufo* or official wholesalers, sometimes private, sometimes state, who were permitted to use the great roads free of charge and without interference. The cost of their goods was high, Wilks suggests a five hundred to six hundred percent mark-up from the coast. The fall in prices of many trade goods, due to the industrial revolution, was not, according to this analysis, passed on to their customers, with the proceeds instead being accrued as rents by the treasury. Austin (1996) questions this, arguing for a far greater involvement of smaller traders, but in any case, the situation was accepted by most Asantes as demonstrated by the ever-increasing imports of goods throughout the century. Households could buy slaves with kola and then use this additional labour to produce gold. This gold allowed them to increase their social status, either through display or the purchase of prestigious luxury goods. Alternatively, slaves might be used to grow more food, or simply afford more leisure time, thus increasing living standards.

Over the *longue durée* the patterns of trade in the Asante and Fante areas of the Gold Coast region were overwhelmingly dominated by commodity exports, in particular gold, produced by a combination of household and unfree labour. It seems that ultimately the event of abolition only hastened an existing trend away from slave exports towards a more intensive use of captive labour for production. There is little evidence to suggest that had the Asante wished to continue selling slaves to American, Spanish or Portuguese traders, the British could have prevented them. Instead, this chapter has argued that the mid-to-late eighteenth-century should be seen as an interregnum when slaves briefly supplanted commodities as the most important exports. The region's initial trade contacts with Europe were very different to those of the Bight of Biafra and, more importantly, to the Bight of Benin. The initial expansion of Akan states in the fifteenth and sixteenth centuries was dependent on the importation of slaves for forest clearance, and then firearms for more effective armies, both of which were paid for by gold. This in turn meant the region's various polities in the seventeenth century were always focused on the control of gold producing areas and the application of labour to mining and extraction. As will be seen later for the Bight of Benin, states instead focused their efforts on the control over the acquisition and marketing of people for export. Within Asante society, the possession and distribution of gold became the most important means by which both elites and common households could demonstrate and improve their social status and how the monarch could tax its subjects and maintain its own position.

Demand for gold in Africa had the additional consequence that the Asante already had well developed trading links with the interior powers of the savannah by the end of the eighteenth century. They were therefore never entirely dependent on the Atlantic markets for their exports, and were fortunate that an Islamic revolution created huge demand for kola around the time of abolition. As the eighteenth century wore on, the evidence suggests that gold became scarcer, possibly due to the export of potential productive labour. It seems that the decline in slave exports in the 1780s, noted by Austin (2013), was because labour was already being diverted to the mines of Asante. The increase in the production of both gold and kola would almost certainly have required far more labour. A rise in commodity output was certainly to the advantage of households and lineage groups, who could profit far more from production than export slavery. For the elites, the absence of military threats meant that wealth creation through trade did not threaten their position or power. Instead, increased output of both gold and kola meant they gained through taxation and other rents.

Appendices

APPENDIX 4.1 Estimates of the value of the kola trade at Salaga in the nineteenth century and estimated number of kola tress in Asante in the first half of the nineteenth century

No. headloads low estimate	No. headloads high estimate	No. headloads median estimate	Number of kola nuts/apakan or headload (Wilks p. 268)
1	2	3	4
1200	15000	8100	2000

Kola nuts produced low estimate Col 1 * Col 4	Kola nuts produced high estimate Col 2 * Col 4	Kola nuts produced median estimate Col 2 * Col 4	Av yield/tree 1916/1917 (abaka p. 33)
5	6	7	8
2400000	30000000	16200000	765

No. of kola trees in Asante Low estimate Col 5/Col 8	No. kola trees in Asante High estimate Col 6/ Col 8	No. kola trees in Asante Median estimate Col 7/Col 8	
8	9	10	
3137	39216	21176	

Source: see page 159

APPENDIX 4.2a Estimated per capita consumption of British imported goods into the Gold Coast region

	Clothes (lbs)	Glass (lbs)	Metal manufactures (lbs)
Grand Total: 1827–1849	7,355,688	1,484,678	1,248,807
Per capita consumption, population Ghana 1850: 1,981,047 (Jervan & Frankema 2014)	4	1	1
Per Capita consumption, population Metropolitan Asante 1860: 350,000 (Austin 2005, p. 59)	21	4	4
Per capita consumtion, population Southern + Metropolitan Asante 1860: 800,000 (Austin 2005, p. 50, Wilks 1975, p. 243)	9	2	2

Source: Imports: TNA CUST

Appendix 4.2b Sources on Asante Population

Sources on the population of the region in the nineteenth century are far from reliable, although this is the case for all pre-colonial Africa with the possible exception of the Cape Colony. Wilks (1975, pp. 87–95, 126, 127, 243) based his estimates for the metropolitan, southern and northern provinces of the Asante empire in the nineteenth century on number of men each district was required to muster for army campaigns and 20th century census figures. These were criticised by both Johnson (1978) and Austin (2005) as being far too high. In his review of the available evidence and research Austin (2005, p. 59) concludes the first census in 1911 was almost certainly not accurate:

> We can assume that the real figure for 1911 was higher than the recorded one, meaning that there were probably between 300,000 and 350,000 people within the colonial boarders of Asante, and more riskily that the real number for 1860 would have been similar to that for 1817 and probably quite close to the 1911 level.

Soap (lbs)	Metals (lbs)	Cotton manufactures (yards)	Earthenware (pieces)	Gunpowder (barrels)	Woollen manufactures (pieces)	Guns (pieces)
782.724	19,606,829	86,514,756	2,177,872	7,733,948	68.787	276.308
0	10	44	1	4	0	0
2	56	247	6	22	0	1
1	25	108	3	10	0	0

The metropolitan region of the Asante empire contained some of the gold producing areas and it is likely that much of the production and consumption of export commodities occurred there. However, many of the gold fields were also located in the southern provinces and it was here that other export commodities, especially palm oil was also produced, so the populations of these regions should be taken into account for per capita consumption. Three figures are taken to provide high, median and low estimates. Jerven and Frankema (2014) have calculated a figure for the area of what is today Ghana, which therefore assumes that all the provinces of the empire were engaged in export and consumption of Atlantic goods. The median figure combines Austin's estimate of the population of the metropolitan region with Wilks' figure for the southern region which is also based on observations by European officials. For the low figure, only Austin's number for the central area are used. These figures naturally assume that consumption was spread evenly across the population, which is of course in reality unlikely to have been the case. The intention is primarily to illustrate the relative importance of different imports to the region's consumers.

CHAPTER 5

The Bight of Biafra: From Export Slavery to Slave Production

> King Peppel (of Bonny) was said to be rich. He had inherited his father's wealth, reputed great, in Spanish doubloons and dollars, the price of slaves. And by his own palm-oil trade he had accumulated much, which he did not know what to do with.
>
> Recorded in 1846 during a visit to Bonny by WADDELL, 1863, p. 273

∴

The previous chapter has shown that the Gold Coast region reacted swiftly to the economic shock of Britain's withdrawal from the slave trade. The Asante effectively halted their export of captives and instead used their slaves in the production of commodities for both African and Atlantic markets. The case of the Biafran region has both similarities and differences. Here, export slavery continued in conjunction with a growing commerce in palm oil for sale mainly in Britain, until the latter effectively eclipsed the former in the 1830s. In common with the Asante, households in Biafra took advantage of the opportunity to engage and benefit from the Atlantic market, but demanded a very different selection of products. Numerous studies have examined the commercial transitions in the region, although most have framed their analysis around the 'crisis of adaption' hypothesis set out by Hopkins (1973). The general consensus seems to be that the region's palm oil and slave trades were relatively compatible and that the elites, who had previously dominated the slave trade, were able to remain in control of the commerce in palm oil, until at least the mid-nineteenth-century.[1]

Far fewer studies have specifically investigated the pre-abolition roots of palm oil production. Northrup (1976 pp. 361–64), supported by Dike and

1 See particularly Northrup (1976), Manning (1986), Korieh (2000), Ejiogu and Njoku (2015) on compatibility of the two trades and the initial retention of power by elites. Ohadike (1998), Martin (1988), Lovejoy (2011, pp. 177–84), Law (1995a, pp. 12, 15) on involvement of small producers. Wariboko (1998) on developments in the region's commercial organisations. Nwokeji (2010, pp. 178–203) and Dike and Ekejiuba (1990 pp. 251–60) on the later nineteenth-century, which did see an increase in competition, militarisation and violence.

 | DOI:10.1163/9789004417120_007

Ekejiuba (1990, p. 255) argues that the region was in "a state of economic preparedness" for the transition from slave to palm oil exporting. This was due to a combination of the networks and markets developed for and by export slavery in the eighteenth century, the region's ecological suitability and, more specifically, by the fact that inland farmers were already supplying the coast with large quantities of foodstuffs for the provisioning of European and American ships. This view has recently found support in the volume by Law et al. (2013, p. 13), whose Chapters 2, 3 and 4 provide quantitative support to the idea that there was a strong and growing pre-abolition export trade in non-slave products in the Bight of Biafran region. The palm oil sector grew rapidly, both before; and after 1808 (Lynn 1997, pp. 61–63), surpassing nominal value of the slave trade at its 1790s height in the 1850s (Eltis 2013, Nwokeji 2010, p. 180, Eltis and Jennings 1998, p. 946). This chapter will argue that commodity exports were becoming more attractive than slaves to the merchants of this region, especially from the 1820s as demand was more stable and the costs of key trading goods were falling. It will also investigate why households, the main unit of production, responded so actively to increased demand for palm oil, as was also the case in Asante. It will also ask why the traders and merchants who had previously profited so handsomely from the slave trade were prepared to transport and market palm oil, while the monarchy and aristocratic elites in Dahomey were unwilling to give up export slavery except under conditions of extreme duress in the 1850s.

It will be argued that there are two factors which so far have not been given sufficient attention in the literature of the commercial transition in Biafra. The first is with regards to the region's trade relations with Britain, its principal trading partner for slaves in the eighteenth, and palm oil in the nineteenth century. Lynn (1997, pp. 83, 84) has noted that many of the first British palm oil merchants had previously operated as slave traders and used their existing contacts and networks to enter into the new trade. However, it will be argued that the role of the British state, particularly its policy on excise and import duties, may have played a more influential role than previously thought in stimulating investment in the palm oil business.

Secondly, long-term political and institutional development in the Bight of Biafra was very different to the Bight of Benin and the Gold Coast, which were dominated by large, relatively centralised states. The expansion of export slavery was made possible by the trading network developed by the Aro people, who were to act as the crucial middlemen between the interior and the coast. However, this network was only to realise the full potential of the region's slave exporting capacity from the 1730s. While export slavery had been a feature of the region's economy for several centuries, it did not experience the enormous influx of European manufactures in the seventeenth century that had such an impact on the development of larger political entities on the Gold Coast and the Bight of Benin. Instead, a different form of economic and social organisation developed to handle the traffic in people, based on existing trade routes between the coast and the interior. The region was famous for having no 'states', although this did not mean that there was no authority or the ability to organise long distance trade (McIntosh 1999, pp. 11–13). However, as a result of its later entrance into the big leagues of slave exporters, the Bight of Biafra did not develop large scale, centralised polities with elite hierarchies dependent on external trade for the purchase of luxury goods, or slave raiding, as an organising principal of state power. In the Bight of Biafra, elite status was based largely on wealth creation through trade of all kinds. This chapter will argue that, as in the Asante kingdom, the region's 'big men' benefited at least as much from household involvement in palm oil production as they did from the previous trade in slaves, which was not the case in Dahomey. They were therefore willing to use their commercial networks and power to facilitate the growth of the palm oil trade.

The layout of the chapter is as follows. Firstly, it provides an overview of the patterns and value of external trade across the eighteenth and nineteenth centuries. It then examines the role of the British state in promoting the palm oil trade, before considering how the region's specific institutional development influenced both internal demand for labour and household production.

1 Area of Study

This chapter focuses on the area which can roughly be defined as east of the Niger River and South of the Benue river and contained three distinct types of terrain (Nwokeji 2010, p. 183). Firstly, the low lying coastal regions which had little fertile land and traditionally relied on small scale agriculture, fishing and salt, which could be traded to inland regions that lacked natural sources of both salt and protein. Next, a broad belt of tropical rainforest which could support a much denser population. The indigenous staple crops were yams and the oil palm, which were usefully supplemented by those introduced from other world regions such as cocoyams, bananas and plantains from Asia, as well as tomatoes, cassava, maize and peppers from the Americas.[2] The fertility of the soil of this region was quickly depleted in the rainforest environment so its inhabitants practised either long fallow agriculture, where land-extensive conditions made this possible, or engaged in regular migrations to new areas

2 Isichei (1976) believes all of these crops might have been introduced by the Portuguese in the fifteenth and sixteenth centuries (p. 7).

(Dike and Ekejiuba 1990, pp. 36–28). These migrations required the clearance of the dense rainforest, helping to scatter palm kernels on fallow or abandoned land. This was to account for the density of wild oil palm trees across the region in the eighteenth and nineteenth centuries (Northrup 1979, p. 8, Martin 1988, p. 22). Further north, the area generally referred to as the middle belt, consisted of more savannah like territory unable to support the population densities of the south due to its more unpredictable rainfall and poorer natural resources.[3]

Populations living in the central area of the Bight of Biafra are referred to as Igbos and the area as Igboland, and the area to the south as Ibibioland (Nwokeji 2010, p. xi, Kolapo 2004, p. 124). These terms are not precise and cover a multitude of different, but related, cultures and language groups living under a wide variety of institutional arrangements (see below). They are also controversial terms, as some have argued that they are a European construction stemming from the overgeneralisations of slave traders and colonialists (Byrd 2010, pp. 20, 21). However, others have suggested that the region did possess a degree of cultural unity based on shared history, traditions and language.[4] The chapter takes the view that, while acknowledging that both identity and borders were fluid concepts in this period, there is sufficient evidence to speak of this area as having a broad 'Igbo' or 'Ibibio' identity.[5]

2 External Trade

The first account by a European of the Bight of Biafra was written between 1501 and 1508 by the Portuguese explorer Duarte Pacheco Pereira. He noted that a large village, which Fage (1980, p. 71) suggests was Bonny, was already engaged in significant trade with the interior. Salt produced at the coast was exchanged for yams, cattle and slaves, which were transported from the interior in canoes carrying up to eighty men. The Portuguese were able to participate in this trade through the exchange of 'copper manillas' for captives and provisions. It was ultimately based on the requirements for salt and fish in the interior, and for agricultural produce on the coast which did not have a suitable ecology for

3 Nwokeji (2000), quotes one author as saying that the area "…has all the diseases and problems of forest and savannah, but not compensating advantages, except a general absence of population pressure." (p. 628).

4 To get an idea of how contentious this debate can be, refer to a series of articles and responses in the journal Slavery and Abolition. See Northrup (2000), Chambers (2002), Kolapo (2004).

5 See Isichei (1976), Dike and Ekejiuba (1990), Ohadike (1994), McIntosh (1999).

farming. Similar circumstances were observed around 150 years later by the Dutch physician and traveller Olfert Dapper (1676, p. 136–137). He wrote that at Elem Kalabari: *"The blacks bring their slaves for sale on the Calabar river, and take their boats up to our ships, the same traders also deal in food and sell yams, bananas, palm oil, goats and dogs."*[6] In addition to slaves and provisions, Dutch merchants could also buy akori (coral beads), ivory and locally made knives. In terms of numbers of slaves exported into the Atlantic, the region averaged around 1,200 per year during the seventeenth century. As noted in Chapter 1, this was very like other regions of West Africa until the 1670s, when slave sales from the Bight of Benin increased rapidly.

In the Bight of Biafra, it wasn't until the Aro trade network expanded into the central and southern regions of Igboland in the 1730s, that the region became a major exporter of slaves (Lovejoy and Richardson 1999, pp. 382, 383, Nwokeji 2010, p. 20). Between 1700 and 1720 an average of 1,711 captives were embarked from Biafran ports, compared with an average of 13,388 in the last twenty years of the century. Throughout the period under study, the three ports of Bonny, Old Calabar and Elem Kalabari were responsible for over ninety percent of slave departures, with Bonny by far the most important at the time of abolition.[7] Lovejoy and Richardson (1999, 2004) argue that Bonny's success lay in more efficient institutions for the regulation of credit with Europeans, and for greater efficiency in terms of provisioning and loading times. While agreeing with this assessment, Nwokeji (2010) and Behrendt et al. (2010, p. 107) argue that it was principally due to Bonny being better positioned on the trade routes from central Igboland, which contained the region's densest concentrations of people and most efficient riverine connections to the coast (Chuku 2015, p. 43). Largely as a result, the Bight of Biafra had become West Africa's most important slave embarkation point by the 1780s.

As noted above, all of these ports were in areas unsuited for the cultivation of yams,[8] and were always dependent on importing their food from the

6 This is the author's translation. The original reads: *"De zwarten, die de slaven in reiere Kalbarien in hun kanoos te koop brengen, en daer mede aen boort van onze schepen komen, voeren ook eten voor dezelve mede, dat zy verkopen, als Injames, Bananessen, oil de Palm, Verkens, Bokjes en Hoenderen."*

7 Europeans sometimes referred to coastal town of Elem Kalabari as 'New Calabar' to distinguish it from 'Old Calabar' on the Cross River estuary (Lovejoy & Richardson 1999, p. 335). This is actually a misnomer as Elem Kalabari is in fact an older settlement (Dike & Ekejiuba 1990, p. 33), but will always be referred to as 'Old Calabar'.

8 Icichei (1976) writes of the central place of the yam in both the diet and culture of the region. She notes that in Biafra, the 'hunger season' did not necessarily indicate that there was no food, but that there were no yams available (p. 28).

surrounding regions (Northrup 1979, p. 6).[9] The existence of established trading networks for food goes a long way to explain why and how the region was able to develop the extensive provisioning trade for slave ships that was outlined in Chapter 2. From the middle of the eighteenth century, Old Calabar began to increase its output of commodities, perhaps in reaction to the growing dominance of Bonny in the slave trade and the impact of the American revolution on merchant shipping in the Atlantic (Behrendt et al. 2010, pp. 80–97 and Appendix 5.1). As shown in Chapter 3, sales of ivory and redwood grew rapidly from the 1760s, which was probably due to the establishment of trade links with Duala merchants who had access to larger herds of elephants, and trees, on the Cameroon grasslands (Behrendt et al. 2010 p. 92). From the 1770s, palm oil started to be exported from Old Calabar in response to increased European demand, which was initially met by households in the Ibibio region who had also supplied slave traders with yams and other provisions since at least the early eighteenth-century.[10]

After abolition, palm oil exports increased and, while slave sales did not rise to the levels reached at the end of the eighteenth century, they still recovered due to the return of vessels from Portugal/Brazil, France and Spain/Uruguay. Most importantly, until at least the 1840s, the palm oil and slave trades were largely compatible, as they were transported along Aro trade routes and handled through either the canoe house trading organisations at Bonny (Wariboko 1998, Manning 1986, p. 224, Lovejoy 2011, p. 180) or the 'mercantile oligopoly' at Old Calabar (Lynn 1997, p. 61). The region's geography was a crucial factor in the rapid expansion of the palm oil trade. Not only were palm trees grown in abundance, but oil could be easily transported to the coast along navigable rivers and waterways (Lynn 1997, p. 37). As already noted, the region had developed an inland to coast trade on the 'largest canoes in West Africa' before European contacts (Northrup 1976, p. 362).[11] During the era of the slave trade

9 This was known to British traders at the time. For example, one trader, a Mr Penny, related to a Parliamentary Committee on the slave trade in 1788 that : "*At Bonny the country produces a few yams etc, but not sufficient for their subsistence. A great quantity of yams are produced at Andomey and Creek, which supply the town of Bonny, and are brought in canoes for the supply of the ships in the trade. At New Calabar the produce is much the same, and the inhabitants are obliged to be supplied with their provisions from the neighbouring countries.*" (p. 70).

10 Northrup (1976, p. 363) quotes Barbot (1699) as saying that Old Calabar was being supplied with provisions by the kings of Agbisherea, a form of the Efik word for Ibibio. In the 1820s, Bold (1823, p. 78) says that the people of 'Egboshery' were still among the major suppliers of palm oil.

11 In the 1670s, the Dutch traveller and physician Dapper (1676, p. 136) saw "*...zeer grote kanoos daer in twintigh roeiers of scheppers op ieder zijde roeien, en wel zestigh ja tachtich*

the waterways and canoes were a crucial part of the region's ability to rapidly transport large numbers of captives to the coast (Byrd 2010, p. 28). In the nineteenth century, this riverine network was crucial to the development of the palm oil trade. Household producers could leave relatively small quantities of oil at bulking depots, which could then be loaded and transported in quantity down to coastal trade towns (Isichei 1976, p. 95, Northrup 1978, p. 195, Oriji 1992, p. 542).

Until the 1820s Old Calabar was the region's principal exporter of palm oil, but around this time Bonny entered the trade, and by the 1840s it had become by far the most important centre for oil exports.[12] In the interior, the increased production of palm oil, especially in Ibibio and Igbo areas, created an important market for food imports from other regions. Igbo merchant adventurers began creating new settlements in the north eastern middle belt region, where slave villages were established for yam production (Northrup 1979, p. 10, Manning 1986, p. 217, Lovejoy 2011, p. 179). Along the coast, the growth of towns also encouraged more intensive use of slaves in agriculture (Manning 1986, p. 12) and also for the transportation of palm oil and slaves. By the late 1830s the slave trade began a decline from which it did not recover, so that by the time of the parliamentary report on trade with Africa in 1842 the witnesses were able to state that the era of the slave trade was over.[13]

The next question is whether this switch entailed significant opportunity costs for those involved with slave exports. In the following section, this will be examined from a purely monetary/financial perspective. In Sections 5 and 6, the wider impacts on labour and production in the region will also be analysed.

---

mannen in kunnen gevoert worden..." In the nineteenth-century Wariboko (1998, p. 146) notes that these canoes could carry up to 80 people in addition to large quantities of palm oil.

12 Lynn (1997, pp. 20, 21) has made the most extensive study of output from Biafran ports. The earliest reliable statistics he quotes are from the early 1850s. These give Bonny as providing 36.6% and Old Calabar providing 13.9% of all British palm oil imports. Another report from 1855 suggests that, within the Bight of Biafra, Bonny exported around 65% of oil and Old Calabar 16%.

13 1842 (551) (551-II) Report from the Select Committee on the West Coast of Africa; together with the minutes of evidence, appendix, and index. Part I. – Report and evidence. R. Levinge *"Formally at Bonny I have seen 20 vessels in the river all engaged in the slave trade; now there is not such a thing there."* 4000, p. 227/228. Midley *"A great number of the principle slave dealers in the Bonny river...have given all their energies to palm oil."* 4121 p. 233.

3 The Value of the Commodity Trade and 'comey'

In her study of the slave trade at Bonny, Hargreaves (1987, pp. 196–198) suggests that the decline of slave exports was financially harmful, at least to the elites, as palm oil did not bring in as much revenue as captives. By contrast, Northrup (1978, p. 182) writes that "…the ports of the Bight of Biafra hardly seemed to miss an economic heartbeat…" and made a relatively painless transition into the era of 'legitimate commerce'. This section compares the nominal value of the slave trade at its height with that of palm oil during the first half of the nineteenth century to test the extent to which the wider region's economy suffered or thrived. The new estimates are based on the average prices of slaves from 1795 to the 1850s on the coast, using data on the number of captives from the TSTD and prices from Lovejoy and Richardson (1995). Admittedly, the set of data on prices and estimated output of palm oil from Bonny and Old Calabar is limited (for sources see Figures 5.2a, 5.2b). The figures for palm oil are conservative as they only include output to Britain, and there is some evidence that other nations, especially the Americans, were also beginning to enter the market.[14]

When comparing the nominal prices of slaves and commodities, it was only in the 1850s that palm oil overtook the late eighteenth-century value of slave exports (Figures 5.1.a, 5.1.b), which confirms earlier estimations made by Eltis & Jennings (1988, pp. 939, 946). There are, however, two important aspects to

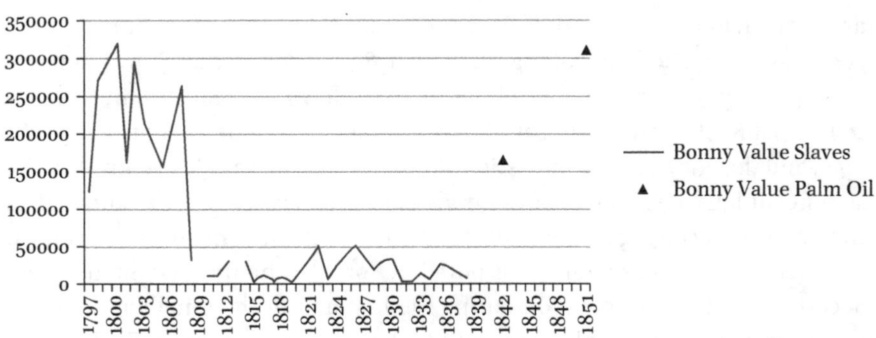

FIGURE 5.1a Estimated nominal value (GB £) of the slave and commodities trade at Bonny 1795–1850

14 In the 1842 report, one merchant interview stated; "*I believe a great deal of it goes to America, but nearly so much as to England*" 2220 Dring, p. 113. It is possible that French ships may have come as they were starting their involvement in the palm oil trade at Whydah during the 1840s (see Chapter 6).

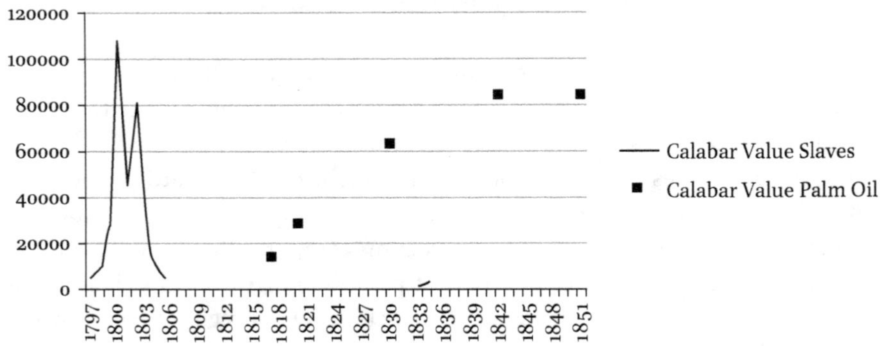

FIGURE 5.1b Estimated nominal value (GB £) of the slave and commodities trade at Old Calabar 1795–1850
Sources: Slave Prices at the coast from Lovejoy and Richardson (1995). Slave numbers from TSTD, variables 'Principle Port of Embarkation/Slaves embarked'. Palm oil prices: Old Calabar 1820 Bold (1822), p. 81, Bonny 1821 Adams (1823), p. 245, Old Calabar 1821 Adams (1823) p. 247, 1830 Old Calabar / Bonny Lynn (1992), p. 80, Bonny 1842 1842 (551) (551-II) Report from the Select Committee on the West Coast of Africa; together with the minutes of evidence, appendix, and index. Part I. – Report and evidence. Clegg Evidence 1652 p. 92, Old Calabar/Bonny 1855 Latham (1973), p. 71. Palm Oil quantities: Lynn (1997), pp. 13–21

be taken into consideration. Firstly, palm oil was not traded for specie but for an assortment of trade goods.[15] As noted in Chapter 4, the price of British trade goods to Africa had been falling since the 1780s. Recent research by Frankema et al. (2015, p. 37) has shown that terms of trade with Great Britain for those selling palm oil in Africa improved by just under a factor of 4 between 1800 and 1850, and this may be an underestimation as it does not take into consideration significant falls in the value of key trade goods such as salt. As a result, African traders were receiving significantly more goods for the same nominal value of products traded and therefore, as noted by some at the time, profited more.[16] Secondly, demand for palm oil during the first half of the nineteenth century was subject to considerably less volatility than the trade in slaves. For example,

15 See for example Bold (1823, p. 81) for the articles of trade commonly used to purchase palm oil.

16 1842 Report on the slave trade: Clegg (Supercargo for Tobin and Horsfall) Evidence p. 92 1649 *"You have stated that the supply of goods from this country to the coast of Africa has greatly increased in your experience; has the tendency of that increased supply in your opinion been to lessen or increase the slave trade? To lessen the slave trade; they scarcely take the trouble of buying slaves in Bonny now, they get so well remunerated by palm oil."*

around 15,000 slaves were embarked on ships from the Bight of Biafra in 1774, which fell to 294 in 1779. In 1794, more than 25,000 captives left the area, while just over 2,000 did just one year later. In the nineteenth century, volatility was less, but still significant with differences of up to 5,000 from year to year even before the equipment act of 1839 made British abolition efforts more effective (Appendix 5.2). By contrast, demand for palm oil rose steadily, and with few significant fluctuations throughout the first half of the nineteenth century.

The elites and workers of coastal ports also benefited from various taxes and payments for services which Europeans were obliged to pay in order to trade (these were often referred to as 'customs' or 'comey'). These were in operation throughout the slave and palm oil trades, but there are so far no estimates about the relative value of these payments in the late eighteenth and nineteenth centuries to the people of the ports. The only reference to the income gained by coastal elites comes from a letter written by the commander of the anti-slave trade patrol who suggested that King Pepple of Bonny earnt £4,000 a year "*...arising from the tonnage duty levied upon British merchant vessels trading in the river.*"[17] Other traders and local citizens could also demand 'comey', so to estimate a figure for the port of Bonny as a whole, some approximations of how much each ship visiting would have had to pay are used. There are currently few accurate figures regarding exactly how many palm oil ships were trading and where exactly they went. The 1842 parliamentary report on West African trade states that in 1840, 36 British vessels visited Bonny for palm oil, which are assumed to have stayed constant in the following two years.[18] Adams (1823, p. 245) states that in the 1820s every ship had to pay £150 'comey' for the right to trade. Lynn (1992, p. 83) suggests that in the 1830s this may have been as high as £200 or as low as £50. Let us stay with a figure of £150, as reports at the time suggested the trade was becoming more, not less, expensive.[19] Lynn (1997, p. 73) notes that in addition traders had to pay 'custom' on each puncheon of palm oil at a rate of 1 bar (equivalent to a British shilling in the

17 Capt Tucker to the Secretary of the Admiralty May 25 1841, 1847–48 [970] Papers relating to engagements entered into by King Pepple and the Chiefs of the Bonny with Her Majesty's naval officers, on the subject of the suppression of the slave trade, p. 15.

18 1842 (551) (551-II) Report from the Select Committee on the West Coast of Africa; together with the minutes of evidence, appendix, and index. Part II. – Appendix, Index and Map, p. 33.

19 1842 Parliamentary Report on the Slave Trade pt1. Capt T Midgley interviewed: "*4110 There has been a great increase of palm oil and it has got much dearer than it was some years ago, owing to the opposition in the trade a great number of merchants being embarked in it. 4112 The natives have become more aware of its value? – They have.*"

TABLE 5.1 Nominal value of palm oil customs at Bonny (GB £) 1840–1842

Year	Tons of palm oil exported	Puncheons of palm oil exported	Custom bar £	Work bar £	Dashes £	Comey £	Total customs palm oil £
1840	6.703	8.379	3.491	175	3.491	5.4	*12.557*
1841	8.438	10.547	4.395	220	4.395	5.4	*14.409*
1842	8.929	11.161	4.65	233	4.65	5.4	*14.933*

Sources: see pages 189–190

1840s[20]), as well as a 'work bar' for every 20 puncheons loaded. Furthermore, 'dashes' or tips were expected around every transaction amounting to around 5sh/puncheon (Lynn 1997, p. 73). Lynn (1997, p. 19) estimates that Bonny was providing between thirty five and fifty percent of Britain's palm oil in 1840. Using the CUST records, and working with the 'Bonny Puncheon' of 240 gallons/¾ ton (Law 1995b, p. 13) gives a rough estimate how many puncheons were exported from 1840 to 1842, which can be seen in Table 5.1.

During the apogee of the slave trade the value of customs/comey was likely to have been higher, but probably not significantly so. Behrendt et al. (2010, p. 67) give a high figure of £1,800 paid by the Bristol merchant James Rogers in the late 1780s at Old Calabar. This however is unlikely to be representative for Bonny, as it was known to charge lower customs (Lovejoy and Richardson 2004, p. 371), and Rogers himself was known as a rather inefficient trader (Morgan 2003). There are also figures available for two Old Calabar bound ships, the Dobson and Fox in 1769/1770, who paid around £900/ship (Behrendt et al. 2010, p. 67). An estimate of £1000/ship for comey, dashes etc and, for lack of other data is taken and it is assumed that this remained the same over the period. This meant that the average for the period from 1797 to 1840 was £10,119. If it is to be assumed the amounts paid remained the same after abolition, the average income earned from custom from 1808 to 1830 was £6,304. However, as demonstrated by Figure 5.3, this masked a good deal of variation, with some years generating a lot of income and others very little. Furthermore, in the nineteenth century, the customs from slave ships was an additional income to that of palm oil to brokers who traded in both captives and commodities. In this respect, we must assume that the ending of export slavery did financially

20 1842 Parliamentary Report on the Slave Trade pt1. Clegg evidence p. 89 1581.

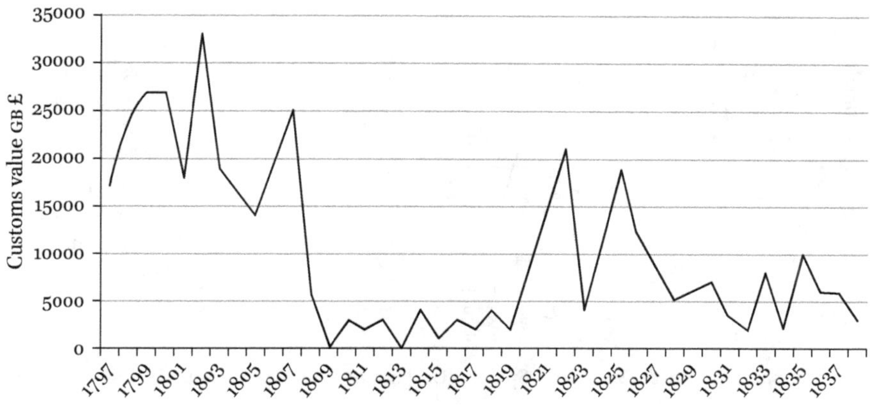

FIGURE 5.2 Estimated nominal value of customs from slave ships at Bonny GB£ 1797–1840
Sources: TSTD (variable Principle Place of Embarkation/Voyage ID), Table 5.1 see pages 188–189

impact coastal merchants, although this was unlikely to have been severe, due to the rising demand for palm oil and because income from the non-slave trade had the considerable advantage of being far less volatile.

The benefits of palm oil trading were not equally spread across the region. For example, the town of Elem Kalibari, which had previously been a major exporter of slaves, was not able to begin exporting oil in significant quantities until the 1850s due to competition and military aggression from Bonny (Wariboko 2014, pp. 106, 107). However, for Bonny and Old Calabar and for the region as a whole, the costs associated with the region's involvement in palm oil trade over the first half of the nineteenth century were certainly not high from a financial perspective. One reason for this was, as noted above, that demand from Great Britain grew rapidly, and steadily, especially from the 1820s. The next section examines the role of exogenous factors, in particular the role of British foreign and economic policies, on the development of the palm oil trade and the decline of slave exports.

4 Britain and Palm Oil Trading

In terms of the output of slaves from the region, British abolition efforts had a modest impact for the first 25 years. Post abolition numbers were lower due to the slave trade shifting to the southern Atlantic (Eltis 2009), but recovered in the 1820s as prices in West Africa became more competitive (Appendix 3). However, the specific *timing* of Biafra's exit from the Atlantic slave trade was at least partly influenced by British anti-slavery policy. The imposition of the

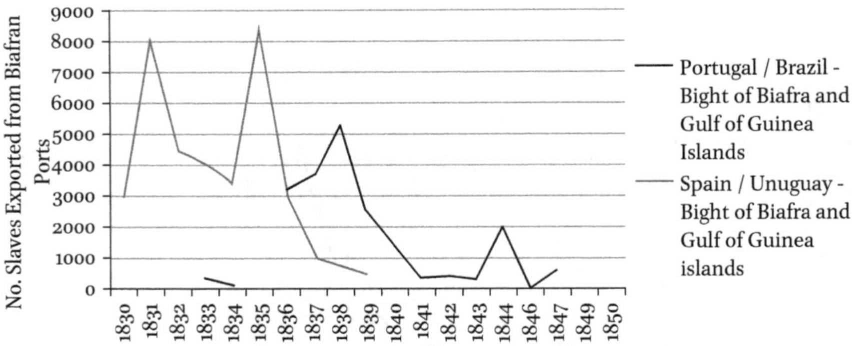

FIGURE 5.3 Portuguese/Brazilian + Spanish/Uruguayan slave exports from the Bight of Biafra 1830–1850
Source: TSTD

'equipment clauses', a policy which allowed British naval vessels to board and detain ships on the grounds that they contained the necessary equipment for carrying slaves, seems to have had some impact. After Spain reluctantly agreed to submit to this policy for their vessels in 1835, slave numbers fell precipitously (Figure 5.3). The equipment clause was then imposed unilaterally on Portuguese/Brazilian ships in 1839, but slave exports had already been falling since the previous year. This may have been due to the fact that in 1837, the ruling elite at Bonny had signed a treaty with the British agreeing to the cessation of slave exports.[21] This is unlikely to have been because they were unable to export slaves, as numbers of captives on Brazilian ships were rising at the time, and British merchants with some knowledge of Bonny admitted that ultimately there was little that could be done to prevent determined slave ships from taking captives.[22] Officers from the slave trade patrol squadron made numerous complaints that the King of Bonny was regularly violating his agreement with the British and exporting slaves through other ports from 1838 to 1842.[23]

21 PP. 1847–48 [970] Papers relating to engagements entered into by King Pepple and the Chiefs of the Bonny with Her Majesty's naval officers, on the subject of the suppression of the slave trade: April 9th 1837, p. 1.

22 In 1842, John Clegg and Richard Baily, both British merchants who traded at Bonny, told a parliamentary committee that if the chiefs at Bonny wished to resume slave trading then British cruisers would be unable to stop them 1842 (551) (551-II) Report from the Select Committee on the West Coast of Africa; together with the minutes of evidence, appendix, and index. Part I. – Report and evidence.

23 One set of parliamentary papers provides the correspondence between naval officers and the British government during the period when the King of Bonny was negotiating a treaty to end his involvement in the slave trade (PP. 1847–48 [970] Papers relating to

However, what is striking is that even though the Bonny elites had the ability to continue their involvement in export slavery, the numbers sold were far less than the previous decade. Thus, while the slave trade patrols almost certainly played some role in reducing slave exports, there must have been other factors at play.

With regard to the development of the non-slave trade in the Bight of Biafra, demand side factors had some role in encouraging supply. During both the American War of Independence and French Revolutionary Wars, the Biafrans saw the most extreme fluctuations in the number of ships visiting their ports, as English merchant shipping was particularly affected by these conflicts (Appendix 5.1). Behrendt et al. (2010) argue this was a factor influencing merchants at Old Calabar to diversify their output. However, Bonny, the most important port, did not undergo the commercial transition to palm oil until the early 1820s, so these conflicts were not a decisive factor. More important was the fact that the British were the most significant customers for Biafran slave traders in the eighteenth century. As argued in Chapter 4, slave merchants trading in Biafra were already beginning to buy significant quantities of palm oil and other commodities in addition to slaves after the 1770s. In the post abolition-period many former Liverpool slave traders such as the Aspinall family, John Tobin, Jonas Bold and James Penny became successful oil traders by using their existing networks and contacts at Bonny and Old Calabar (Lynn 1997, p. 83). More importantly, many of these merchants had previously taken most of their slaves at Bonny and therefore focused their post abolition efforts on this port, thereby helping stimulate supply.[24] However, regardless of whatever advantages they may have enjoyed in this market, unless the economic climate was favourable to their interests there was nothing preventing them from investing in other markets outside of Africa.

---

engagements entered into by King Pepple and the Chiefs of the Bonny with Her Majesty's naval officers on the subject of the suppression of the slave trade). After the agreement was signed there were numerous complaints that he and other traders were still engaged in the export slave trade. For example; Lieutenant Burslem to Commander Tucker September 1840 "*…a constant supply of slave are sent by canoes through the creeks to the Rivers Brass and Nun for shipment….*" Commander Tucker to the Secretary of the Admiralty February 1841 "*…the King has the power to suppress the Slave Trade, but will not it being too lucrative…*" Capt. Foote to the Secretary of the Admiralty August 1842 "*….the more I see of these Kings and chiefs, the more I am convinced of the utter uselessness of entering into Treaties with them, for they will take all they can grasp from England and only carry on the slave trade to a greater extent with it….*"

24 The TSTD indicates that of the important early pioneers of the palm oil trade, George Case, the Aspinall family and John Tobin all focused their pre-abolition slave trading operations on Bonny.

FIGURE 5.4 Index of palm oil prices £/cwt 1770–1850 (1770=100)
Sources: To 1816 see Chapter 4, 1816–1850 *Prices Current Liverpool Mercury*

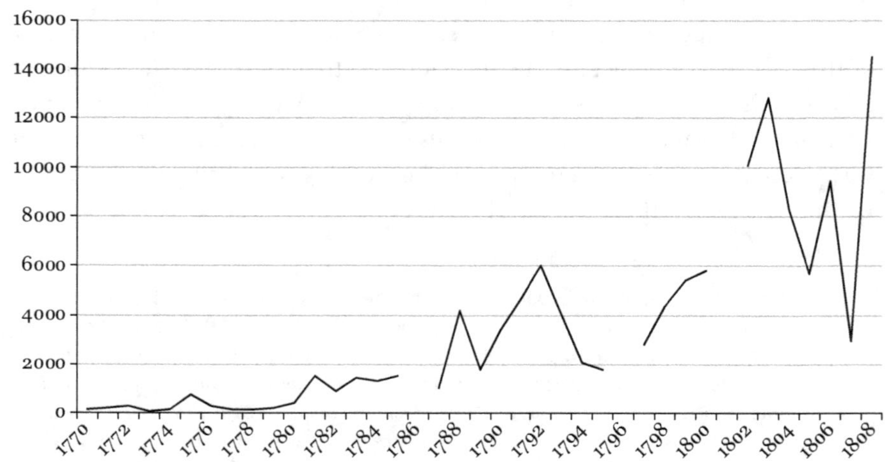

FIGURE 5.5 Index of the volume palm oil imported into Great Britain 1770–1808 (1770=100)
Sources: TNA CUST 17/1–17/30

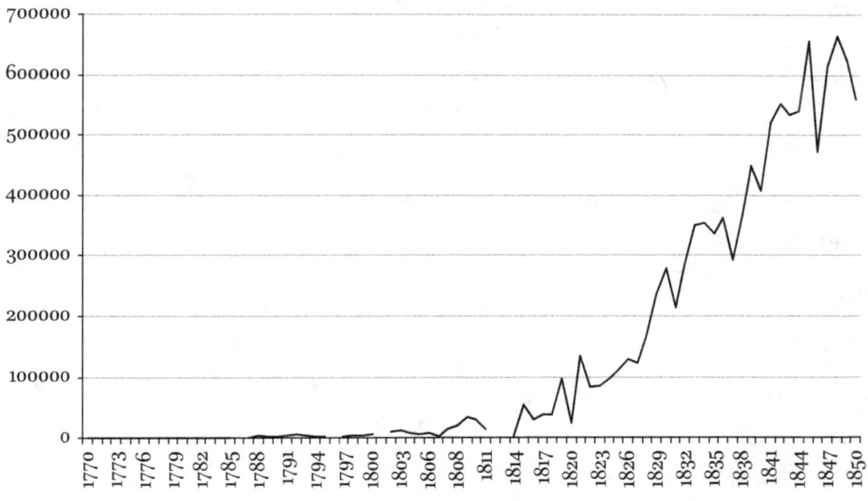

FIGURE 5.6 Index of the volume of palm oil imported into Great Britain 1770–1850 (1770=100)
Source: TNA CUST 17/1–17/30, 4/5–4/45

As can be seen from Figures 5.5 to 5.7, from 1770 to around 1808 increased output was matched by rapidly rising prices. There was then a sharp fall in price, which was briefly interrupted after the end of the Napoleonic wars. However, from the early 1820s prices went through a relatively stable three-decade period characterised by a slow upwards trend. Clearly, rising demand played a role and the stability of prices was also an important consideration, but increased mark-ups, which had been a feature of the palm oil trade from 1770 (see Chapter 3), were no longer a potential motivating factor. Yet there is another possible element in the equation that has so far gone unremarked in the literature. The British government's policies with regards to import and export duties, either deliberately or inadvertently, did much to support the growing British palm oil trade in the first half of the nineteenth century.

In 1818, a parliamentary committee put forward new duties on African products, which required adjustment after the end of the Napoleonic conflict (Table 5.2). The price and quantity of all major African commodities fell quite substantially in British markets in the period 1814–1816 and this led to a fall in the amount of some imported commodities (Appendix 5.4 and Appendix 5.5). While there is currently no direct evidence, it appears that the committee decided to increase or maintain the duty payable on items being imported in smaller quantities, while decreasing that paid on commodities which were bought in greater volumes. This makes sense as duties were charged by weight,

TABLE 5.2 Parliamentary papers: Committee for trade: Statement of proposed duties on African imports, 1 December 1818

		Present duty			Proposed duty			% increase/ decrease
Articles of African produce	**Duty weight**	**£**	**sh**	**d**	**£**	**sh**	**d**	
Elephants teeth	cwt	3	19	2	4			1
Gold Dust		Duty free			Duty free			n/a
Guinea pepper	lb		1	7		2	6	58
Gum Senegal	cwt		11	10		12		1
Hides	piece			4			6	50
Beeswax	cwt	3	6	6	3	6	6	0
Camwood	ton	1	18			15		-61
Ebony	load	1		7		15		-27
Palm oil	cwt		6	4		2	6	-61
Redwood	ton	1	18			15		-61

Source: From Newbury (1965), p. 84

so to maintain its income the government needed to charge more for imports that were becoming relatively scarcer. However, for products such as palm oil, which was being imported in greater quantities, they could afford to decrease the duty by an impressive sixty one percent (Table 5.2). Thus, for the Liverpool merchants who had dominated the trade with Biafra since at least the 1760s (Morgan 2007, Lynn 1997, p. 83), there was a positive circle of increased demand leading to lower duties, which helped to offset the falling prices in British markets after 1818 (Figure 5.8).

Duties continued to be reduced after 1839 and this again coincided precisely with a period of falling prices on British markets. There is some evidence that the reduction in duties was directly linked to the wider policy of eradicating the slave trade through the promotion of 'legitimate commerce'. In an 1840 report on trade duties, the commissioners make the explicit link between the growth of 'legitimate commerce', the decline of slavery and the rates of duty imposed on African products. One merchant interviewed was no doubt acting in self-interest when he reported that the reduction in the duty on palm oil was

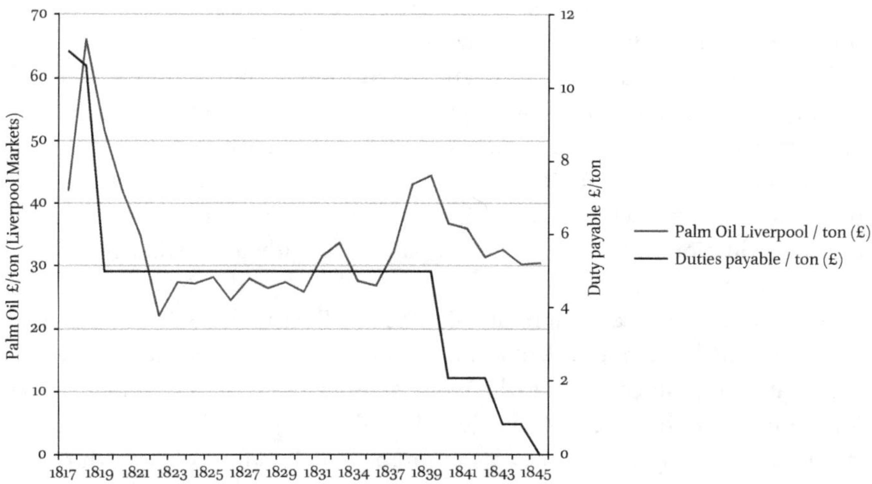

FIGURE 5.7. Palm oil prices £/ton + duty paid in £ on a ton of palm oil 1818–1845
Sources: Prices: Liverpool Mercury: Prices Current 1817–1845, Duties: 1818/1819 Newbury (1965), p. 84; 1834, 1840 1840 (601) Report from the Select Committee on Import Duties, Forster pp. 129 512–519; 1843 Newbury (1965), p. 84; 1845 LYNN (1997), p. 97

responsible for a rise in quantity purchased by merchants, but it also seems logical that a decrease in transaction costs would be beneficial to traders.[25] This issue was also raised in the 1842 parliamentary report on the slave trade. The report's author was clear that promoting 'legitimate commerce' was a key strategy designed to stop the Atlantic slave trade,[26] and another merchant also

25 Parliamentary Papers, 1840 (601) Report from the Select Committee on Import Duties; together with the minutes of evidence, an appendix, and index, p. 129. Mr Ewart to Mr Forster: "*1509 In a moral point of view is not it of great consequence as respects the question of slavery? Undoubtedly, because if ever slavery is to be done away with, you can only do away with it by introducing commerce and cultivation. 1510 The high duty puts a stop to the introduction of commerce in that article? – Clearly so. 1511 Have not the productions of that part of the coast of Africa very much increased when they have been allowed to come in on equitable terms; for instance, palm oil? – Considerably, there are persons still living I believe, who can recollect when the quantity of palm oil introduced into this country annually did not exceed a few tons. Now, I believe, it is from 15,000 to 20,000 tons a year.*"

26 Parliamentary Papers, 1842 (551) (551-II) Report from the Select Committee on the West Coast of Africa; together with the minutes of evidence, appendix, and index. Part I. – Report and evidence. Mr Aldam to Madden, 9817, p. 638 "*Do you think that the legitimate trade of the Bonny was one great cause of the slave trade being put down there? It had a very great influence there…*"

urged the commissioners to lower the duty on goods on the grounds that this was essential in the fight against slavery.[27]

Even more important was the cut in the duty paid on salt, *the* essential trade good for Biafran palm oil following parliamentary recommendations in 1818.[28] Largely due to the reduction of duties, the price of salt dropped by over 7 times between 1820 and 1825 (Table 5.3) which further offset the falling price of palm oil in the home market. Whether this support was intentional or not is unclear, but the reduction of duties on salt and palm oil greatly reduced business costs for British merchants.

External factors were therefore significant. Firstly, there were merchants with relevant human and economic capital who were motivated to expand their palm oil businesses, and who could cater to an expanding British market for African commodities, especially palm oil. These merchants were in turn supported by fairly significant cuts in import and export duties. With the old duties on palm oil and salt, a merchant in 1816 was paying around seven point three percent of the selling price of a ton of palm oil in Liverpool to the British treasury for importing oil and exporting salt. By 1825, this figure had reduced to

TABLE 5.3 Salt exports from Britain to Africa 1780–1825

Year	Salt exports Africa (bushels)	Salt price/cwt (pence)
1800	66.537	388,506
1805	82.559	466,308
1812	60.452	553,245
1815	64.408	550,449
1820	130.72	540,384
1825	290.932	75,871

Sources: TNA CUST 17/22, 17/27, 9/1, 9/3, 9/8, 9/12, Clark (2006)

27 Parliamentary Papers, 1842 (551) (551-II) Report from the Select Committee on the West Coast of Africa; together with the minutes of evidence, appendix, and index. Part I. – Report and evidence. Campbell 8879, p. 561 "*….I think every restriction should if possible be taken away from the legitimate trader, in the way of tax or duty, making him give good security that he would in no way barter with, or introduce any of the usual article for the slave trade, more particularly spirits, gunpowder, arms.*"

28 Parliamentary Papers, 1818(393) Report from the Select Committee on the Laws Relating to the Salt Duties.

one point six percent of the price of a ton in domestic markets.[29] Secondly, abolition efforts in the 1830s put some pressure on Biafra's main slave-trading centres. However, unlike in Dahomey (Chapter 6), there is little evidence that local merchants sought to develop alternative methods to evade or circumvent the slave trade patrols, even though this would have been more than feasible. For a full explanation, it is therefore necessary to turn to the endogenous factors that were influencing the region's export trade patterns.

5 Institutional Development in Biafra

Since at least the ninth century, the region was settled by groups with complex political arrangements, practising long distance trade and supported by advanced iron working technology (Isichei 1976, pp. 7–14). As noted above, the trade in slaves did not become substantial until the mid-eighteenth-century. This was for a number of reasons; firstly, local trade networks could not deliver sufficient numbers of slaves. Secondly, European traders and plantation owners in the Caribbean felt that slaves from the Bight of Biafra were more unhealthy and weaker than those from other regions (Nwokeji 2010, pp. 34–36).[30] Thirdly, the expanding demands for export slaves from Northern European nations with recently acquired American possessions were being met by other areas, in particular the Bight of Benin and West Central Africa. Moreover, there were no gold deposits to attract commodity traders. Therefore, unlike the two other case study areas, the region did not experience the same degree of trade contact with European nations until relatively later. These contacts were one of the most significant spurs to the development of more centralised states in the Gold Coast and Bight of Benin (see Chapters 4 and 6). By contrast, the Bight of Biafra developed more decentralised political institutions, which shaped its trade relations with the Atlantic world. Along the coast, and in particular at Bonny and Old Calabar, towns developed that had a particular focus on trade. In the interior, there were a plethora of village level groups which projected their power over a limited territory. Finally, there was the Aro confederacy, whose pan regional trading network was a necessary component in

29 Calculation based on the quantities of salt needed for a ton of palm oil from Bold (1823, p. 82) and the duties in Table 2. Palm oil prices from Price Current, Liverpool Mercury 1816 and 1825 (see Chapter 3).

30 Recent scholarship has shown that this bias was based on solid evidence as the mortality of captives embarked from the Bight of Biafra was higher than for other West African regions (Eltis 1989, Klein & Engerman 1997, Klein et al. 2001).

the transformation of the Bight of Biafra into the most important slave exporting region in West Africa by the 1750s.

The Aro rose to prominence for two reasons. Firstly, their capital at Arochukwu lay close to major regional markets, such as Bende, and was also only 6 hours by canoe to Old Calabar, and 2 days to Bonny and Elem Kalabari (Dike and Ekejiuba 1990, p. 44). Even more importantly, Arochukwu was home to one of the region's most important religious centres, the Inbiniukpabi oracle. This functioned as '*highest court of appeal, including for the coastal city-states and communities on the west side of the Niger River*' (Nwokeji 2010, p. 6), and gave the Aro a unique authority that transcended political and social boundaries (Northrup 1978, Dike and Ekejiuba 1990). Those taken to the oracle and judged guilty were metaphorically 'eaten' and taken by the Aro for sale as slaves. This authority was crucial, as a high proportion of the region's export slaves found themselves in the holds of American bound vessels resulting from judicial proceedings, as opposed to capture through violence (Nwokeji 2010, pp. 130, 179, Martin 1988, p. 27). Individuals did engage in the kidnapping of others in order to sell them to other traders, but this was a risky strategy as the penalties if they were caught were severe (Nwokeji 2010 p. 131, Ejiogu and Njoku 2015, pp. 11–15).[31] Furthermore, the Aro did employ various Cross River and Aboh Igbo groups as mercenaries who they used both to gain additional captives and enforce their authority (Nwokeji 2010 pp. 6, 131).[32] They also occasionally encouraged local communities to attack other villages.[33] However, unlike in the other two case study regions, slave raiding did not contribute significant numbers of slaves, although small scale kidnapping was quite common (Behrendt et al. 2010, p. 103).

The reason deserves some explanation. In both the Gold Coast and Dahomey the introduction of firearms on a large scale led to significant military

31 The former slave Olaudah Equiano, whose autobiography was a key testimony for abolitionists (1794), was captured in this way, see pp. 31, 32. However, he also notes his village sold "*...such among us has had been convicted of kidnapping, or adultery and some other crimes we esteemed heinous.*" pp. 12, 13.

32 These groups had developed a social distinction between *ufiem* (heroes), who had seen battle and brought home heads from a campaign, and *ufo* (cowards) who had not. The latter group were seen as social outcasts until they had brought home heads. The Aro typically took any survivors as slaves (Oriji 1992, p. 179).

33 Equiano (1794) noted that such conflicts were more common during times of famine or were encouraged by slave traders. However, the consequences of failure were high for those engaging in such actions "*If he prevails and takes prisoners, he gratifies his avarice by selling them; but if his party is vanquished, and he falls into the hands of the enemy he is put to death...*" (pp. 15, 16).

revolutions in the seventeenth century, which involved mass deployments of musket wielding soldiers capable of large-scale military campaigns. By the time the Biafran region became an important slave exporting area, a very different set of institutions had developed, which allowed for the efficient 'production' of slaves to meet growing American demand without the raids common in the Gold Coast and Dahomey (Nwokeji 2010, p. 127). Thus, while the Aro did use guns, their mercenaries typically did not, relying instead on more traditional weapons and the element of surprise. Military operations were more successful in the semi-savannah areas of northern Igboland, but further south; the dense forest environment hampered coordination, and raids provoked effective defensive responses (Oriji 1992, pp. 179, 180). In addition, local communities did not generally engage in raids or warfare that 'produced' slaves. Furthermore, the region was relatively densely populated (Nwokeji 2001), and the literature has suggested that this encouraged the development of social and legal institutions to manage conflict, further discouraging the use of large scale violence to acquire captives (Dike & Ekejuiba 1990, p. 162, Anywanwu 1992, Noah & Ekpo 1992, Ohadike 1992,1998). In such circumstances, slave raiding expeditions under the command of powerful elites were not an option. Instead, the region's captives were acquired through the development of a complex trade network, which relied on effective cooperation between the Aro, local 'big men' and the commercial towns at the coast. This meant that the region's elites developed a very different set of priorities to those in Dahomey.

The Aro established themselves as slave traders in the seventeenth century by developing strong ties with elite groups in Old Calabar, and a trading network that allowed captives to be taken from regional markets to the coast. In the later seventeenth and early eighteenth centuries they began a pattern of expansion in which groups of Aro would migrate and set up Aro communities in other areas, known as *mmuba* or proliferation (Nwokeji 2010, p. 2). The first settlements were established around the Arochukwu and then spread eastwards into Ibioland and Central Igboland in the 1720s. Each community was linked back to the capital through their lineage group and was required to regularly return for festivals, to pay tribute and recognise the authority of their lineage heads and the king (Dike & Ekejiuba 1990, pp. 64–70, Nwokeji 2010 p. 96). In the interior and at the coast they forged links with local elites through shared membership of secret societies, such as the Okonko in the Ngwa region (Martin 1988, p. 27), the Ekong in Ibibio territories (Noah and Ekpo 1992, pp. 189, 190) and the Ekpe at Old Calabar (Behrendt et al. 2010, p. 31). These societies were common across many regions of Africa, providing horizontal or cross cutting lines of authority to manage disputes and enforce legal punishments

(McIntosh 1999, Osafo-Kaako & Robinson 2013). Within Biafra they played an especially important role in the enforcement of contracts, which allowed Europeans to provide goods 'on trust' to coastal merchants, who could in turn rely on their ties to the Aro and interior elites to provide either commodities or slaves (Nwokeji 2010, pp. 6, 78).

The extent to which the Aro represented a pan region 'state' is debated. Northrup (1978) and McIntosh (1999, p. 11) argue that the Aro created nothing more than a trade network that allowed goods to be traded from the coast to the interior. By contrast, Dike & Ekejiuba (1999, p. 55) suggest that this organisation had 'state like structures', while Nwokeji (2010, p. 14) suggests that "*The Aro were the only group in the region that deliberately and consistently established settlements abroad for the purposes of trade that were tied to the homeland through system-wide institutions.*" He argues that while the various Aro settlements had a good deal of autonomy, they nevertheless were willing to submit to the distant authority of the capital to benefit from the prestige of representing the capital, and to deter enemies who were wary of offending the wider community. Another guide to understanding the nature of the Aro is through the work of North et al. (2009). They note that in pre-industrial societies most states did not contain strong institutions, relying instead on coalitions of elites which were, according to the context, passably effective at maintaining power. A 'fragile order state', which corresponds closely to the Aro, can be characterised by *"…simple institutional structures /private elite organizations that can extend to province level….elites that only commit to observe laws to facilitate trade and in the face of external threats….patron-client networks….elites capable of organizing violence against internal threats and to maintain trade…. simple laws that govern the relationships among individuals based on social identity and stipulate a set of rules that patrons can use to make decisions."* (pp. 42–43). However, one characterises the Aro, they were highly efficient at managing the flow of people, commodities and trade goods to and from the coast, through their contacts and relationships with village elites and traders at the ports.

Therefore, across the region the most common forms of political organisation contained elites, whose power and prestige did not rest on the maintenance of state structures such as bureaucracies, armies or the enforcement of tribute over dependent territories. The more common form of institutional organisation rarely went above village level. Here, rank and social prestige could be achieved through the purchase of titles in secret societies, and by acquiring wealth through trade (Ohadike 1994, p. 87). There were some exceptions; on the Niger River at towns like Aboh and Attah there were kings, although their authority seemed to have also largely rested on trade and it was unlikely they could project power much further than the banks of the Niger.[34] Along the coast, while certain families tended to monopolise power, individuals were never able to make their positions hereditary, and success depended on their continued wealth-generating capacities. For example, in the nineteenth century Duke Ephraim of Old Calabar had managed to secure lifelong positions as both head of the Ekpe secret society (*Eyamba*) and the town council (*Obong*), but was unable to pass these positions onto his children (Latham 1973, p. 115). During the eighteenth century one family or 'trading house', the Pepples, were able to gain an ascendancy over the other elites, but were still only first among equals and needed to rule in cooperation with other houses. In the nineteenth century, the Pepples remained the most powerful house, but no single individual was ever able to gain ascendancy over both trade and politics without provoking determined opposition (Hargreaves 1987, pp. 174, 193–196).

What linked these elites and regions was trade, be it in palm oil or people. Trade was not only beneficial but essential to elite power. However, there are two further important questions to consider. Firstly, did the region have sufficient labour available to both increase its output of palm oil and to continue exporting captives? Secondly, how did the focus on palm oil production impact on the Aro and their slave network?

6 The Demand for Labour and the Internal Slave Trade

Martin (1988) has argued that production of palm oil was carried out largely by households through a greater exploitation of female labour. This has been criticised by Korieh (2000) and Lovejoy (2011) who argue that slaves were an essential labour component, even in the more densely populated areas of central Igboland that had largely avoided the negative demographic consequences of the eighteenth-century slave trade (Nwokeji 2000). This is an important, as the Aro had built their wealth and influence on the slave trade. If palm oil production in the nineteenth century required more coerced labour, then any fall in

34 The explorers Laird and Oldfield (1837) described meeting the Kings of both Attah and Aboh. In the case of Aboh, they note that the king's power came from his controlling the flow of palm oil and provisions on a key point of Niger (pp. 97, 101, 103). A more recent study by Nwaubani (1999, pp. 102–06) agrees that Aboh political economy was based on their ability to act as a market for trading coastal and interior products, and that the king's power was limited to the river and could not be enforced much further inland.

slave exports to the Atlantic would have been compensated by rising internal demand. Conversely, if households did contain sufficient labour capacity then the Aro would have suffered a fall in income.

Most of the literature indicates that the expansion of the palm oil trade did require a corresponding increase in the number slaves. Palm oil production was extremely labour-intensive and the task fell disproportionately on females, who also had numerous other tasks including childcare, cooking, cleaning, agriculture and trading (Nwokeji 2010, p. 182). To get some idea of the scale of the increase it is possible to calculate roughly how many additional days' labour were required. Palm oil during this period was classified as either 'soft' or 'hard', depending on how much free fatty acid (FFA) it contained. Low levels of FFA meant it was soft and could be used for the manufacture of soap, glycerine and for machine lubrication. Hard oil with higher levels of FFA was used for candles and lower quality soap. The softer the oil the more labour-intensive the production process (Lynn 1997, pp. 46, 47, Maier 2009). Northrup (1976, p. 361) quotes a study from the 1930s,[35] which suggests that semi-hard palm oil required around 250 days' labour to produce a ton. Reid (1986, p. 348) takes estimates from the (unpublished) Phd dissertation of Patrick Manning to give a figure of 315 days' labour per ton, but does not specify if this is for hard or soft oil. An observation from the first half of the nineteenth century gave a rough estimate that a slave along the Niger could produce a ton of oil in a year.[36] Lynn (1997, p. 49) is more specific, giving a figure of 132 days for hard oil and 420 for soft, which roughly corresponds to Maier's (2009 p. 15) estimation that the production of soft oil required five times as much labour. Since we do not know exactly what proportion of oil was soft or hard, a middle figure of 250 days' labour/ton is taken.

Labour was also required to transport oil from villages to bulking centres next to the rivers, from where the oil would be transported to the coast (Martin 1988, p. 28, Lynn 1997, p. 48).[37] Ohadike (1998), quoting a text from the 1920s,

---

35 A.F.B. Bridges, 'Report on Oil Palm Survey in the Ibo, Ibibio and Cross River Area', 1938, Appendix VII, MSS. Afr.s. 679, Rhodes House Library, Oxford; Daryll Forde and Richenda Scott, The Native Economies of Nigeria (London, I946), 52.

36 *"An able- bodied slave is at present worth about four pounds' worth of British goods, and when he is shipped he can produce nothing more. But supposing he was kept in his native country, he might be very slight exertion produce one ton of oil per annum, which would be worth eight pounds or purchase double the quantity of British goods."* Oldfield & Laird (1837) Narrative of an expedition into the interior of Africa, by the river Niger, p. 361.

37 This was described by Captain Becroft and his surgeon Mr King (1841), who described such a centre north of the Calabar on the Cross River. Palm oil was "*….disposed of to the Eboes on the opposite side of the river, who at present dispose of it to the native traders from New Calabar and Bonny.*"

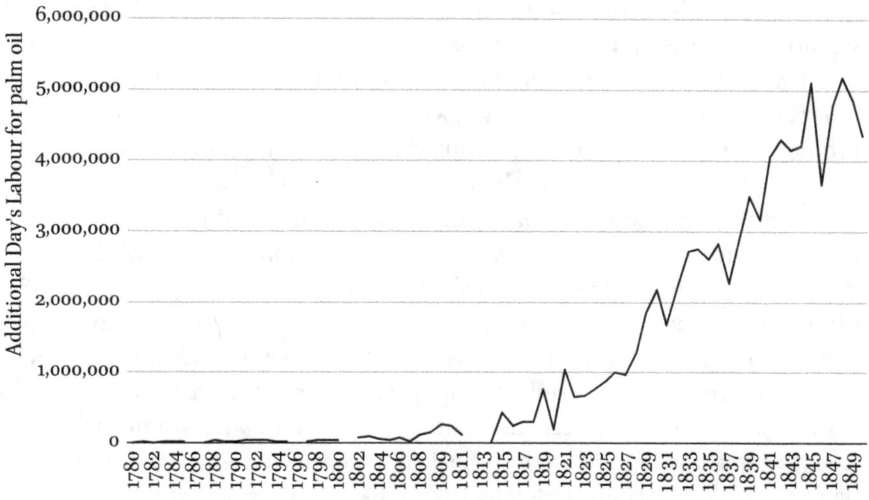

FIGURE 5.8. Additional days' labour in the interior of the Bight of Biafra to produce palm oil for the British market
Sources: See pages 204–206

suggests that "*...a carrier could carry a head-load of between 50 and 60 pounds.... between 15 and 25 miles a day.*"[38] Reid (1986) in a study on Dahomean palm oil suggests 35 lbs of oil (around 4 gallons) in containers weighing around 15 lbs, which seems reasonable as Lynn (1997, p. 48) suggests that most oil was carried in earthenware containers. Lynn's (1997, p. 48) own estimations are that that oil may have been carried in multiple journeys with each load between 1 and 5 gallons. For the purposes of this study it will be conservatively assumed that porters took 4 gallons or 35lbs per trip, and that it took around a day to get to and from the bulking centre. Therefore, a day's labour was required for every 4 gallons of palm oil, and 64 days for each ton. In terms of the quantities of palm oil, Lynn (1997, p. 20) quotes published figures showing that sixty five percent

38 Reference: Alan McPhee The Economic Revolution in West Africa (1926 pp. 54, 55). This estimate seems relatively accurate. Studies among the Luo in Eastern Africa have shown that women can carry up to 70% of their bodyweight through headloading. Modern experiments show that both men and women can carry 20% of their bodyweight on their heads, without expending additional energy, so long as they are skilled by learning this from childhood (Heglund et al. 1995). An estimation of 50% is taken. Eltis (1990) estimates that the mean height of Biafrans during this period was 163.7cm. Taking a modern height/weight and, making the reasonable assumption that slaves were generally likely to be on the border between a healthy weight and underweight, this would give a rough weight of 50kgs. This means each person could carry around 25 kilos or 55 lbs/trip.

of Great Britain's oil was coming from Biafran ports in 1851. This is a very conservative figure as, in the 1830s, areas such as the Bight of Benin and the Gold Coast were not exporting oil in great quantities, nor does it include exports to other countries. Taking these figures, we can estimate that by the 1830s palm oil production for the export trade required at least an additional 2,000,000 days' labour. This was equivalent to the full-time labour of around 5,500 people per year and the figure was to more than double by the 1850s (Figure 5.8). To put this into context, in the twenty years before abolition the Bight of Biafran region exported an average of 13,524 slaves a year. In the twenty years *after* 1807 the annual average was 5,641, which meant that captives who would previously have been exported were instead diverted into a growing internal economy.

The *degree* of slave labour almost certainly varied from region to region. Korieh (2000, p. 603) suggests that outside of the Ngwa area studied by Martin (1993), many Igbo regions were enthusiastic users of slaves in the production of palm oil. This view is supported by Dike & Ekejuiba (1990, p. 257) and Ejiogu & Njoko (2015, p. 257) who argue that slaves were purchased in greater numbers in Igboland throughout the nineteenth century, either to augment household labour in the production of palm oil, or to grow food for areas where household labour was more fully engaged in palm oil production. This latter activity seems to have been especially important for the supply of captives in the internal market. Food shortages were reported in the coastal region in the late 1820s (Northrup 1979, p. 9) and European travellers were meeting farmers in the Niger delta region with up to 200 slaves, in the 1840s, who were at work growing yams for towns to the south (Ohadike 1992, p. 191). In Northern Igboland slave villages were set up to provide food for those in the palm belt region, often with direct Aro support and supplies (Northrup 1979, p. 10, Nwokeji 2010, p. 183). There was also increasing demand for slaves from households with rising levels of incomes, and from elites who wanted people for sacrifices at the funerals of wealthy men and women (Dike and Ekejuiba 1990, p. 256),[39] and for coastal canoe house trading organisations in need of labour to man canoes or head-load the oil (Lovejoy 2011, p. 180). Thus, even areas with denser populations would have required additional coerced labour as argued by Lovejoy (2011, p. 144), and it should be noted that the falls in slave prices in the early nineteenth-century (at least for male slaves) would have made fulfilling this requirement more feasible for a greater number of people (Nwaubani 1999, p. 101, Lovejoy and Richardson 1995b). In addition, these figures also show that the

39 For a fuller discussion on the role of human sacrifice across West Africa see Law (1985). For his analysis of the increase in human sacrifice in the Biafran region, and his criticisms of an earlier paper by Isichei (1978, p. 469), see pages 70–72.

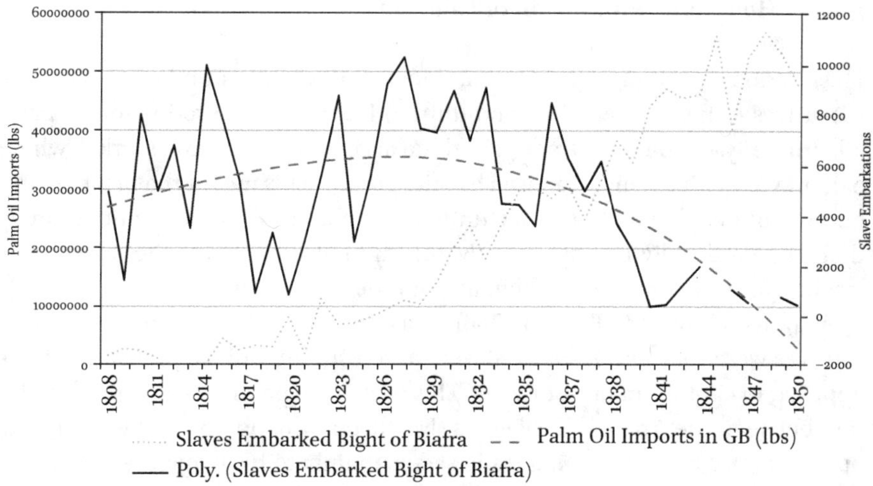

FIGURE 5.9 Palm oil imports (lbs) into Great Britain and slave embarkations from the Bight of Biafra with trend line 1808–1850
Source: TSTD, TNA CUST 4/5–4/45

region could therefore not have continued to simultaneously export slaves and increase its output of palm oil. Indeed, a tipping point was reached around late 1820s when exports of captives to the Atlantic began an irreversible decline (Figure 5.9).

Importantly, the literature strongly suggests that it was the Aro who were providing these slaves, and continued to do so until the British invasion in 1902 (Northrup 1979, p. 10, Korieh 2000, p. 599, 608, Dike and Ekejuiba 1990, p. 235). This is not to say that the nineteenth century was not to cause problems for the Aro. As new producers entered the market, new trade routes opened that began to bypass the Aro (Dike & Ekejiuba 1990, p. 257, Martin 1988, p. 28). When Europeans began to establish factories in the 1860s and use steamboats to connect directly to local suppliers, the Aro began to lose control over the middleman trade (Dike & Ekejiuba 1990, p. 257, Kolapo 2002, pp. 24, 25). In addition, the slump in oil prices and the economic recession of the 1870s was extremely disruptive (Manning 1986, p. 226, Lynn 1997, p. 151). However, for the period under study, the Aro's slave-trading network was still just as busy transporting the higher value slaves, either for the external or internal markets, as it was palm oil. The material power and interest of the region's trading elites were therefore not affected by the development of the palm oil industry. The next question is, why were households prepared to invest so much labour into the production of oil (Northrup 1976, p. 361)?

7 Household Production of Palm Oil

This section will argue that non-elite households had a number of powerful incentives to invest their (free and unfree) labour in the production of palm oil. Primarily, the palm oil trade gave them access to the Atlantic market, which had previously been monopolised by elite groups. This meant that a far greater number of people had the opportunity to purchase goods that could improve their standard of living. Importantly, this did not mean that elite households lost out, as they continued to benefit from the commodity trade.

As noted above, the Bight of Biafra was unusual in that the majority of its captives were sent into Atlantic slavery as a result of judicial punishments, as opposed to capture in raids or wars. This was made possible through cooperation between the Aro and local elites (Northrup 1978, pp. 70–73, Nwokeji 2010, pp. 134–135). The provisioning trade seems mainly to have operated relatively close to Old Calabar and Bonny and was controlled by local elites running large plantations (Behrendt et al. 2010, p. 93). Therefore, during the period of the slave trade, participation in long-distance exchange was probably not an option for the majority of people living in the palm oil belt.

Palm oil production led to non-elite households entering the market, which is suggested by changes in trade products brought to the region. One way to illustrate this is to examine the cargoes of different types of merchant ships from the port of Bristol. As noted in Chapter 3, the city was unique in the 1790s for sending both specialist slave and commodity ships to Africa. The Bristol port authorities published a twice-monthly newsletter called the *Bristol Presentments*, which detailed the import and export cargoes of ships entering the ports, in addition to their clearance and arrival dates. An analysis of the average quantity of different types of goods loaded onto commodity and slaving vessels heading to ports in the Bight of Biafra, shows that commodity vessels required a very different selection, which suggests that they were intended for a different group of consumers (see Appendix 5.6). The slaving vessels provided the same kinds of cargo that was demanded by elites in other regions, namely a large quantity of cloth, metals, guns, gunpowder and ammunition. By contrast the commodity vessels seem to have carried less expensive foreign cloth, and greater amounts of cheaper British fabric. There is far less metal and almost no gunpowder, weapons or ammunition. The most striking difference is the huge quantity of salt, which became the most important item of trade for palm oil, but was of little importance to the slave trade.[40]

40 In their analysis of trade goods on Biafran slaving vessels in the late 1760s/early 1770s, Behrendt at el. (2010, pp. 58–68) make no mention of salt. Latham (1973, p. 73) also notes that it was a product entirely associated with the palm oil trade.

One trader in the 1790s noted that at Old Calabar "*Palm Oil is very plentiful. Ships carry very large quantities home of late from place – It is in general bought for salt, one measure or crew of salt for one of palm oil* (p. 52)" and advises traders to "*...take care and reserve as much salt as will do your business for palm oil...*".[41] Capt. Thomas Cobb, writing to Bristol merchant James Rogers from Old Calabar in 1792, informs his employer that "*I have discharged all the salt and taken on board nine butts four pipes ninety-one puncheon and three hogsheads of palm oil. It far exceeds your order for oil but the salt would not command redwood nor scarce any one article but oil...*"[42] This situation remained unchanged at Old Calabar until at least the 1820s, when Capt. Edward Bold (1823) noted that every assortment of trade goods used to barter for oil required salt at a ratio of around 4:6 and that "*Salt is a very profitably and commanding article here, therefore you cannot bring too much....*" Adams (1822 p. 263) writing about the expanding trade for palm oil at Bonny noted that "*...as the palm oil trade increases...salt, in all probability will become more in demand, vessels trading there take at present about fifty tons each.*" The customs records also show that the expansion of the palm oil trade was accompanied by a corresponding increase in salt exports to Africa (see Table 5.1 above).

This trend continued into the nineteenth century. From 1828, the British customs records begin to provide more accurate geographical information, both for goods going to and coming from Africa. Goods coming from the Gold Coast region were grouped under "Cape Coast Castle and the Gold Coast from Cape Apolonia to the Rio Volta" and it is fairly certain that most of the trade goods going to the region "Coast South of the Volta with the Island of Fernando Po" were destined for Biafra to be exchanged for palm oil.[43] A sample from 1828 to 1832 is taken to compare the types of products that were being sent to the two different regions. Valued in current prices in British markets, the value of commodities from Biafra (around eighty four percent of which were palm oil) was around 1.75 times greater than those from the Gold Coast (see Appendix 5.7). The differences in the goods that were exchanged for these products is striking

41 British Library, Add Mss 12131, 'Mr Parfitt's information on Trade between Sierra Leone and Cape Lopez w. Islands St Thomas etc' and 'Extract of a Diary Kept by E.L. Parfitt on the Board of the Sierra Leone Company's Ship *Calypso*', Papers Relating to Sierra Leone, ff. 174–320, p. 83.

42 C107/6 Letter from Thomas Cobb, Captain of the Triton, January 19th 1792 Old Calabar.

43 South of the Volta essentially meant all of Africa from the borders of modern day Ghana to the Cape of Good Hope. However, as noted in Chapter 2, neither the Bight of Benin nor West Central Africa were exporting commodities during this time and therefore had very little trade with Britain. Palm oil dominated exports and the vast majority was bought in Biafra.

(Table 5.4). The Gold Coast region, despite the lower value of its exports, bought relatively more cloth and clothing and had a preference for iron manufactures. Ships going to Biafra catered for both the elites and non-elites. Thus, there are large numbers of iron bars, guns and gunpowder but also more low quality material ('Slops and Negro Clothing'), as well as half a million pounds of salt, which is absent from trade goods going to the Gold Coast.

TABLE 5.4 Quantities of goods imported into the 'Gold Coast' and 'Coast South of the Rio Volta' regions 1828–1832

Product	Unit	Gold Coast	Coast South of Rio Volta
Apparel	pieces	243.628	36.176
Calicoes	pieces	867.381	1,588,744
Cotton Manufactures	yards	2,663,696	2,742,946
Woollens Manufactures	yards	5.243	517
Hats	pieces	10.78	60.013
Muslins	pieces	28.316	520
Slops and Negro Clothing	*pieces*	*28.224*	*196.896*
Brass	lbs	62.374	96.826
Copper	lbs	0	5.04
Iron Bar	pieces	1,157,248	8,816,640
Iron Wrought	lbs	130.676	20.048
Tin	lbs	8.988	4.256
Glass	pieces	107.093	183.128
Salt	*lbs*	*0*	*515.78*
Soap	*lbs*	*21.651*	*121.845*
Staves	pieces	4.73	62.684
Gunpowder	lbs	1,191,867	6,847,205
Guns	pieces	70.263	195.69

Source: TNA CUST 8/27–8/36, 10/19–10/23

The differences indicate that the Gold Coast region was far more interested in what might be termed luxury items, which had a role in signalling status and wealth. By contrast in the Bight of Biafra, there were large numbers of customers who were more interested in items that improved more basic standards of living, such as soap for cleanliness, cheap clothes for themselves or perhaps their slaves and of course, salt. The latter item would have had a significant impact on the lives of less privileged households. In his study of salt in Western Sudan, Lovejoy (1986) notes that "*Salt satisfies a physiological need, and it may well be that salt is also man's earliest addiction.*" (p. 1). In the rainforest belt of West Africa, this need may have been much higher for two reasons. Firstly, the heat of the tropics means people sweat more, which raises the craving for salt. Secondly, the tse-tse fly, with its debilitating impact on livestock production, meant that people living in this region had far less meat in their diet, which is a natural source of salt. Isichei (1976, p. 31) and Martin (1988, p. 28) note that the only alternative in the forest zone was potash (vegetable ash), a far less appealing source of salt than sodium chloride which was beginning to be mass produced cheaply in Britain at the turn of the nineteenth century (Lovejoy 1986, p. 18, Latham 1973, p. 74). More salt also allowed for the possibility of importing greater quantities of salted preserved meat to supplement the protein-deficient diets of those in the forest. Martin (1992, p. 28) notes that until the mid-twentieth century farmers in the Ngwa region spent a good deal of their income on salted fish from the coast, Europe or Northern Nigeria and that "... *this scarcity of salt, cloth, meat and fish did not prejudice the survival of Ngwa farmers, but it did provide them with a strong incentive to engage in regional trade.*" Equiano (1794, pp. 12, 13) also suggests that dried, salted fish was "*...esteemed a great rarity...*" in Igboland and was an important part of regional trade.[44]

The general patterns of trade indicate that more households were entering the palm oil market to buy goods that could improve their standards of living. However, this phenomenon did not threaten the power of existing elites who were able to benefit even more than commoner households (Manning 1986, p. 227, Lynn 1997, p. 58, Korieh 2000, p. 599). Village heads often had power over the allocation of communal land, where wild palms were common. In addition, they enjoyed access to greater resources of labour, as they generally had

44 There has been some doubt over whether Equiano was actually from Africa. Carretta 2005 has suggested that he was in fact born in Carolina and his African heritage was an invention to help promote the abolitionist cause. However, both Nwokeji (2006) and Lovejoy (2006) have argued strongly against this hypothesis, saying that it is far more likely that Equiano was born and raised in Igboland.

more wives/children and/or slaves. They were also more likely to be members of secret societies, such as the Okonko in the Ngwa region, whose contacts with local Aro merchants afforded easier access to more coerced labour, which in turn allowed them to increase production (Martin 1988, p. 32). Of course, these conditions were not unique to the Biafran region, but what was different was that, while local village-level elites probably gained more from the new trade, they did not dominate or monopolise it. The demand for goods was therefore not driven by a status conscious elite looking to preserve the existing hierarchy, as was the case in Dahomey and, to a lesser extent, Asante.

These changes were not positive for everyone. By the mid-eighteenth-century salt production at the coast, which had long been the basis of the local economy, was crowded out by cheaper foreign imports (Northrup 1978, p. 213).[45] However, over the nineteenth century foreign imports greatly benefited producers of palm oil. Martin (1992, p. 29) and Lynn (1997, pp. 68, 69) note that during this period the region saw an increase in cheaper products which, in addition to salt, included Lancashire textiles, tobacco from America and gin from the Netherlands. These became accepted as forms of currency for small scale transactions in the region, thus helping stimulate more market activity. In addition, like Asante, production for the market gave previously poorer households the possibility of acquiring additional labour in the form of slaves (Ohadike 1998, p. 192). This labour could be used to either gain more wealth or provide more leisure time to free members of the household. For the Aro, it had the additional benefit of bringing many new customers for their principal product (Dike & Ekejiuba 1990, p. 257). In short, there were plenty of very good reasons why households were motivated to greatly expand their production of palm oil in the late eighteenth and early nineteenth centuries.

Chapters 2 and 3 showed that in the Bight of Biafran region, the transatlantic slave trade did not crowd out other forms of commercial exchange, even after the rapid expansion of exports from the 1740s. Producers in the interior responded to demands for provisions and, from the 1770s, for commodities. This was partly the result of having long established commercial networks between the interior and the coast, which were facilitated by efficient riverine trade routes. Furthermore, the region was particularly well endowed with natural resources, in particular oil palms and tropical hardwoods, for which there

45 Adams (1823, p. 139) noted that salt was still being produced in the western half of the Niger Delta and at Bonny and Calabar (pp. 118, 122, 139), and members of one of the Niger Expeditions saw that it was still an industry in Brass (Lander & Lander 1832, Vol 3, p. 237), but after this, sources do not list it as one of the local industries.

was a growing demand in the expanding industrial economies of Europe. However, this chapter has argued that these factors do not by themselves explain the nature and timing of the region's commercial transition.

Just as importantly, institutional development in the area was very different to that of either the Gold Coast or the Bight of Benin. Until the Aro opened the central Igbo region to transatlantic slavery in the early eighteenth-century, embarkation numbers had never been high. Without the stimulus of luxury trade goods and military technology, the political competition and military revolutions that marked the other regions did not occur. Instead, systems of elite order developed that were able to monopolise external trade, without strongly hierarchal systems of order based on military power. For the Aro traders, the powerful 'big men' of the interior and the merchant elites at the coast, power and wealth were always ultimately dependent on trade of all kinds. The broadcast of authority, enforcement of tribute or military reputation, all of which were facilitated by slave raids, were never as important. Slaves were generally not acquired through large-scale, organised violence and were always traded alongside commercial agricultural products and commodities.

This institutional setting meant that at the start of the nineteenth century, the region was not, like Dahomey, economically or politically dependent on the transatlantic slave trade. The unilateral and sudden withdrawal of the British was of course an economic shock, but the transition to palm oil was relatively smooth for three key reasons. Firstly, those who had previously grown rich from slave trading did not, in the long run, lose out financially and probably gained. The Aro could continue to sell slaves to a growing internal market, while still controlling the trade routes that handled palm oil. The 'big men' of the interior became the largest producers of oil and the merchants at the coast continued to gain from marketing a new product that was significantly less volatile than slaves. Secondly, commoners, who had previously been largely excluded from trade with the Atlantic, gained access to trade goods that could materially improve their standards of living. Thirdly, the British government helped to incentivise ex-slave traders to invest in palm oil, which ensured that the new market grew steadily over the first half of the nineteenth century.

While the diplomatic and military campaign against transatlantic slavery remained relatively weak, both captives and commodities could continue to be traded side by side, as had been the case in the eighteenth century. However, a combination of increasing labour demands for the production of palm oil and food, combined with the impact of more effective measures against slavers in the 1830s, was sufficient to bring the export of captives to an end. This was a largely positive choice, where merchants decided to focus on an export sector that had already been growing for more than 60 years. By contrast, the Dahomean monarchy and ruling elite only grudgingly began to support the development of palm oil exports in the late 1830s, and strove to maintain their output of captives for as long as possible. The reasons why are the subject of the next chapter.

Appendices

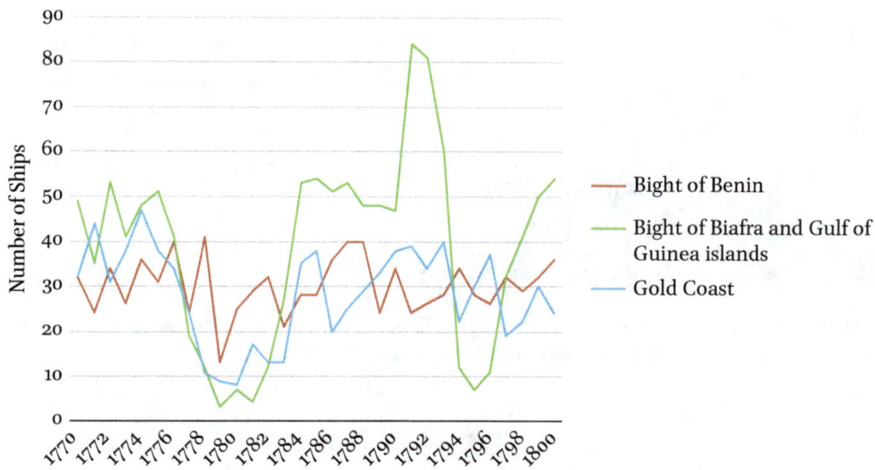

APPENDIX 5.1 Number of slaving ships visiting the three case study regions 1770–1800
Source: slavevoyages.org

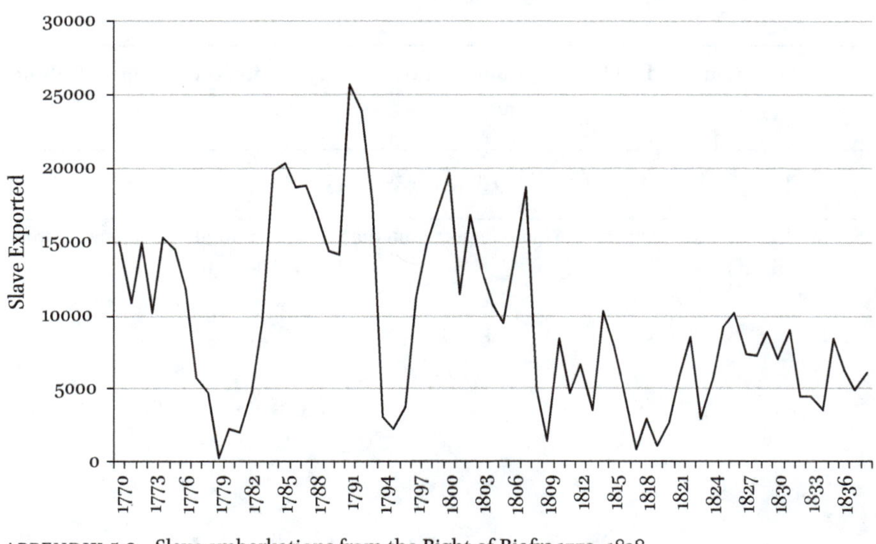

APPENDIX 5.2 Slave embarkations from the Bight of Biafra 1770–1838
Source: slavevoyages.org

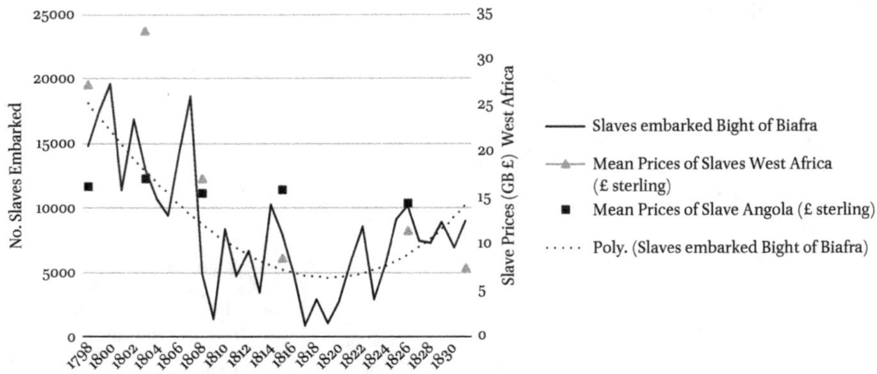

APPENDIX 5.3 Slave exports Bight of Biafra + Slave prices West Africa and Angola 1798–1830
Source: slavevoyages.org, Lovejoy & Richardson 1995a

APPENDIX 5.4 Percentage fall in the value of the principle African commodities imported into Britain between 1814 and 1816

Beeswax	Camwood	Ebony	Gum Senegal	Hides	Ivory	Palm Oil	Pepper	Redwood
-67%	-40%	-70%	-83%	-71%	-27%	-38%	-79%	-67%

Source: Parliamentary Papers 1816 (506) Report from the Select Committee on Papers Relating to the African Forts

APPENDIX 5.5 Index of the quantity of goods imported into Great Britain from Africa (1811=100)

Year	Beeswax	Camwood	Ebony	Gum Senegal	Hides	Ivory	Palm Oil	Pepper	Redwood
1811	100	100	100	100	100	100	100	100	100
1812	93	99	138	16	83	46	49		144
1814	81	89	63	59	318	53	8	47	143
1815	6	116	228	67	320	65	175	198	191
1816	1	42	164	61	64	46	101	194	140
1817	12	15	201	37	52	34	126	136	136
1818	8	89	169	35	165	50	124	42	84
1819	48	99	63	6	0	54	314	47	53
1820	34	90	0	0.1	236	56	76	39	2

Source: CUST

APPENDIX 5.6 Average quantity of trade goods on Bristol ships trading in the Bight of Biafra 1790–1791

Cloths and Clothing (puncheons)

Year	Slave/ Commodity	Linen	British cotton	India goods
1790	Slave	3.6	8.6	18
1790	Commodity		6	0.125
1791	Slave	25	1	13
1791	Commodity	0	0	13

Wrought and Unwrought Metals

Year	Slave/ Commodity	Iron bars	Lead bars	Wrought iron chests	Copper/Brass manufactures chests	Iron pots/ Brass pans
1790	Slave	1791	487	48	47.5	637
1790	Commodity	160	0	31	0	0
1791	Slave	911	294	35	19	994
1791	Commodity	140	0	28	40	50

Weapons and Ammunition

Year	Slave/ Commodity	Kegs Gunpowder	Bags Lead and shot	Chests Muskets	Casks Gunflints
1790	Slave	1194	167	11	11
1790	Commodity	0	0	0	0
1791	Slave	9237	37	3.5	5.5
1791	Commodity	100	0	0	3

Other				
Year	**Slave/ Commodity**	**Chest Bugle**	**Punch Spirits**	**Salt**
1790	Slave	3	45	482
1790	Commodity	0	2	9306
1791	Slave	3	40.5	334
1791	Commodity	4	37	4380

Source: Bristol Presentments

APPENDIX 5.7 Value (GB £) of commodities from the two case study regions 1828–1832

	Beeswax	Camwood	Ebony	Palm oil	Pepper	Redwood	Ivory	Gold	Total
Coast South of the Rio Volta with the Island of Fernando Po	2126	1767	1844	1143628	150	134966	82447	0	*1366929*
Cape Coast Castle and the Gold Coast from Cape Apolonia to the Rio Volta	420	1003	45113	87313	9455	14	39185	593880	*776384*

Sources: CUST, Liverpool Mercurcy Prices Current. Ivory price from Parliamentary Papers 1816 (506) Report from the Select Committee on Papers Relating to the African Forts

CHAPTER 6

The Bight of Benin: Dahomey and the Dominance of Export Slavery

> It was the slave trade that made him terrible to his enemies, and loved, honoured and respected by his people. How could he give it up?
>
> King Gezo of Dahomey, as reported by the British diplomat, THOMAS CRUIKSHANK, 1848, p. 7

∵

This chapter will tackle the question of why the region of the Bight of Benin that came to be controlled by Dahomey remained focused for so long on the export of captives, in contrast to the Gold Coast and the Bight of Biafra. The evidence presented in Chapter 2 suggests that an aversion to the non-slave trade characterised this area throughout the seventeenth and eighteenth centuries. In Chapter 3 it has been argued that the region never seriously engaged in the provisioning trade throughout the long eighteenth-century. In Chapter 4 it has been shown that Dahomean merchants did not respond to the rising European demand for African commodities in the late eighteenth-century. Other studies of the region have also pointed out that the Dahomean elites remained committed to export slavery for longer than other areas of West Africa during the nineteenth century (Thomas 1999, Klein 2010, p. 65, pp. 695–996, Lovejoy 2011, pp. 171–172). This chapter will show that the slave trade in the Bight of Benin developed earlier, and with far greater intensity, than in either the Bight of Biafra or the Gold Coast. It will argue that this early engagement encouraged the development of more centralised, militarised states with elites, dependent on the slave trade to maintain their political and economic power. In addition, the region's ecology ensured that states could not easily gain the kind of regional ascendancy enjoyed by Asante. As a result, even the most powerful state along the coast, Dahomey, was continuously threatened by powerful neighbours until the 1820s, and always faced competitors for slave exports in the region. These conditions reinforced a state ideology based on military power and expansion in order to acquire more captives.

The state of Dahomey thus developed an institutional rigidity which affected the late commercial transition in the nineteenth century. Greater centralisation

 | DOI:10.1163/9789004417120_008

and powerful elites monopolised much larger shares of the available female and coerced male labour force to serve their economic and political agendas. The kingdom's armed forces were more professionalised, and mobilised far more regularly, than in the other case study areas, which meant that a greater amount of labour was required to produce food for larger numbers of non-productive people. Furthermore, warfare disrupted agriculture by taking away producers from the land when the military required extra manpower. In addition, the demographic impacts of the slave trade and its attending violence led to a severe demographic decline across the region. While the kingdom of Dahomey may not have suffered as much as the areas that its armies raided, the fall in population limited the pool of both free and coerced labour available for other forms of economic activities. Therefore, households and lineage groups, which had driven the commercial transition in the other case study regions, had far fewer opportunities here to expand their output of export commodities.

This interpretation goes against the 'crisis of adaptation' argument put forward by Hopkins (1973) and supports the broader conclusions of Soumonni (1995) that the gradual abolition of the transatlantic slave trade did not fundamentally undermine the power basis of the Dahomean elites. At the same time, however, this case confirms the intuition of Hopkins' thesis, namely that a change from a slave export based economy would weaken the foundations of elite authority and provided non-elite households with the opportunity to increase their wealth and influence. The chapter will argue that without elite support, an alternative export sector would not have emerged, and that the elites changed their focus only after the abolition policies of the British effectively shut down the transatlantic slave trade. Finally, it seems plausible that the high demands of the state and its army were the reason why the Dahomeans abstained from exports of food provisions to slave ships during the long eighteenth-century.

The chapter is organised as follows. It presents an analysis of the long-term trade contacts, beginning in the seventeenth century when the region first became important for slave embarkations, and which supports the analysis of the region's long-term commitment to slave trading given in Chapters 1 and 3. It then provides an analysis of the comparative value of the palm oil and slave trades, suggesting that the palm oil trade was less valuable to the Dahomean elites than the slave trade. The next section argues that the most important slaving nations in the region, Portugal and France, were not significant buyers of commodities, but that this was not a key variable. Instead it will be argued that the development of a highly stratified military state, and the labour demands of the elites and their armies, were the primary determinant of the continued focus on slave export trading up to the 1840s.

1 Area of Study

Geographically, the Bight of Benin was a 200 mile/320 km stretch of coast extending from the Cape of St Paul on the Rio Volta in the west to Cape Formosa in the east (Law 2004, p. 51).[1] The area was geographically united through what is known as the Benin Gap, where the rainforest belt is interrupted by a savannah landscape that was more characteristic of West Africa's interior (Law 1991, p. 19). Nonetheless, as argued in Chapter 1, the region's ecology was suitable for oil palms, with the potential to transport them to the coast. The origins of the Dahomean kingdom are unclear, but it was probably initially formed in the early seventeenth-century by refugees or settlers who displaced or conquered the original inhabitants of the Abomey plateau. The plateau was situated around 100 km from the coast, bounded on two sides by the Koufo and the Zou (which became the Weme) rivers. The Dahomean state had initially expanded across the Abomey plateau during the seventeenth century, as a tributary of the more powerful kingdom of Allada. Under one of the first Dahomean kings, Wegbaja (1650–1680), a number of military reforms were carried out, including the adoption of and more effective use of firearms, and a centralization of warfare and justice under the king (Thornton 1999, p. 82, Reid 1986, p. 26). This process of political centralisation was continued by subsequent monarchs and the kingdom developed a level of military organisation that was far more potent than any of its southern neighbours (Reid 2012, pp. 82, 83). Dahomey became the major inland supplier of slaves to the Alladans and Huedans (Law 1991, p. 185), and under King Agaja defeated and conquered these two states in the 1720s. The motives for Agaja's expansion have been debated, but there seems to be a consensus that this move was designed to at once protect his own people from slave raiding, while also ensuring that the state could control both the supply and sale of captives to Europeans.[2] Most of the kingdom's slaves and goods were transported along the main road which began at the capital Abomey and went south through Cana and Agrime, the latter town marking the end of the plateau and state's core region of power (Law 2004,

1 The region was also referred to as the Slave Coast, which was a term to denote a trading region between the Volta River and the port of Lagos.

2 Akinjogbin (1967) initially proposed the idea that Agaja's intentions had been to secure control of the coast in order to abandon slave trading. Manning (1982), whilst agreeing that this would have been beneficial to the region's long-term development, argues that his intentions were probably more likely to have been to ensure security from raiding for his own people and to gain control over the supply and sales of slaves. This interpretation is supported by Law (1991) and Bay (1998).

pp. 117, 120). Travellers were then obliged to pass through the Lama swamp in order to proceed to the coast. The Dahomean state was the pre-eminent political and military power on the coast from the Popos to Seme from the 1720s until the onset of formal French colonial rule in 1892. Its control over both the key coastal port of Whydah, and the interior regions from which most slaves were captured, meant that the state exported the majority of the region's slaves for the period from the seventeenth to the nineteenth centuries.[3]

2 Long-term Trends in Dahomey's Trade

The most significant difference between the Bight of Benin and the two other case study regions was that here the slave trade grew to significant proportions far earlier, and dominated the trade in captives in the late seventeenth and early eighteenth centuries (Figure 6.1).[4] The area had long been known as a source of slaves to Europeans, who had imported slaves from the region into the Gold Coast from the sixteenth century (see Chapter 4). The British, French

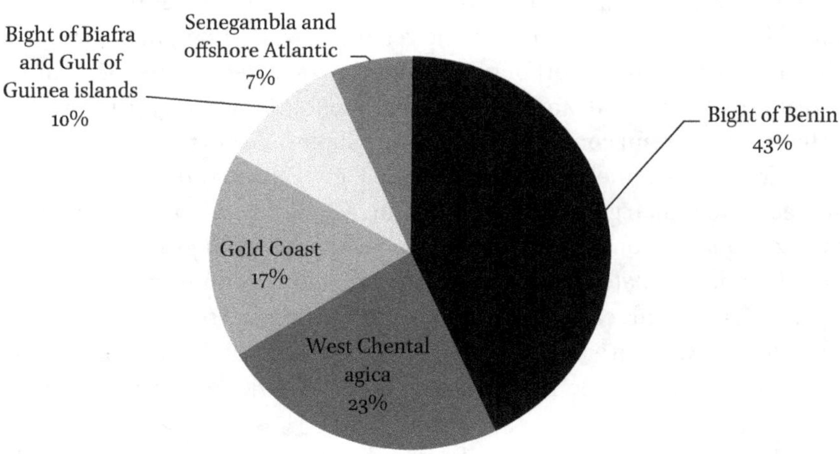

FIGURE 6.1 Percentage of slaves embarked by region 1650–1730
Source: TSTD

3 Although in the nineteenth-century, the port of Lagos was to overtake Whydah as the most important port for the transatlantic slave trade in the Bight of Benin (Mann 2007, pp. 39, 40).

4 Slaves from the Bight of Biafra may have been traded earlier than those from areas of the Bight of Benin which Dahomey came to control. There is evidence that the Portuguese were taking slaves from *Old* Calabar from at least the early seventeenth century, but the numbers were relatively small (Behrendt et al. 2010, p. 48).

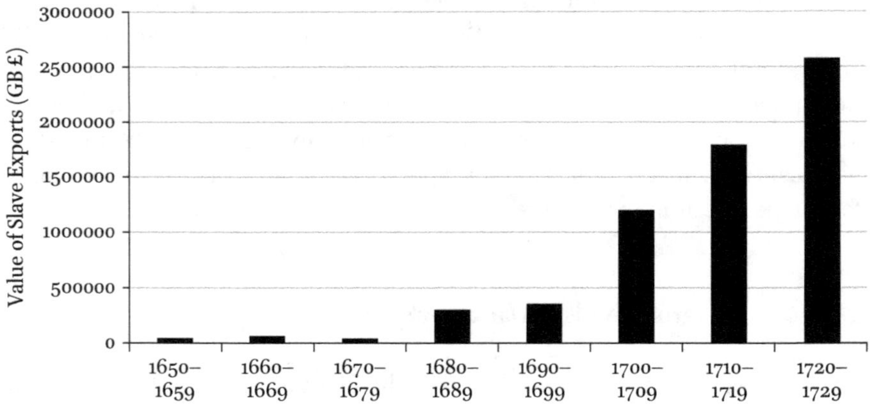

FIGURE 6.2 Nominal value of slave exports from the Bight of Benin 1650–1730
Sources: Slave Prices from Manning (1982, p. 332), Slave Embarkations from TSTD

and Dutch began to demand labour for their growing American possessions in the seventeenth century and, as the Gold Coast was not exporting sufficient numbers of captives, they looked to the Bight of Benin to meet their requirements (Klein 2010, pp. 77–80).[5] As the region possessed no gold, it came to specialise solely in the export of people, which was to determine the nature of the region's Atlantic trade for the centuries to follow (Law 1991, pp. 118–122).

This had important consequences for the people living in this region. Firstly, the trade was extremely lucrative, and led to high quantities of valuable European and Indian goods flowing into the region (Figure 6.2).[6] This simultaneously increased competition for control over a new and growing source of income, and stimulated the development of more centralised, militarised states, geared towards capturing, transporting, buying and selling greater numbers of slaves (Norman 2012, p. 147). Indeed, in the Bight of Benin, the infamous 'guns-for-slaves trade cycle' hypothesis set out by Whatley (2014) came into full bloom.

As will be discussed later in the chapter, slave exports became crucial to the political and economic power of the Dahomean state. As a result, the monarchy and elite groups of the kingdom stuck to a slave raiding model, while their

5 Sources suggest that the introduction of new crops from the Americas led to strong population growth, which meant that the region had a large pool of people who could be enslaved (Manning 1982, p. 7, Law 1991, pp. 59–60).

6 If these figures are converted into 2005 GB£, then the slave coast saw an increase from around £4 million in the decade from 1650 to nearly £220 million worth of goods imported from 1720 to 1730. Calculated using the currency converter from The National Archives: http://www.nationalarchives.gov.uk/currency/default.asp#mid. Accessed 7/6/2016.

counterparts in the Gold Coast and the Bight of Biafra were diversifying their export economies. The difference is most clearly illustrated in reaction to the changed economic environment in the two decades following abolition. As shown in Figure 6.3, the region had seen declining revenues from transatlantic slave exports for some time due to the loss of the French trade in 1794,[7] and Portuguese/Brazilian traders focusing their attention on Angola and South-eastern Africa (Eltis 2009). Rather than exploring alternatives such as palm oil to compensate for the loss of revenue, the state instead focused its efforts on military campaigns and reviving the slave trade. During the 1820s the king, Gezo, took advantage of the collapse of the Oyo kingdom to increase the extent and frequency of military expeditions to capture slaves and extend the kingdom's power (Reid 1986, p. 33). Captives from areas such as Mahi and Yorubaland temporarily swelled the kingdom's exports (Law 2004, p. 160). When British abolition efforts became more effective in the 1830s, the Dahomeans responded by developing more elaborate strategies to avoid the British blockade. These strategies included bringing larger numbers of slaves to the coast and keeping them there for longer periods so that boarding could take place more rapidly,[8]

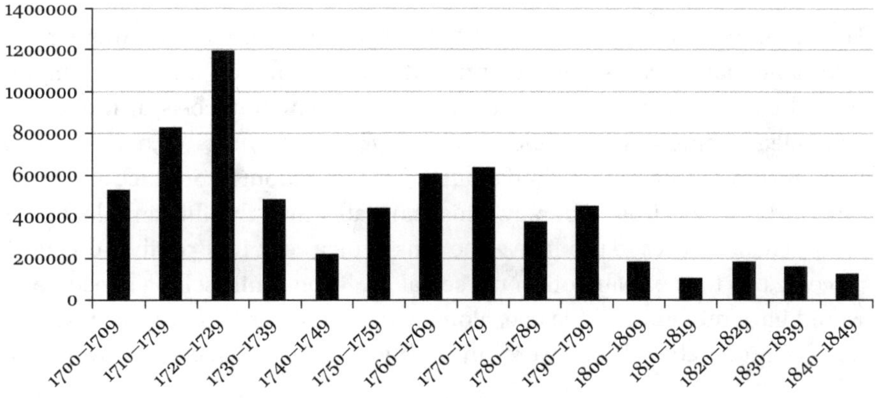

FIGURE 6.3 Income from slave sales at Whydah (British £)
Source: Prices from Manning (1982), slave numbers from TSTD

7 As a result of the French and Haitian revolutions. Although French slaving ships were to re-enter the trade just a decade later, it was in reduced numbers (TSTD).

8 1842 (551) (551-II) Report from the Select Committee on the West Coast of Africa; together with the minutes of evidence, appendix, and index. Part 1. – Report and evidence. F Swanzy to committee, p. 37, para 615 "…there is still an importation of slaves from Dahomey into Whydah; there they are kept till they can ship them; perhaps the half of them may be dead before they can be shipped."

or by taking slaves to other ports such as Little Popo via the coastal lagoons.[9] Alternatively, Portuguese/Brazilian traders would arrange for two ships to be sent to the coast, one with trade goods and another to transport captives, which limited time at the coast and made it easier to evade the anti-slave patrol (Law 2004, pp. 158, 191–193).

Even after the virtual collapse of transatlantic slavery in the 1840s, and when the monarchy had finally begun to invest in the production of palm oil (Manning 1982, p. 17, Law 2004, p. 222) there were still many in the ruling coalition who resisted change. Gezo's successor, Glele, supported by powerful elements within the Dahomean elite, attempted to re-orientate the state back towards a slave raiding model, when demand for coerced labour on the sugar plantations of Cuba led to a brief revival in Atlantic slavery (Bergad et al. 1995, p. 58, Soumonni 1995, p. 90). To explore why, in contrast to the other case study regions, the Dahomean state remained so committed to the export of captives, let us begin by examining the relative profitability of both the commodity and slave trades.

3 Comparative Value of the Slave and Commodity Trades

For the Dahomean monarchy and its elite supporters, palm oil was far less profitable than slave trading. The price of a ton of palm oil was slightly higher than the cost of a slave (Figure 6.4), but the production costs of the former were clearly much higher. Reid (1986, pp. 346–350) calculated, very roughly, that one ton of palm oil required around 795 days' labour to produce and transport to the coast from Abomey. This translates into the full-time labour of around 10,000 slaves to produce 2,000 tons of oil a year. In 1850 silver dollar ($) prices, 2,000 tons of palm oil would sell at $248,000, while selling 10,000 slaves would have brought in $600,000, along with far greater tax/customs revenues for the monarch.[10] There were, in addition, other obstacles to overcome.

9 Ibid. Lt Reinald Levinge RN to committee, p. 227, paras 3996–4000 "…it would be of no use blockading Whydah alone, without blockading the coast 20 miles on either side of it. Could you maintain an effectual blockade to that extent? No, I tried and could not do it, because they communicate by signal; if a vessel comes in the offing, they make a long telegraph to her to proceed to sea for some days, or to come upon the coast at Apee on a given day, where their slaves are waiting for them…."

10 Gezo, the king during the 1840s, wrote to Queen Victoria saying "*At present my people are a warlike people and unaccustomed to agricultural pursuits. I should not be enabled to keep up my revenue were I at once to stop the slave trade.*" This view is restated by the British diplomat Cruikshank who wrote in his report on the negotiations with Gezo over the abolition of the slave trade "*No other trade was known to his people. Palm oil, it was true. was now*

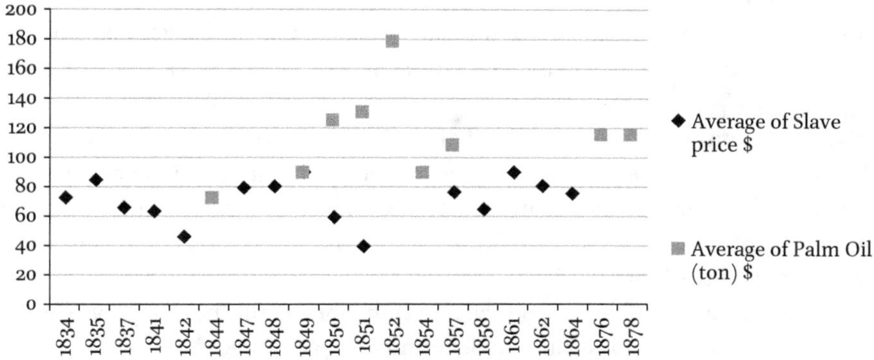

FIGURE 6.4 Average price per slave and ton of palm oil at Whydah 1834–1878
Source: Law (2004, pp. 159, 208)

Whydah was by no means an ideal port for the loading of palm oil as the beach was over 3 km from the town. Once there, the oil needed to be loaded into canoes and transported to ships 2km away through shark infested waters because the currents and waves were too dangerous close to the shore (Law 2004, p. 213). Some of these problems were eventually overcome. For example, the town of Cotonou was developed, which allowed oil from the interior to be transported directly to the coast via the Wembe river, thus reducing transport costs. However, this was unlikely to have made a significant difference, to the fact that slaves remained a considerably more profitable trade. In addition, Dahomean merchants soon faced competition from other ports in the Bight of Benin such as Porto Novo, Badagary and Lagos, which were also very suitable for oil exports due to access to interior markets through water transport, and having hinterlands that were ecologically favourable to palms (Mann 2007, pp. 118–150).

Beyond the fact that slaves could make more money for the king and his elites, there were other reasons why palm oil was not a complement to the Dahomean slave trade in the same way it was for the elite merchants in the Bight of Biafra, or as gold was for the Asante. Firstly, the Dahomean monarchy and its elite supporters were able to control and monitor the trade in slaves far more effectively than the trade in palm oil. While private merchants collectively sold the majority of the region's slaves, the king was always the single

---

engaging the attention of some of them, but it was a slow-method of making money and brought only a small amount of duties into his coffers." Quotes in Reid (1986, pp. 317, 318).

largest seller because of his key role in the military campaigns during which most captives were acquired. All merchants had to pay the king for permission to trade, and their rights could be withdrawn (Bay 1998, pp. 104–106, Law 2004, pp. 113–118). Alternatively, the state could act as a middleman for trade in captives from other areas such as Yorubaland (Law 1989b). Their movement from the interior was closely monitored and subjected to tolls along the routes from plateau to the coast (Law 2004, p. 117). This kind of centralised control was much more difficult to achieve for palm oil, which was largely a result of the geography of the kingdom.

While it was possible to produce and transport oil on the Abomey plateau, the area south of Lama swamp had a number of advantages. For a start, water was much scarcer on the plateau. In the capital of Abomey all sources of fresh water lay outside the city. Therefore, acquiring sufficient water was always a much more labour-intensive process, especially outside the rainy season (Reid 1986, p. 51). Costs were also lower nearer to the coast, due to shortened transportation times and the fact that palm production was compatible with existing patterns of agriculture. However, the kingdom's southern provinces always saw the Dahomeans as foreign occupiers and so the state's power was much weaker than in its 'core areas' of power on the plateau (Law 2004, p. 276). Even on the plateau, extending royal power was costly and may have provoked resistance (Monroe 2007, 2012, 2015). Small-scale theft and illegal production, especially from the larger estates, and tax avoidance by the larger Whydan merchants, were common. It was ultimately far more difficult to monitor and control economic activity at the coast due to its distance from the capital and as a result, the monarchy could not control the revenues stemming from palm oil trading as effectively as it could with the slave trade (Law 1992, pp. 8–9).

There was one further commodity that might also have been better exploited by the Dahomeans. Lovejoy's (1980) study of the kola trade between the Asante and the Muslim savannah markets asks why the states around the Bight of Benin did not export this product until the early twentieth century (pp. 20, 21). Lovejoy's focus is on Oyo, and he suggests that the restrictions on the movement of Muslim merchants, together with hostilities between them and the southern caliphates of Ilorin and Nupe, may have been responsible. Dahomey also possessed kola trees in its southern regions (Manning 1982, p. 60) and there is evidence that merchants from the kingdom were active in northern states such as Borgu for the purpose of purchasing slaves (Law 1989b, p. 57). Kola trees did not need to be specifically cultivated as they grew naturally, so any production could occur in the context of existing agriculture (Agiri 1972, p. 34). This meant that there was the potential for exchanging kola for slaves (as was the case with the Asante at Salaga) during the periods when Dahomeans bought captives as well as raiding for them (Law 1989b).

However, with the exception of the small quantities exported to Brazil in the 1860s, there is no evidence that such a trade developed.[11] One unpublished thesis suggests that in the context of Oyo, the kola nuts had some religious significance to the Yoruba who were therefore unwilling to export them to their northern neighbours (Agiri 1972, pp. 54, 55). There is no evidence that this was the case in Dahomey, but other reasons may have been more significant. One such reason was that the type of kola which grew around the Bight of Benin was the genus *c.acuminata*, as opposed to the *c.nitida* cultivated by the Asante, and greatly valued on the savannah (Abaka 2005, pp. 18, 19). Secondly, the instability caused by the conflicts between Oyo and its northern, Muslim neighbours, and the chaos that ensued when the Oyo kingdom fell, disrupted trade to the savannah (Law 1977, pp. 284–288). However, the explorer Clapperton, in 1829, noted that Dahomean slave merchants were operating on trade routes to Hausaland and therefore could have traded kola with the interior (Clapperton 1829, pp. 83, 84, 123). During the twentieth century kola nuts, including *nitida,* were traded between south eastern Nigeria and Benin and Hausa provinces to the north (Tachie-Obeng et al. 2001[12]). The absence of such a trade reinforces the idea that the Dahomean state was, at the very least, not focused on the expansion of other sectors of its economy besides slaves.

While it is clear that the Dahomean elites would likely always to have suffered a fall in revenue had they switched to an export economy based solely on palm oil and perhaps kola nuts, they could yet have developed the kind of dual model of the kind seen in Biafra in the 1820s. It is therefore necessary to look at other factors influencing the rigid attachment to export slavery.

4 Trading Partners

In contrast to the Gold Coast and the Bight of Biafra, the Portuguese and the French, rather than the British, were the most important customers in the long eighteenth-century (Table 6.1). The Portuguese dominance of trade can at least

11 After the British occupation of Lagos, the Blue Books indicate that there was export trade of kola nuts to Brazil, possibly for the large numbers of slaves or former slaves from Oyo / Dahomean territories (Agiri 1972, pp. 58–62). However, this trade was very limited in the 1860s and 1870s, worth only £4,000 in 1871 (the highest figure for the period) compared to nearly £200,000 of exports of palm kernels in the same year. TNA CO151/2–11, Blue Books Lagos 1863–1873.

12 "COLA NITIDA & COLA ACUMINATA A State of Knowledge Report undertaken for The Central African Regional Program for the Environment," Tachie-Obeng, E. & Brown, N Brown, Oxford Forestry Institute Department of Plant Sciences, University of Oxford (2001).

TABLE 6.1 Percentage of slave embarkations from the Bight of Benin by nation

Years	Portugal/Brazil	Netherlands	France	Great Britain
1680–1720	43	17	11	26
1721–1760	61	3	28	8
1761–1808	57	0	23	19
1761–1791[a]	49	0	33	17

Source: TSTD

a 1791 was the year the French revolutionary government temporarily withdrew from the slave trade

partly be explained by local preferences for Portuguese exchange goods. Bahian merchants were particularly motivated to expand their presence in the region as they exported a certain kind of low grade tobacco soaked in cane spirit that was greatly prized in the Bight of Benin, but essentially unsellable in European markets. Pipe smoking was a symbol of elite status and Ribeiro (2008, p. 142) has argued that '*…the large expansion of the Bahian slave trade, and especially the traffic from the Costa da Mina, coincided with the establishment of the traffic in tobacco*'. A further advantage for the Portuguese was that, during the first half of the eighteenth century, they were able to pay with the gold mined in the Minas Gerais mines (Law 1990b, pp. 106–111). The Dahomeans were eager purchasers of gold, perhaps due to the declining value of cowries, the region's principal currency (Law 1991, pp. 307–308). While this trade only lasted until the mines were largely exhausted in the 1760s (Bergad 2006, pp. xvii, 6), it did give Brazilian/Portuguese traders the status of Dahomey's preferred trading partners. The reasons for the French to prefer trading in the Bight of Benin are less clear, but British dominance in other areas of West Africa may have been a contributing factor.

The dominance of France and Brazil/Portugal had two possible consequences. Firstly, neither nation was a significant buyer of either provisions or commodities from the case study areas, instead focusing almost exclusively on the purchase of human captives. Chapters 1,2 and 3 showed that demand for provisions and 'legitimate commerce' in the pre-abolition period were largely driven by British traders, especially from the 1770s. A relative lack of demand may have been a reason why the Dahomeans remained so focused on the slave trade to the detriment of developing other types of exports. This was certainly the analysis of one British trader in 1842, who argued that the relative lack of British traders at Whydah was the reason for the weak development of 'legitimate commerce'.[13] Secondly, in the post-abolition era, it was probably easier for Brazilian/Portuguese vessels to circumvent British abolition efforts, at least until the 1830s. Slavers leaving Brazil could take legitimate passports to trade in Molembo or Cabinda in West Central Africa, which was in theory a legal slave-trading zone until the Equipment Act was passed in 1839 (Thomas 1999, p. 659). These passports allowed them to stop at Sao Tome and Princes Island to provision themselves, and from there they could easily sail the short distance to Benin where they already had well-established trade contacts (Ribeiro 2008, p. 139). As a result, Dahomey did not suffer the same kind of shock experienced by the withdrawal of the British from the transatlantic slave trade.

Although demand of course influences supply, Lovejoy and Richardson (2007) argue that, ultimately, regional patterns of slave/non-slave exports were driven by what local markets were able or willing to provide.[14] As shown in Part 1, the Bight of Benin never supplied a large quantity of provisions or commodities even when, from 1680 to 1730 it was Britain's second most important region of slave embarkation, supplying around a third of its slaves. RAC ships usually stocked up on food at the Gold Coast before sailing on to Arda, Jakin or Whydah. In the mid-eighteenth-century, the commodity vessels of the MCC did stop at some ports in the Bight of Benin but never bought more than small quantities of ivory. Furthermore, during the apogee of the transatlantic slave trade in the second half of the eighteenth century, one in five slaves from the Bight of Benin found themselves in ships that sailed from Bristol, London or Liverpool. Throughout the period under study there were therefore relatively large numbers of ships landing in harbors along the Slave Coast which would have been prepared to buy commodity exports or food provisions had these been available. Thus, while the nationality of Dahomey's main trading partners may have had some role to play, it was certainly not a decisive one. Of far greater importance was Dahomey's military culture.

5 Dahomean Militarism

Dahomey's continued focus on slave exports, against the long-term trend of revenue decline, cannot be fully appreciated without first understanding the

13 1842 (551) (551-II) Report from the Select Committee on the West Coast of Africa; together with the minutes of evidence, appendix, and index. Part 1. – Report and evidence. F Swanzy to committee, p. 45, para 758.

14 "In every region the supply of captives for sale to European carriers remained essentially under African control…" Lovejoy and Richardson, 2007, p. 50.

institutional lock-in effects of slave-trade based militarism. In Dahomey, the military ethos of the ruling elite was, according to one recent analysis, the most extreme of any in pre-colonial Africa (Reid 2012, p. 113). While Asante was a highly-militarised society, Chapter 4 has argued that there were several reasons why alternative 'peace parties' could emerge, and the elite could both tolerate and support the development of commodity exports. In contrast, factors unique to the Bight of Benin prevented the ruling elite from tolerating the development of policies or factions supporting commodity exports. These factors are the region's specific ecological make-up, and path-dependent institutional development, in the context of early specialisation in a centrally coordinated slave trade.

5.1 *The Seventeenth-century Roots of the Dahomean Military State*

The Dahomean state, unlike that of Asante or polities of the Biafran area, developed and expanded in a region in which the Atlantic slave trade played a pivotal role in the economy and society. Law (1991, p. 267) has argued against early interpretations by Akinjogbin (1967) that the Dahomean state was radically different from its predecessors. Instead he suggests that its policies were based to a great degree on the traditions and ideologies of the seventeenth and early eighteenth-century slave coast polities that preceded it. Three legacies were of particular importance. Firstly, the slave trade had been growing steadily for nearly 80 years and was providing ever greater quantities of valuable foreign goods (Figures 6.1 and 6.2). In contrast to Asante, the Dahomean state came to power in a region where slaves were the only commodity exchanged for important imports such as guns and cloth. Even more importantly, they inherited a tradition in which the monarchy benefited most from the trade in people. For example, the kings of Hueda (the territory that included the port of Whydah) had the right to sell their slaves first, at set prices that were usually higher than the market value. Foreign traders were also expected to buy a certain number of slaves from the kings before they could begin trading with other merchants (Law 2004, p. 117). If one state was able to defeat its rivals and control both the coast and interior it could monopolise the 'production' of slaves, and the associated revenue flows would disproportionally benefit the king.[15]

Secondly, the ability to control this wealth depended on the development of larger, more effective fighting forces. The first major slave exporting kingdom was that of Allada, which dominated the region in the mid-seventeenth-century. However, during the latter half of the century the Hueda Kingdom,

15 Bay (1998, p. 43) states that for Dahomey "...income from the (slave) trade was indisputably a central source of state revenue for at least half the life of the kingdom...".

situated on the coast with its capital at Savi, became the single most important embarkation point of slaves to the Atlantic market on the West Coast of Africa. Having broken free from its former Alladan rulers in the 1670s, the elites of the kingdom developed a more efficient, centrally controlled and taxed, slave export operation (Law 1991, p. 51, Norman 2009, p. 147).[16] Competition between Hueda and Allada further enhanced the focus on "*…funneling war captives to the sea and taxing traders moving through their territories…*" (Norman 2012, p. 147). Conflicts between Hueda, Allada and other powers along the coast also led to a change in the nature of war which was very similar to the military revolutions within the Akan region in the same period. Imported firearms led to a greater professionalisation of warfare. Larger armies needed greater central control to organise, provision and lead. Contemporary sources suggest that the size of Allada's army in the 1670s was between 40,000 to 50,000, out of a total population of around 200,000, which would suggest that virtually all adult males were called up to fight (Law 1991, pp. 58, 97). While Law (1991, p. 235) is cautious in attributing warfare during the period to a desire to simply capture slaves, the possibility of profitably selling your captives certainly made conflict more lucrative than in the past, and also provided the means to keep warfare going. As victory meant gaining a greater share of the slave trade, it heightened the stakes in any conflict (Klein 2010, p. 119).

Finally, the goods imported from the Atlantic allowed these kings and other influential elites to differentiate themselves from the common herd through conspicuous consumption. It also allowed them to develop and maintain systems of patronage and redistribution to maintain the loyalty of the populace. Archaeological studies from the region controlled by the Hueda kings find that from the late seventeenth-century, the monarchy and elites were building large compounds for themselves, and were filling these with imported goods from Atlantic slave merchants (Table 6.2).[17]

In a tradition apparently inherited from Allada, Huedan kings were required to parade annually and redistribute some of the wealth gained from the Atlantic trade to elites and the general populace. This was seen as perhaps a just recompense for the privileges they enjoyed, which, as argued above, allowed

16 However, it was still the case that the majority of slaves were probably still supplied by Allada, and perhaps ultimately Dahomey (Law 2004, p. 48).

17 Norman (2009 pp. 408, 409) suggests that the imports that have survived tend to be '*concentrated in offering and ritual spaces*' which suggests that such items were used by elites to gain the favour of various '*cosmological actors*'. However, this would also signal to the rest of the population that those giving such generous gifts in such quantities were blessed with divine favour and were therefore worthy of their positions.

TABLE 6.2 The number of late seventeenth/early eighteenth-century imported artefacts found at the Savi palace site and Huedan countryside/settlement centres

Artefact comparisons	Imported smoking pipe (#)	Metal objects (#)	Imported Ceramics (#)	Beads (local & imported) (#)	Imported glass (#)
Savi Palace excavations	4.879	542	946	1.031	5.661
Countryside/ Settlement centres	372	52	9	30	83

Source: Norman (2009), p. 404; Palace data from Kelly (1995)

them a far greater share of the profits of the slave trade. However, Norman (2012, p. 149) suggests that the last three Huedan monarchs came to see this as a burden and began to distance themselves from these ceremonies, which in turn alienated them from their subjects and created internal tensions that could be exploited by their enemies. From 1714 on, the Alladans launched a series of attacks and attempted to redirect the slave trade away from Huedan territory. Neither side achieved anything beyond weakening themselves, which gave the Dahomeans the opportunity to attack and defeat both states in the late 1720s.

To conclude, the Allada and Hueda kingdoms bequeathed Dahomey a model of statehood which rewarded military prowess through a growing transatlantic slave trade. Moreover, this history also contained some clear lessons about what might happen to prospective rulers when they ever ceased to distribute sufficient rewards to their followers, or when they failed as military commanders.

5.2 *Regional Politics and the Maintenance of Militarism*

The second major influence on the institutional development of the Dahomean state was the fact that it was never able to achieve the same kind of regional hegemony enjoyed by Asante, until perhaps the 1820s/1830s, after the collapse of Oyo. As argued in Chapter 4, after the 1740s Asante faced no significant threat from neighbouring states and also held a near monopoly over their most important export product, gold. By contrast, the Dahomeans always faced threats to both their territorial integrity and their control over their key export, slaves. Both conditions provided a clear incentive to strengthen the formal and informal institutions underpinning the slave trade.

After King Agaja had conquered the states of Allada and Hueda in the 1720s, he was unable to enjoy the relative security enjoyed by the Asantahene, in large part due to the unique ecology of the region. To the north east of Dahomey lay the territories of the Oyo empire. The heartlands of this kingdom lay in the savannah belt of the Dahomean gap and were therefore largely free of the trypanosomiasis carrying tse tse fly (Alsan 2015, p. 386). This allowed the Oyo to import horses of sufficient size and strength from their northern neighbours and maintain the region's only cavalry based army (Law 1976, p. 184, Reid 2012, p. 80). This force was a far superior military tool to the musket wielding infantry forces fielded by the states nearer the coast, and until the nineteenth century the Dahomeans were never able to devise an effective strategy to resist it.[18] Oyo firstly invaded after Agaja's victories in 1727, supposedly on behalf of the Huedan kings, and continued to launch attacks until the late 1740s (Law 1991, pp. 288–295, 318–323). In every case the Dahomeans were forced to retreat into the bush, and let their territories be plundered. However, shortages of provisions and the presence of the tse tse fly, especially during the rainy season, meant that Oyo could never keep its army in the field for long, not least because the horses were extremely expensive to import and maintain (Law 1976, p. 186, Reid 2012, p. 80). Around 1748, the Dahomeans had to agree to become a tributary of Oyo and therefore, until the collapse of Oyo in the 1820s, always suffered a significant existential threat to its existence.

Meanwhile on the coast, the Hueda leadership fled westwards where they eventually settled around Lake Aheme and remained a threat to Whydah until defeated in the 1770s (Law 1991, p. 286). While the Dahomean military had a reputation for both ferocity and effectiveness (Law 1991 p. 270), geography again played a role in ensuring that its conflicts with these coastal rivals took so long to resolve. Firstly, Dahomey's enemies had the option of calling on assistance from Oyo, which often prevented them from applying sustained military pressure in other conflicts. Secondly, the new towns founded by refugees and members of the royal houses of Allada such as Apa, Badagary, Porto Novo

18 This had been the case for earlier states as well. Oyo had invaded and defeated Allada in 1698, apparently due to the murder of an ambassador sent by the former power (Law 1991, p. 237). According to Bosman (1705, p. 397) "*…in a short time mastered half of the King of Ardra's* (i.e. Allada) *territories, and made such a slaughter amongst his subjects that the number of the dead being innumerable, was commonly expressed by saying they were like the grains of corn in the field.*"

and Epe were on the eastern side of the Slave Coast. They were generally situated around lagoons and waterways, requiring canoe-based warfare, which the Dahomeans never effectively developed as their forces mainly came from the drier Abomey plateau (Smith 1989, p. 52, Law 1991, p. 314).[19] Thornton (1999, p. 76), sums up this position "...*Dahomey...could never control the coast because it lacked an adequate fleet...it was constantly harassed from the north because it could not maintain a cavalry. It is not surprising that Dahomey's rulers lived so much by war for they were almost incapable of winning any war decisively and were constantly vulnerable.*"

There were two main consequences over the long term. Firstly, the threat of invasions meant that the state needed to continue to devote considerable resources to the army and therefore retain the highly-militarised structure it had developed in the seventeenth century. Secondly, it always faced considerable competition in the trade for slaves from other areas of the Slave Coast and from Oyo, who could send slaves through other ports in the east hostile to Dahomey. The state had to maintain a high slave output through raiding and military expeditions otherwise Whydah would lose its position as the region's main port, and the state would lose crucial revenues and goods.[20] It did of course use its military forces to weaken the opposition. For example, after 1770 the port of Badagary, supplied with captives from Oyo, was beginning to export more captives than Whydah, which led to a Dahomean invasion and the destruction of the town (Ribeiro 2008, p. 143). However, Dahomey was still not free of external threats until after the fall of Oyo in the 1820s.

The Dahomeans did initially benefit by expanding their raiding activities into the previously closed areas of Yorubaland.[21] However, the increased violence and instability also created opportunities for the new Yoruba states, in particular Ibadan, Ijaye and Abeokuta, to participate in the transatlantic slave trade. These new states switched from cavalry-based warfare to gun-wielding infantry commanded by warriors whose power, like that of the Dahomean

---

19 This is mentioned by Norris (1789) who noted that during a campaign against the exiled Huedan king in the 1770s, their enemies were able to escape by fleeing to an island in the coastal lagoons and were safe because "...*the Dahomeans had no canoes, and indeed know nothing of the management of them....*"

20 This was largely achieved by Agaja's successor Tegbesu who reversed many of the previously unpopular policies of his predecessor and helped reestablish good relations with Europeans after the wars of Agaja nearly brought trade to a halt (Ribeiro 2008, p. 143). He also helped strengthen the monarchy's control over their core territories on the Abomey plateau, secured peace with Oyo and once again established an efficient and increasing flow of slaves to the coast (Bay 1998, p. 119, Law 1989b).

21 For the first time, Yoruba, as opposed to Aja, captives made up the majority slaves exported (Manning 1982, p. 31).

elites, rested on their military prowess and ability to redistribute wealth acquired through slave raiding (Reid 2012, pp. 7–8). Their main outlet was the port of Lagos which had eclipsed Whydah as the most important slave entrepot by the late 1820s (Mann 2007, pp. 40–42). Not only did Dahomey have to deal with the new competition, they also became involved in a destructive conflict with Abeokuta. This culminated in a disastrous war in 1851 during which most of the Dahomean army was destroyed, and took away their ability to effectively raid for slaves (Reid 1986, pp. 288–289, Reid 2012, p. 113). This was ultimately a temporary set-back as the army was rebuilt and was to begin slave raiding again within a decade in response to the aforementioned demand from Cuba. However, the revival was short lived after British-led efforts eventually forced the closure of this last American market for slaves in the early 1860s (Klein 2010, pp. 206–211).

5.3 *Militarism and Elite Power*

This militaristic culture provided a remarkably effective and stable basis for elite power. There were just 9 kings from 1645 to 1889 who ruled for an average of around 27 years, comparing favourably to Asante whose rulers stayed on the Golden Stool for an average of 15 years each during the period 1720 to 1884. Bay (1998) sets out in detail how successive kings used both religion and developed a unique role for powerful women to legitimise and cement their rule. However, time in office was ultimately dependent on military prowess, legitimacy in the eyes of the elite military caste, and effectively rewarding supporters through wealth generated by the slave trade (Smith 1989, p. 53). Successful military campaigns were thus crucial to the monarch and the ruling elites. Royal officials and dependants could be granted land and villages in new territories, which provided them with food and wealth for distribution to support their own dependants (Bay 1998, p. 103). Captives taken in war were, by Dahomean law, the property of the man who controlled the soldiers. As the king controlled the largest army he could expect the most slaves for sale, sacrifice or capture, but as all his leading officials were also required to contribute soldiers, they too had plenty of motivation to take an active role in the annual campaigns (Reid 1986, p. 69).[22] Common soldiers also benefited as they were paid a certain amount in cowry shells for each head and live captive they brought back to their commanders (Reid 1986, p. 70). Thus, the monarch was able to

22 A British diplomat estimated that 40% of captives in late 1840s were taken by the king (Parl. Papers Col. Africa Vol. 50., 1849 (399), vol. XXXIV: Mission to the Kings of Ashantee and Dahomey, Report by B. Cruickshank 9/11/1848, quoted in Reid 1986, p. 70).

harness the potential for violence of his elites and their dependents and channel it into an economically rewarding pursuit under his control.[23]

Another institution dependent on the transatlantic slave trade inherited from the Alladans and Huedans was the annual 'customs'. This was an event at which the ruling coalition of the king and elites could publically display their military might through parades, their devotion to ancestors though the sacrifice of slaves and prisoners of war, and their wealth through conspicuous displays of gift giving to both commoners and elite supporters. Both Law (1991, p. 277) and Bay (1998, pp. 66–67, 128) argue that these ceremonies formed the core basis of the legitimacy of the rulers. The king in particular needed to show that he sat firmly at the apex of a pyramid of power and wealth. He needed to prove that he was not only able to distribute more largess and sacrifice greater numbers of people[24] than those around him, but that he also exceeded his predecessors in terms of riches and generosity (Law 1997b, pp. 215–216). Hosting insufficiently impressive customs could be very costly to the monarchy. As already noted, the final Huedan kings may have provoked internal opposition to their rule by their failure to adequately redistribute their profits from the slave trade (Norman 2012, p. 149). Soumonni (1995, p. 80, 81) suggests that one of the principal reasons for the deposition of King Gezo's predecessor, Adanzan, in 1818, were his '*irregular and unimpressive Annual Customs*'.

This is to be compared with the Asante kings and elites whose wealth, power and prestige was ultimately based on gold, which required that they supported the application of labour to production. The absence of gold within the Bight of Benin, and the early impact of the transatlantic slave trade, meant that

23 As King Gezo told the British diplomat Cruikshank in 1848 during negotiations to abolish the slave trade: "*It was the slave trade that made him terrible to his enemies, and loved, honoured and respected by his people. How could he give it up? It had been the ruling principle of action with himself and his subjects from their earliest childhood. Their thoughts, their habits, their discipline, their mode of life had been formed with reference to this all-engrossing occupation; even the very songs with which the mother stilled her crying infant, told of triumph over foes reduced to slavery. Could he, by signing this treaty, change the sentiments of a whole people? It could not be*" (quoted in Law 1992, p. 10). It should be noted that this statement was made in the context of negotiations about the compensation that would be paid to Gezo by the British government to give up slave exports. Therefore, it is natural that his negotiators would want to emphasise the difficulties of such a request in order to increase the potential pay-off. Nonetheless, it still does reflect the fact that most contemporary and modern literature has argued, that Dahomean rulers did rely on the revenues accrued from the Atlantic and the ideology of militarism.

24 Bay (1998, p. 66) notes that "*…in a society where wealth was measured in terms of the numbers of dependants under a person's control, human sacrifice signalled the greatest possible expenditure of wealth. It also signalled military power and an implicit threat to Dahomey's neighbours, for those who were sacrificed were captives of war.*"

the region's elites developed a very different attitude towards both free and coerced labour, which will be the subject of the next section.

6 Militarism and Labour

The institutional development of the Dahomean state had a very significant impact on the allocation of labour within the kingdom. Firstly, warfare and the slave trade greatly reduced the population in the region as a whole, thus decreasing the pool of both free and coerced labour. Secondly, the powerful elite could exert a far greater control over scarce female labour and direct it towards its own needs and priorities. Thirdly, military activities and slaving activities took farmers away from their land, while at the same time requiring labour for food production for non-productive soldiers and slaves. This meant that, unlike in the Gold Coast and Biafra, there was far less free or coerced labour available to develop an export commodities trade. In the absence of elite support, such a trade was not feasible.

6.1 *Demographic Impact*

The early intensity of the slave trade had a major demographic impact. At least until the nineteenth century, the majority of slaves, were captured within around 200 km of the coast[25] and enslaved by violence[26] (Klein 2010, p. 119, Law 1991, p. 182). Manning (1982, p. 32) estimates that from the 1680s to the 1730s the area around the Bight of Benin experienced an annual population loss of around three percent. This resulted in a fall of the population in the entire region from around 511,000 in the mid-1680s to around 280,000 at the beginning of the nineteenth century. It should also be noted that the kingdom of Dahomey was spared the worst excesses of this demographic decline. There was firstly the rule, apparently instituted by the founding king of the dynasty Wegbaja, that no native born Dahomean could be sold outside of the kingdom. While this rule was occasionally broken, such as during the reign of Tegbesu, Dahomeans were far less likely than their neighbours to end up in the holds of European ships (Bay 1998, pp. 145–146). Secondly, the Dahomeans (and the

25 Manning (1982, p. 32), although Law (1991, pp. 182–190) suggests that many slaves may have been captured from further afield, especially in Yoruba areas where they were sold in a succession of markets until they reached the coast. However, the evidence is not conclusive, especially so before the nineteenth-century. Lovejoy (2011, pp. 79–80) supports Manning's view that until at least the mid-eighteenth century nearly all slaves were coming from Aja areas no more than 200km from slave ports.

26 I.e. slave raiding, taken as captives during war or kidnapped.

Alladans and Huedans before them) also retained considerable numbers of slaves to work in the domestic economy (Law 1991, p. 67). Exact numbers are not available but they probably made up a substantial proportion of the population.[27]

However, even in Dahomey there was a decline in population (Bay 1998, pp. 145–146). As well as regular warfare having a destructive impact on agriculture/food production, many were killed during conflicts which were more or less constant, given the lack of regional hegemony and the material and ideological demands of the elites (Law 1991, p. 61). For example, Bay (1998, pp. 58–59) estimates some 5,000 were killed and 10,000 to 11,000 were taken prisoner during the conquest of Whydah by Agaja. Armies risked heavy losses through diseases such as smallpox, and the Dahomean army suffered a number of serious defeats against Oyo and coastal states such as Popo, which saw them lose large numbers of men (Law 1991, p. 62, 319). Warfare was a damaging activity, not only because of the potentially high numbers of casualties, but also because of the premium placed on young adults of both sexes as soldiers and captives.[28] They were disproportionally targeted during raids and wars and as a result probably suffered higher rates of mortality, either during combat or due to the harsh conditions during transportation for sale as slaves, thus reducing the general reproductive potential of the population (Bay 1998, p. 146).

To put this population decline in comparative perspective, the metropolitan region of Asante was around 16,000 km^2 (Wilks 1975, p. 80) and probably contained a population of around 350,000 in the mid-nineteenth-century (see Appendix 4.2b) which gives a population density of 21.7/km^2. This was hardly crowded, and far lower than the figure for England and Wales of 35/km^2 in 1700.[29] Law (1991, p. 58) gives a figure of around 200,000 people in the kingdom of Dahomey in the mid-nineteenth-century, and also suggests that there were fewer people than two centuries before. During the same period Dahomey had an approximate area of 29,000 km^2, which gives a far lower population density

27 Norris (1789, p. 157) notes that "*...the bulk of the people are slaves to a few freedman...*" Forbes (1851 Vol. 1, p. 14) writes that "*...of the whole population* (of 200,000) *not more than 20,000 are free, the remainder slaves.*" Both of these are likely exaggerations, based on their belief in the absolute power of the king over his subjects (Norris 1789, p. 157 and Forbes 1851 Vol. 1, p. 37). However, they do probably reflect the fact that there were considerable numbers of non-free people within the kingdom.

28 The so-called 'Amazon' regiment of female soldiers became increasingly important during the nineteenth-century and may have made up around half of the Dahomean forces who battled French forces at the end of the 1880s (Ross 1971, p. 156).

29 Based on a population of 5,290,000 from Floud et al. 1994, 151,013 km^2 from www.ons.gov.uk, accessed 25/10/2016.

of 6.9/km^2.[30] Thus, there was a greatly reduced pool of labour available to produce either surplus food to provision slave ships or develop the kind of dual-commodity/slave export model seen in the Bight of Biafra. However, a relatively light population density was not the only impediment. Elites in Dahomey monopolised both free and coerced labour to a far greater extent than in the other case study areas, and used it in pursuit of their own wealth and power. This denied commoners the opportunity to engage in production for the Atlantic market.

6.2 *Female Labour*

Law (1991 p. 64) notes that sources in the late seventeenth-century suggest that both men and women were engaged in agriculture, while a century later only females seem to be working the fields. He suggests this was a result of the development of a "*…a warrior ethos which involved a disdain for agriculture, and which might well have discouraged its free males from participation in agricultural work.*". This would have firstly meant there were fewer available sources of labour, in an area experiencing a strong demographic decline. However, this was exacerbated by the fact that elite men in Dahomey were always highly motivated and able to acquire as many wives and female slaves as possible to enhance their wealth and social standing (Law 1991, p. 67). Agaja was said to have had 2,000 wives in 1724 (Bay 1998, p. 50), while Bosman (1705, p. 344), writing about the Huedan kings, suggests they had between four and five thousand, with leading nobles having up to a thousand.[31] Writing in the later eighteenth-century, Norris (1789, p. 99) estimated that the royal wives numbered "*…between three and four thousand; his principal men have from one to three or four hundred wives each and people in humbler stations from half a dozen to twenty…*" Polygamy was the norm, rather than the exception, in all three case study regions but Law (1991, p. 65) argues that it was particularly extreme in Dahomey, especially in the way that females were monopolised by the elites. Norris (1789, p. 99) wrote that the monarchy and aristocracy "*…engross the major part of the women…*" Writers in the nineteenth century noted that the state had the right to demand a daughter from every family in kingdom, who could be assigned to the female regiment in the army, kept in the palace or "*…dashed to the deserving soldiers as wives…*" (Skertchly 1874: 454–455, Law 2004, p. 94). This meant

30 Based on the size of *département* in the modern country of Benin, compared to the approximate borders of the kingdom in the nineteenth-century. Data from http://www.geohive.com/cntry/benin.aspx, accessed 8/9/2016, Manning (1982, p. 60).

31 Law (1991, p. 79) suggests that the Dahomean and Huedan kings had from 800 to 3,000 wives, both in their palaces and around the kingdom.

that common men had a much reduced chance of finding a wife, which is perhaps best illustrated by the existence of state controlled prostitution. In 1705, Bosman noted that:

> In Fida (Whydah) and the country around it and in all the land of Fida, is a very great plenty of whores and at a cheaper price than on the Gold Coast…these countries being very populous, the slaves vastly numerous and the married women kept up very strict….'tis customary for some of the most considerable and rich negro ladies, when lying upon their death bed to buy some of these foreign female slaves and make a present of them to the publick. (p. 214)[32]

This tradition carried on into the Dahomean era. Bay (1998 pp. 148, 149), working on data from Law (1991, p. 54), notes that prostitutes were either provided by the state or endowed to the people by wealthy women, with prices controlled and far below market value.[33] This service was provided because elites were denying younger and lower ranked men the ability to find a wife. It also meant that most of the kingdom's female labour was harnessed and controlled by elite men. Extremely strict rules about adultery for both men and women (Klein 2010 p. 122) meant that many women, even in smaller households, would never produce as many children as they were capable of, simply as a result of sharing their husband with so many others.[34] The result was a lower birth rate which in turn exacerbated the existing problem of a falling population. It also meant that a great share of the kingdom's labour force was exploited by elite men and not by common households. This was important, as elites probably had far less motivation than commoners to use the labour available to them in the production of export commodities.

Wives, after all, might have been used in palm oil production, considering that in the other case study areas, this was primarily the women's responsibility.

32 While this practise was unusual enough for Bosman to note, it was apparently not unique. To the west of the Fante region on the Gold Coast local citizens could apparently petition the local Caboceroes (i.e. wealthy traders) to provide a certain number of prostitutes who, after a truly bizarre ceremony "*…for the remainder of her life obliged to refuse no man the use of her body though he offers never so small a sum…*" (pp. 211, 212).

33 For example, at the end of the seventeenth century, sex cost 3 cowries, and a chicken 96. By 1710 sex had risen to 5 cowries, and chickens to 160. By the 1850s, an 'official' prostitute cost 20 cowries while chickens had risen to 280.

34 We might further speculate that there may have also been problems with the 'quality' of the offspring, if this continues over generations. See Henrich et al. (2012) for some discussion of the downsides of polygamous relationships, albeit in a modern context.

In general, men only cleared the land and harvested the fruits, although there is evidence that in the second half of the nineteenth century male slaves supplemented female labour when production demands were higher (Law 1995c, p. 206). Even so, women seem to have been the principal producers. Why then did elite households not produce more palm oil when there had been a clear demand since the late eighteenth-century? For a start, women were heavily involved in agriculture, child rearing and food preparation, which was crucial given the high number of unproductive men involved in military activities (see below) (Bay 1998, p. 146, 197, Law 1991, p. 66). In addition, the wives of elite men, especially those of the royal family, were also significant producers of wealth for their husbands. The wives of the Huedan monarch had monopolies over certain market activities such as beer brewing (Norman 2012, p. 155). In the time of the Dahomean kings, palace wives and slaves controlled the trade in pottery and the stringing of cowry shells (Bay 1998, p. 210). Women were also heavily involved in the production of goods for local markets such as prepared food and locally dyed cloth (Bay 1998, p. 212), and seem to have been the principal traders in those markets (Law 2004, p. 76). Contrary to what Inikori suggests (2007, 2011), there was a strong market for goods within Dahomey (Law 1991, p. 47). Contemporary sources noted that markets at both Savi, during the time of the Alladans, and Whydah, after the Dahomean conquest, were full of a range of both locally produced goods together with trade items from the Atlantic as well as the African interior (Norman 2012, p. 148, Law 2004, p. 82). Such markets were also an important source of revenue for rulers, who claimed taxes on market sales (Law 1991, pp. 92, 93). Thus, directing available labour towards internal production and trade was potentially very lucrative for elite men.

However, slaves might also have been used in palm oil production. While labour had become scarcer for most of the eighteenth and early nineteenth centuries, the situation changed in the 1820s with the collapse of the Oyo empire. The consequence was that the territories open to Dahomean raids increased dramatically, especially in the Yoruba areas on their eastern borders. It therefore became possible to both export sufficient numbers of slaves, whilst at the same time retaining more for the production of export crops. As argued in Chapter 4, 'foreign' slaves were usually preferred as their labour could be more intensively exploited than slaves who shared a common cultural/linguistic heritage with their masters. The influx of Yoruba slaves into Dahomey led to the development of a clear distinction between *anato* or free commoners and *kannumon* or slaves. The latter category was not fixed and some slaves might have *anato* children or become *anato* themselves. However, some groups of slaves were denied such a possibility and they and their descendants were considered *kannumon* in perpetuity. This was usually the fate of Yoruba slaves (Bay 1998, p. 192) and, as such, it seems that they were not afforded the rights of Aja slaves. Thus, male Yoruba slaves were among the first to be used to increase palm oil production, despite their unwillingness to be involved in what was considered 'female work' (Bay 1998, pp. 188, 196–197). However, although some slaves were used in this way in the 1840s, it was not common practice until the 1850s. There were potential security risks, as slaves imported from outside the Aja areas to work on plantations were likely worked harder than other slaves, and could not be so easily incorporated into local societies. Manning (1982, p. 54) and Reid (1986, p. 420) note that there were rumours (which were taken very seriously by the state) of a conspiracy between the Egba confederacy[35] and Yoruba slaves on the Abomey plateau in 1855.

However, fears of uprisings did not prevent their use in production throughout the second half of the nineteenth century (Law 1995b), so we must look to additional reasons why the kingdom's labour resources were not channelled earlier into the production of export crops. In the next section, it will be shown that the regular military expeditions were a substantial drain on manpower, which further compounded the relative scarcity of surplus labour for production.

6.3 *Production for the Army*

The exact nature of the Dahomean military machine has been debated for many decades. Most literature agrees that the Dahomean military was more effective and more highly trained than other armies in the region (Snelgrave 1734, pp. 77–79, Dalzel 1795, p. 47, Forbes 1851 Vol. I, pp. 19, 20, Law 1991, p. 96).[36] However, there is some dispute as to whether there was a full-time standing army, which would have made Dahomey unique amongst the case study regions. Some contemporary sources certainly suggest that this was the case (Dalzel 1795, px, Forbes 1851 Vol. I, p. 14, 15). Forbes (1851 Vol. I, p. 14, 15), writing in the late 1840s, states that this consisted of 12,000 full-time soldiers, supported by a further 12,000 troops levied from the provinces and a similar number of auxiliaries, although these numbers are likely to be estimates based on a

35 One of the Oyo successor states and a rival for regional power.

36 This is not to say that it was invincible. Battle tactics remained rudimentary, involving lines of men rushing forward to fire volleys before retreating to reload. Most attacks consisted of raids on less numerous or well-armed foes. While effective in the circumstances of the eighteenth and early nineteenth centuries, it wasn't sufficient against the French or Yoruba successor states (Ross 1971, pp. 154, 155, Smith 1989, p. 87).

possible misunderstanding of local languages.[37] Some modern scholars (Akinjobin 1967, p. 38, Smith 1989, p. 56, Thornton 1999, p. 91) have argued that there was indeed a full-time professional force of soldiers, numbering around 3,000 and recruited from the 'core' regions on the plateau and stationed around the capital. However, this assessment has been disputed for some time (Argyle 1966, pp. 81–89). Ross (1971, p. 148) suggests that while there were 2,000 to 3,000 men stationed around the capital, they did not constitute a standing army and outside of the annual slave hunts were mainly engaged in ceremonial duties. Law (1991, pp. 270, 271) suggests that there was no full-time army as the soldiers apparently also engaged in agriculture, but they were nonetheless much better trained than other soldiers in the region.

While it is not possible to say with any certainty that the state maintained a full-time army, it does seem likely that large numbers of non-productive soldiers were employed for a considerable part of the year, and needed to be supported by the kingdom's agricultural labour force. Moreover, unlike in Asante, kings were obliged to go to war on an annual basis, with these campaigns being tied to the aforementioned 'customs' both before and after fighting (Forbes 1851 Vol. I, p. 15–19).[38] The monarchy retained the right to forcibly enlist young boys to act as a kind of page to more experienced soldiers in order to learn how to fight, which took valuable labour away from farms (Norris, 1795, p. 48, Thornton 1999, p. 91). High ranking elites also maintained full-time professional soldiers[39] and all leading officials were required to levy troops for annual military campaigns (or 'slave hunts') (Bay 1998, p. 105). These were raised from their own lands and might be expected to have at least some military training (Smith 1989, p. 56). Numbers vary but there are reports of such contingents being anywhere between 3,000 and 20,000 men (Thornton 1999, p. 92).[40] Providing

---

37 According to Segurola & Rassinoux in the "Dictionnaire Fon-Français" (2000), p. 125, multiples of 4,000, are translated as meaning 'nombre indéfini'. It comes from a unit of cowry currency called a 'cabess' or 'head' which numbers 4,000 cowries. Thus, a force of 24,000 might simply mean "a lot." I would like to thank Robin Law for providing me with this information.

38 For an account based on Dahomean traditions, see Abbé Thomas Moulero, 'Guézo ou Guédizo Massigbe', Études dahoméennes, nouvelle série 4 (1965), pp. 51–59, which says of Gezo, 'Il ne passa aucune année qu'il n'ait fait une guerre annuelle', and gives a complete list of these 'guerres annuelles' (while noting that there were also 'autres guerres') (pp. 52, 53). Thanks are due once again to Robin Law for passing on this reference.

39 For example, an official at Whydah in the 1740s was noted as having a permanent guard of full time soldiers (Thornton 1999, p. 93).

40 The state and their representatives could potentially call on all adult males and a large number of females to fight or act as porters (Law 1995c, pp. 206, 207).

sufficient provisions for these forces would have been exceptionally challenging, and required that elites used the coerced labour at their dispersal to grow food for the army (Smith 1989, p. 58, Law 1991, p. 67).

It is possible to estimate the labour inputs required (see Table 6.3). Wilks (1993 pp. 44–63) has calculated the yields and labour requirements of a typical farm within the Asante region, which produced the staple foods of the forest region, namely plantain, maize, yams, cassava and cocoyams. These, with the addition of beans, are also noted as the principal foodstuffs in Dahomey and Whydah in the eighteenth century.[41] He suggests that a family of five working a single small farm for three years (the length of time the land could be cultivated before it lost fertility) could produce around 12 tons or 14.5 million calories of these staples, which probably made up around eighty percent of a farmer's caloric intake. The intensity of labour varied considerably, with some years requiring much more work to clear and prepare fallow land. However, he also suggests that a family would not work as hard as coerced labour, so it will be assumed that two more intensively exploited slaves could do the work. Active soldiers consume more calories than the 2,500/day recommended by the WHO for a sedentary lifestyle and could expect to be better fed than farmers, who Wilks (1993, p. 59) suggests consumed 1,773 calories/day. Taking an estimate of 3,000 calories a day would mean each soldier would require 3.29 million calories every 3 years. Therefore, one farm or two slaves could provide for 5.5 soldiers, meaning that the monarchy would need to have over 3,403 free, or 1,361 unfree, farmers to keep 3,000 soldiers supplied with staples. However, for each soldier there were also the boys assigned to them, along with any other dependants such as wives and children, and the slaves on farms also needed to eat. Furthermore, the capital Abomey and the second city of Cana had populations of around 15,000 and 24,000 respectively (Law 2004, pp. 72, 73). While there is no data on the precise numbers of courtiers, artisans and other (agriculturally) non-productive people living there, it can be at least assumed that these towns needed to import a significant amount of food.

The burden of feeding the army on campaign was the responsibility of the war leaders, as the king was only responsible for providing ammunition and powder (Thornton 1999, p. 93). Ross (1971, p. 153) suggests that soldiers carried

41 Bosman (1705, 389) notes that at Whydah people ate "*...oxen, Cows, Goats, Sheep, Hogs (also found on gold coast), turkeys, ducks chickens, lots of wild game birds, corn, millet, beer, sweet potatoes, yams, different types of beans, onions, ginger, lemons, oranges, bananas, tamarind trees, peppers...*" Dalzel (1793, p. iii introduction) commenting on Dahomey, mentions "*...maize, millet, or Guinea-corn of different sorts; a kind of pea or rather kidney beans, called callavances, and also a species of beans, called ground-beans...yams, potatoes of two sorts, the cassava, or manioka, the plantain, and the banana....*"

TABLE 6.3 Estimated agricultural labour required to support Dahomean armed forces

Family farm of 5 free/2 unfree	Calories produced every 3 years (million)	Calories produced per year (million)	Calories consumed by soldiers/day	Calories consumed by 1 soldier every 3 years (millions)	Calories consumed by full-time army of 3,000 men every 3 years (millions)
1	2	3	4	5	6
		Col. 2/3		Col. 4*365*3	Col. 5*3
1	14.5	4.8	3	3.29	9.87
Number of free/unfree farmers required for the full-time army	**Number of soldiers on a major campaign**	**Full army calorie requirements/ day (millions)**	**Full army calorie requirements for a month**	**Years taken for one family farm or 2 slaves to produce calorie requirements**	**Yearly labour requirement (free/unfree)**
7	8	9	10	11	12
Col. 6*5/2		Col. 8*3,000	Col.9*30	Col. 11/Col. 2	Col.12*5/2
3,403/1,361	50	150	4.5	932	4,660/1,864

Source: see pages 246–248

around two weeks' worth of provisions although it would also have been possible to grow food during long sieges. It was also possible to 'live off the land' for short periods as soldiers were accompanied by large numbers of 'auxiliaries' who carried their provisions, as well as hunted, looted or scavenged for them, but there was always an acute risk of running out of food and/or water (Reid 2012, p. 86). Any food taken along needed to last, be portable and not require cooking. According to Smith (1999, p. 59) the Dahomeans apparently ate "toasted grains and bean cake" the latter made of beans and maize flour. As these campaigns yielded the captives who formed the basis of the wealth and power of the elites, it is unsurprising that they had little interest in allowing households to become involved in the production of export crops. Feeding the full army of 50,000 soldiers would require 150 million calories of food each day which, going on the above assumptions would have been the equivalent to the 3-year output of around 10 family farms. If we make the rather simplistic assumption that each farm, worked by 5 people or two slaves, produced 4.8 million calories a year, and everything they produced was requisitioned by the army, then it would take the full-time yearly labour of 4,666 free or 1,864 unfree farmers just to keep forces in the field for a month.[42]

This is of course a very conservative estimate as these farmers needed to keep at least some food for themselves. It also does not factor in the highly disruptive impacts of military activities on agriculture, which meant that farmers may not have been able to produce as much as was possible. The manpower requirements of the army meant that labour might be withdrawn from farms at important times during the year. For example, a Dahomean general, after being temporarily defeated in an engagement with the coastal town of Popo in 1763, took farmers away from their fields during the planting season to reinforce his army (Thornton 1999, p. 94). Palm oil was particularly affected as the start of annual campaign in February coincided "*…with the optimum season for the oil harvest, whose consequent deferral meant that the crop actually realized was inferior both in quantity and quality to its potential…*" (Law 1989a, p. 67). In the second half of the nineteenth century the resumption of slave raiding and military activities by Glele which seriously disrupted the palm oil trade by taking away workers (Law 1997b, p. 229).

In Asante and the Bight of Biafra the expansion of the output of commodities depended on households being free to divert their labour into other forms of economic activity, to have access to slaves to supplement or expand their production capacity and to have the willing support of local elites for the transport and marketing of their products. None of these factors were present in Dahomey. The elite monopolised coerced and female labour to enhance their own wealth or to support the military which formed the core of their power. For example, one visitor in the 1850s was told that "*Industry and agriculture are not encouraged…*" because "*…the king is aware that, if the enjoyment of home, and the luxuries of health and happiness, were once obtained, he would fail in volunteers for the annual slave hunt.*" (Forbes, 1851, Vol. 1, p. 21).

This chapter has argued that there were strong path dependent causes as to why the Dahomean state never shifted to commodity export trade until forced under the extreme conditions of the 1850s. This path had developed in the seventeenth century, when elites were able to capture the ever-rising riches from the transatlantic slave trade and significantly increase their own power through

42 From Wilks' estimation that 14.5 million was produced every three years, thus 4.8 million was produced a year. Thus, dividing the total caloric requirement of 150 million by 4.8 we can assume that 31.25 farms were needed. Each farm had 5 workers and there are 30 days in a month, making a total 4,687 people.

the development of a highly militaristic state. Three factors reinforced and strengthened this development. Firstly, there were environmental reasons. As the region lacked gold deposits, slaves became the only 'product' that could be marketed for the guns, cloth and other luxury goods on which their power came to depend, and these were most effectively acquired by mobilising and arming large numbers of professional soldiers and conscripts. The geography of the kingdom also worked against the development of palm oil exports which, from the point of view of the elites on the Abomey plateau, would always be less profitable than slaves. Secondly, the inability to impose any kind of regional hegemony due to the region's unique geography meant the state was always threatened by credibly powerful enemies who were not only capable of threatening their territorial integrity, but were also serious competitors as slave exporters. This meant maintaining a strong army was a matter of survival as much as a means to acquire wealth. Finally, and perhaps least importantly, there were sufficient numbers of slaving vessels that were only interested in buying captives.

The result was that from the seventeenth to the middle of the nineteenth century it was never in the interests of the elites to stimulate a non-slave export trade. Militarism was demographically costly and the elites had high demands on the remaining females and coerced labour to enhance their status and wealth, as well as needing them to produce food for the army. Taking away labour from these activities would have risked both the security of the state and the wealth of elites. This practical consideration was strengthened by the development of an elite ideology that glorified war and opposed any other trade except in slaves. This was strong enough to survive into the nineteenth century in spite of the general decline of the transatlantic slave trade.

Conclusion

This book has presented a new analysis of the commercial transition in West Africa. It has examined from a comparative perspective why the speed and nature of the change from export slavery to 'legitimate commerce' differed to such an extent across West Africa's most important slave-trading regions. Over the seventeenth and eighteenth centuries various interrelated factors evolved and shaped the initial patterns of trade between West Africa and the Atlantic world, and continued to determine the exports of different areas after 1807. These factors are ecology, the regional political context, trade partners, the nature and duration of trade relations and the institutional relationship between elite groups and household producers.

This is the first time that a long-term, comparative analysis has been applied to the Gold Coast, the Bight of Benin and the Bight of Biafra, which together accounted for around eighty percent of all captives embarked in West Africa. Until now the literature on the commercial transition has largely focused on the nineteenth century, with particular attention paid to how those who had previously profited from the slave trade reacted to the economic shock of abolition. In particular, the 'crisis of adaption' hypothesis set out by Hopkins (1969, 1973) has profoundly influenced debates on the topic (Law et al. 1995, 2013). As argued in the introduction, this has stemmed from the fact that scholars have tended to focus on transatlantic slavery and largely ignore the trade in commodities. This means that we have not had, until now, a full picture of West Africa's commercial relations with the Atlantic world.

The impact of the commercial transition has generally only been analysed through studies of individual regions or states.[1] It has therefore not been possible to identify which broader internal or external factors were ultimately most important in determining how and why different areas moved to an export economy based on commodities. The book has outlined a new narrative in which the ecology and local political contexts interacted to shape the nature of external trade, which in turn profoundly influenced institutional development. This was key to determining how the states and societies that had dominated export slavery in the eighteenth century reacted to the changing environment of the nineteenth century.

1 See Introduction, footnote 18.

 | DOI:10.1163/9789004417120_009

1 Long-Term Patterns of Trade

The quantitative analysis in Part 1 showed that the change from slaves to 'legitimate commerce' continued patterns of trade that had been established in the centuries before 1807. In addition, it contributed a number of important new datasets that provide a more complete picture of Africa's trade with the Atlantic during the eighteenth century (Manning 2012, Jerven et al. 2012). Chapter 2 reviews qualitative sources as well as the trading accounts of the British Royal Africa Company (RAC) and the Dutch Middelburgsche Commercie Compagnie (MCC). These indicate that over the course of the eighteenth century, European traders always bought commodities in addition to slaves from the Gold Coast and Bight of Biafran regions, while the area that came to be controlled by the Dahomeans dealt almost exclusively in the export of people. It also notes that gold had been traded in the Gold Coast region since the fifteenth century, and that both gold and slave exports began to decline from at least the 1780s.

Chapter 3 shows, contrary to the conclusions of Eltis (2013), that for most areas of West Africa the trade in provisions was not substantial enough to stimulate the development of commercial agriculture. However, in some areas this was an important economic sector. The Gold Coast supplied provisions throughout the eighteenth century. Merchants in the Bight of Biafra sold substantial quantities of yams, pepper and palm oil for the middle passage and this may have been a factor in its growth as a major slave exporting centre. There was no evidence that traders going to the Bight of Benin ever bought significant quantities of food.

In Chapter 4, the shift in commodity trading from the western to eastern side of the West African coast is explored and explicitly linked this to the commercial transition. The chapter shows that there was a huge expansion of commodity exports in the late eighteenth-century, bought mainly by slave traders and focused on the Bight of Biafra. Again, the region controlled by Dahomey did not respond to the new demand for palm oil, ivory and sylvan products. This finding is based on a new dataset that provides the most accurate current overview of Western Africa's commodity trade with Great Britain in the eighteenth century, and provides an important update to the work of Johnson et al. (1990).

After 1807, these long-term patterns of trade continued to influence export behaviour. The Gold Coast quickly abandoned slave exports, increased gold production, and therefore reverted to the system of trade that had dominated external relations for most of the region's history. The Bight of Biafra gradually expanded its already growing palm oil industry, eventually abandoning export slavery in the late 1830s. By contrast, in the Bight of Benin slavery was the sole export until the late 1830s, when the increasing effectiveness of the slave trade patrol forced the development of alternative exports.

2 Diverging Trajectories

Chapters 5–7 examines the variables that explain these long-term patterns of export in the three case study regions. In each case the direction of the interaction was similar and is set out in the modified explanatory model (Figure C.1). The nature and duration of external trade relations were a product of each region's ecology, the regional political context and its external trade partners. In addition, local politics were themselves highly influenced by the very different ecologies of each area. External trade in turn had a profound influence on institutional development and in particular on the attitudes of monarchies, aristocratic elites and wealthy merchants towards household production for the

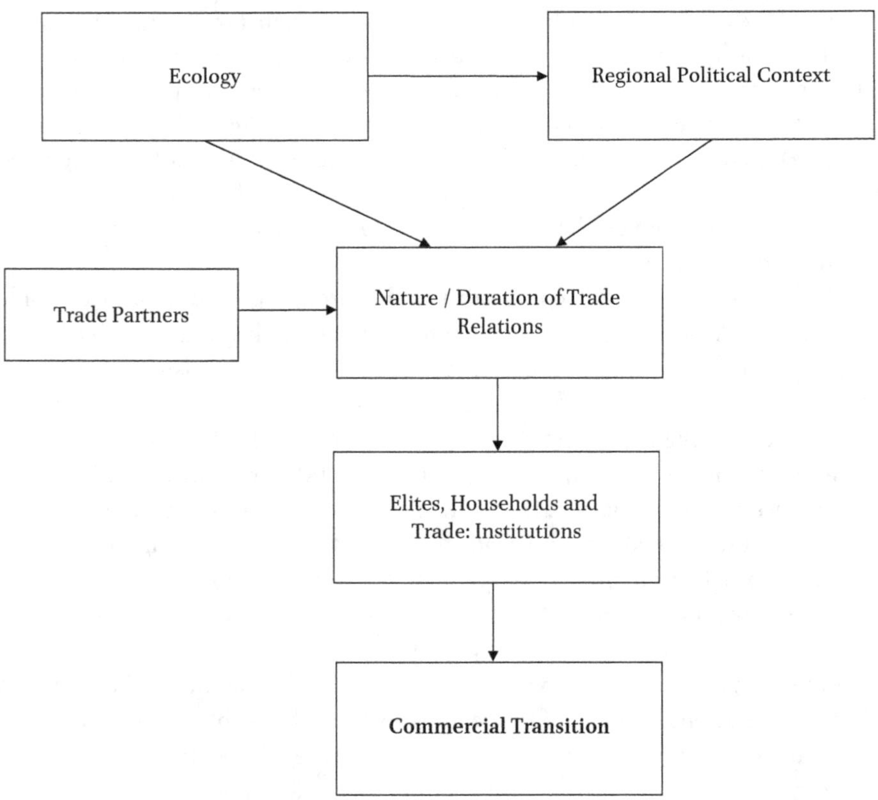

FIGURE C.1 Modified explanatory model for region-specific commercial transitions.

Atlantic and external interior markets. This determined the output of commodities and slaves over the eighteenth century and, more importantly, drove the region-specific commercial transitions in the nineteenth century.

For the Gold Coast region, the seams of gold within the territories that came to be held by the Asante state were key to understanding both long-term trade patterns and the nature of the commercial transition. It was, with the exception of the relatively short eighteenth-century interregnum, the region's most important export for nearly four centuries and led to a 'trajectory of gold'. The struggle over the possession of gold fields was a key factor fuelling political conflict and consolidation in the seventeenth century. Sales of the precious metal also bought the guns that led to a revolution in warfare allowing for mass mobilisation of larger numbers of troops. Eventually these two factors led to Asante becoming the region's superpower and gaining a monopoly over gold output. In the Bight of Benin, the rapidly increasing demand for captives at the end of the seventeenth century also encouraged political competition and military innovation in the states of Allada, Hueda and Dahomey. However, the presence of the Benin Gap and the coastal lagoons meant that no single state could ever fully monopolise power or external trade. This led to a 'slave raiding trajectory' for the kingdom of Dahomey. The particular ecology of the Bight of Biafra meant that there had always been a sophisticated trade network connecting the coast and interior. This always handled a range of commodities, foodstuffs for the agriculturally unproductive coastal towns and slave provisions in addition to captives. Crucially, it was not until the Aro expanded their network into central Igboland in the early eighteenth-century that slave exports could significantly expand. This saw the region experience a 'trajectory of trade'. In all three areas, the major trading partners helped reinforce these trends. The British, who were always more enthusiastic buyers of both provisions and commodities, focused their efforts on the Bight of Biafra and the Gold Coast. By contrast, the French and Portuguese / Brazilians, who were generally only interested in captives, did most of their trading in the Bight of Benin.[2]

This all led to very different institutional outcomes. In Asante, gold became the most important marker of status and wealth. The quantity an individual possessed was a key determinant of rank for everyone from commoners to the king. As a result, there was always a need for captive labour to mine or pan for gold, or to support free households engaged in these activities. While the transatlantic slave trade generated considerable wealth, the export of captives could

2 The French did buy African commodities but almost all of them came from Senegambia

never take away so much coerced labour that it threatened gold supplies. It therefore meant that the monarchy and aristocratic elites always had a vested interest in the commodity trade. At the turn of the nineteenth century, the Asante economy was already undergoing significant adjustments. Europeans saw declining sales of both gold and slaves, while at the same time the state was already beginning to invest in trade to the markets of the savannah. The withdrawal of the British from the transatlantic slave trade was sufficient to accelerate the process of reversion to more traditional external trade relations based on the export of gold and the expansion of kola sales to the newly formed Sokoto caliphate. This changing economic environment was also favourable to commoners, who by engaging more in production of both kola and gold, gained more access to external markets than was possible during the era dominated by slave exports.

In the Bight of Biafra trade relations led to a very different type of institutional arrangement. With no early expansion of external trade to stimulate the development of states, the region remained characterised by decentralised political entities, with long distance trade organised largely by the Aro. The lack of competing states also meant that trade did not have to generate wealth to maintain the hierarchal political orders characteristic of the other case study regions, or to cover the costs of military expenditure. Furthermore, status was not acquired through prowess on the battlefield, and was instead predicated on wealth generated by all kinds of trade. From the 1770s, the increasing demand for palm oil provided opportunities to households to access the Atlantic market for goods that could improve their living standards. Those who had previously grown rich from the transatlantic slave trade were prepared to support the expansion of palm oil, as it in no way undermined their social status or power and furthermore offered a less volatile form of trade.

In the Bight of Benin export slavery generated great wealth and, for the Dahomeans, it stimulated the development of institutions that very effectively maintained the power and prestige of its elites. Regular warfare allowed the monarchy to monopolise the capacity for violence of its elite supporters. The sale of captives meant that all those involved in warfare could profit from the fighting, while also allowing the king to ensure that his share was always greatest. Militarism also provided the spiritual and ideological cohesion to the elite coalition that supported the monarchy, and kept the commoners obedient. However, maintaining this military machine was extremely costly in terms of expenditure and labour. It also demanded continuous success or the monarch risked being overthrown. Mobilising the army for slave raiding was the most effective means of keeping sufficient wealth flowing into the state's coffers and satisfying the demands of a militaristic culture. There was therefore no real incentive for those in power to develop or support any other form of commerce except under the extreme conditions of the 1840s.

3 The Real Impact of Britain's Abolition Campaign

The book thus sheds a new light on the actual impact of abolition on West Africa's economies. It argues that the military and diplomatic campaign waged primarily by the British had very different impacts depending on the region. It is true that the act of forcibly withdrawing its merchant shipping from transatlantic slave trading was an economic shock, especially in the Gold Coast and the Bight of Biafra. However, as noted above, this predominantly served to accelerate existing trends. There were always opportunities for African merchants in these areas to sell more slaves, given the relative ineffectiveness of the early slave trade patrol and the hostility towards abolition on the part of other slave-trading nations. However, in both areas exports of captives were already in decline, and more coerced labour was being harnessed for production, long before the military campaign became a success. Thus, it was the decision of local rulers and merchants to move away from export slavery, not external pressure, that was responsible for the rise of 'legitimate commerce' in the Gold Coast and the Bight of Biafra.

Only in the case of Dahomey was the abolition campaign responsible for finally halting slave exports. While of dubious legality, measures including the Equipment Act of 1839, attacking shipping in Brazilian territorial waters and sustained diplomatic bullying, were a necessary precursor to the ending of transatlantic slavery in the region. Without such efforts, the continued demand for African slaves in Brazil and, from the 1850s in Cuba, would have ensured that the Dahomeans continued to sell captives to the Atlantic market.

4 Implications and Future Research

This study has shown the value of data driven, comparative studies for precolonial West African history. It demonstrates that archival sources still offer considerable potential to provide new insights into the long-term paths of economic development in different regions in Africa. In addition, it shows that the impact of the *non*-slave trade on the economic and political trajectories of different regions has been undervalued in the literature. Only by considering the entirety of West Africa's trade with the Atlantic world can we gain the full picture of its impact on the societies and peoples of the region.

The model of analysis could also be extended to other areas along the West African coast which traded both slaves and later commodities with the Atlantic world. Regions such as the Windward Coast and the Loango Coast of West Central Africa have been the subject of study, but not specifically in relation to the commercial transition, and not in a broader comparative perspective.[3] The Angola region, responsible for the largest number of slave embarkations, has largely been studied in isolation. The change from slave to commodity exports has not been investigated in relation to other areas. Furthermore, the nature of trade from Angola was markedly different from the case study regions as it was largely dominated by Portuguese / Brazilian merchants sailing directly between Brazil and Africa. It would be interesting to investigate whether the model developed in the context of West Africa would be suitable in this context, or if it would require significant adjustment and, if so, why. This could reveal much about the impact of different external trading relations on economic and institutional development in Africa. Finally, the model could also be applied to other slave-trading regions of the world, in particular Asia, to see the extent to which local reactions to increased demand for slaves from the British, French and Dutch in the same period (Allen, 2015) differed or resembled those in West Africa.

3 See, for example Hawthorne 2003, da Silva & Sommerdyk 2010, Sommerdyk 2012, 2015, Martin 1972, 1986.

Bibliography

Published Contemporary Sources

Adams, J. (1822). *Sketches Taken During Ten Voyages to Africa Between the Years 1786 and 1800: Including Observations on the Country Between Cape Palmas and the River Congo, and Cursory Remarks on the Physical and Moral Character of the Inhabitants, with an Appendix Containing an Account of the European Trade with the West Coast of Africa*: Hurst, Robinson and Company.

Adams, J. (1823). *Remarks on the Country Extending from Cape Palmas to the River Congo: Including Observations on the Manners and Customs of the Inhabitants*: G. & WB Whittaker.

Atkins, J. (1735). *A Voyage to Guinea, Brasil, and the West-Indies*: Ward and Chandler.

Barbot, J. (1732). A Description of the Coasts of North and South Guinea, and of Ethiopia, vulgarly Angola. In A. Churchill (Ed.), *Collection of Voyages and Travels* (Vol. 5).

Becroft, C. (1841). On Benin and the upper course of the river Quorra, or Niger. *The Journal of the Royal Geographical Society of London, 11*, 184–192.

Bold, E. (1823). *Merchants and Mariners African Guide*: Cushing & Appleton.

Bosman, W. (1705). *A new and accurate description of the coast of Guinea, divided into the Gold, the Slave, and the Ivory Coasts*: Alfred Jones.

Bowdich, T. (1819). *Mission from Cape Coast Castle to Ashantee*. London: John Murray.

Burton, R. (1864). *A Mission to Gelele, King of Dahome*. London: Tinsley Brothers.

Buxton, T. (1840). *The African Slave Trade, and its Remedy*. London: J. Murray.

Clapperton, H. & Lander, R. (1829). *Journal of a second expedition into the interior of Africa: from the Bight of Benin to Soccatoo*: Carey, Lea and Carey.

Clarkson, T. (1788). *An essay on the impolicy of the African slave trade: In two parts*. London: J. Phillips.

Cruikshank, B. (1853). *Eighteen Years on the Gold Coast of Africa, in two volumes*. London: Hurst and Blackett.

Dalzel, A. (1793). *The History of Dahomy, An Inland Kingdom of Africa; Compiled from Authentic Memoirs; with an Introduction and Notes*. London: T. Spilsbury & Son.

Dapper, D. (1676). Naukeurige Beschrijving der Afrikaensche gewesten, van Egypten, Barbaryen, Libyen, Biledulgerid, Negroslant, Guinea, Ethiopiën, Abyssinie… Getroken uit verscheyde hedendaegse Lantbeschrijvers en geschriften van baereisde ondersoekers dier Landen. *Amsterdam, Jacob van Meurs*.

De Montesquieu, C. (1748). *Montesquieu: The Spirit of the Laws*. Paris.

Dupuis, J. (1824). *Journal of a Residence in Ashantee*. London: Henry Colburn.

Equiano, O. (1794). *The Interesting Narrative of the Life of Olaudah Equiano or Gustavus Vass, The Africa, Written by Himself*. London.

Forbes, F. (1851). *Dahomey and the Dahomans Being the Journals of Two Missions to the King of Dahomey, and Residence at His Capital in the Years 1849 and 1850* London: A. and W. Galignani.

Laird, M. & Oldfield, R. (1837). *Narrative of an expedition into the interior of Africa, by the river Niger in 1832, 1833 and 1834* (Vol. 2): Richard Bentley.

Lander, R. & Lander, J. (1832). *Journal of an expedition to explore the course and termination of the Niger: with a narrative of a voyage down that river to its termination*: J. & J. Harper.

Livingstone, D. (1858). *Missionary Travels and Researches in South Africa: Including a Sketch of Sixteen Years' Residence in the Interior of Africa, and a Journey from the Cape of Good Hope to Loanda on the West Coast; Thence Across the Continent, Down the River Zambesi, to the Eastern Ocean*. London: Harper & Brothers.

Meredith, H. (1812). *An Account of the Gold Coast of Africa with a Brief History of the Africa Company*. London: Longman.

Norris, R. (1789). *Memoirs of the Reign of Bossa Ahádee: King of Dahomy, an Inland Country of Guiney. To which are Added, the Author's Journey to Abomey, the Capital; and a Short Account of the African Slave Trade.* W. Lowndes.

Parfitt, 'Mr Parfitts information on Trade between Sierra Leone and Cape Lopez w. Islands St Thomas etc.' and 'Extract of a Diary Kept by E.L. Parfitt on the Board the Sierra Leone Company's Ship *Calypso*', Papers Relating to Sierra Leone, ff. 174–320. British Library, Add Mss 12131.

Phillips, T. (1693). Journal of a voyage in the Hannibal of London, ann. 1693, 1694 *Awnsham and John Churchill, Collection of Voyages and Travels*, VI. London, 1732.

Postlethwayt, M. (1774). *The universal dictionary of trade and commerce* (4th ed. Vol. II). London: John and Paul Knapton.

Robertson, G.A. (1819). *Notes on Africa: Particularly Those Parts which are Situated Between Cape Verd and The River Congo: Containing Sketches of the Geographical Situations, the Manners and Customs, the Trade, Commerce, and Manufactures, and the Government and Policy of the Various Nations in this Extensive Tract: Also a View of Their Capabilities for the Reception of Civilization, with Hints for the Melioration of the Whole African Population*. Sherwood, Neely and Jones, Paternoster Row.

Rousseau, J. (1762). *The Social Contract*. Paris.

Skertchly, J. (1874). *Dahomey as it is: Being a Narrative of Eight Month's Residence in that Country: with a Full Account of the Notorious Annual Customs, and the Social and Religious Institutions of the Pfons*: Chapman and Hall.

Smith, A. (1776). *An inquiry into the wealth of nations*. London: Strahan and Cadell.

Smith, W. (1745). *A New Voyage to Guinea*. London: J. Nourse.

Snelgrave, W. (1734). *A New Account of Some Parts of Guinea: And the Slave-trade*. London: James, John, and Paul Knapton.

Stedman, J. (1796). *Narrative of a Five Years' Expedition, Against the Revolted Negroes of Surinam, in Guiana, on the Wild Coast of South America: From the Year 1772, to 1777* Johnson & Edwards.

Waddell, H.M. (1863). *Twenty-nine years in the West Indies and Central Africa: a review of missionary work and adventure, 1829–1858.*

Secondary Sources

Abaka, E. (2005). *"Kola is God's gift": agricultural production, export initiatives & the kola industry of Asante & the Gold Coast c. 1820–1950*: James Currey.

Adu-Boahen, K. (2010). Abolition, Economic Transition, Gender and Slavery: The Expansion of Women's Slaveholding in Ghana, 1807–1874 *Slavery and Abolition, 31*(1), 117–136.

Agiri, B. (1972). *Kola in Western Nigeria, 1850–1950: A History of the Cultivation of Cola Nitida in Ẹgba-Owode, Ijẹbu-Rẹmọ, Iwo and Ọta Areas.* (Phd), University of Wisconsin.

Aidoo, A. (1977). Order and conflict in the Asante empire: a study in interest group relations. *African Studies Review, 20*(01), 1–36.

Akinjogbin, I. (1967). *Dahomey and its Neighbours, 1708–1818*: Cambridge University Press.

Allen, R. (2001). The great divergence in European wages and prices from the Middle Ages to the First World War. *Explorations in economic history, 38*(4), 411–447.

Allen, R. (2009). *The British industrial revolution in global perspective.* Cambridge: Cambridge University Press.

Allen, R., Bassino, J., Ma, D., Moll-Murata, C. & Van Zanden, J. (2011). Wages, prices, and living standards in China, 1738–1925: in comparison with Europe, Japan, and India. *The Economic History Review, 64*(s1), 8–38.

Allen, R,B. (2015). *European slave trading in the Indian Ocean, 1500–1850*: Ohio University Press.

Alsan, M. (2015). The Effect of the TseTse Fly on African Development. *American Economic Review, 105*(1), 382–410.

Anyanwu, U. (1992). Kinship and Warfare in Igbo Society. In T. Falola & R. Smith (Eds.), *Warfare and diplomacy in precolonial Nigeria: essays in honor of Ṛobert Smith*: University of Wisconsin Press.

Argyle, W. (1966). *The Fon of Dahomey: a history and ethnography of the Old Kingdom.* Oxford Clarendon Press.

Arhin, K. (1990). Trade, accumulation and the state in Asante in the nineteenth century. *Africa, 60*(04), 524–537.

Austen, R. (1987). African Economic History. James Currey.

Austen, R. (1990). On Comparing Pre-Industrial African and European Economies. *African Economic History*, (19), 21–24.

Austen, R., Derrick, R., & Derrick, J. (1999). *Middlemen of the Cameroons Rivers: the Duala and their hinterland, c. 1600–c. 1960* (Vol. 96). Cambridge University Press.

Austin, G. (1996). 'No Elders Were Present': Commoners and Private Ownership in Asante, 1807–96. *The journal of African History*, *37*(01), 1–30.

Austin, G. (2005). *Labour, land and capital in Ghana: From slavery to free labour in Asante, 1807–1956*: University of Rochester Press.

Austin, G. (2008a). Resources, techniques, and strategies south of the Sahara: revising the factor endowments perspective on African economic development, 1500–20001. *The Economic History Review*, *61*(3), 587–624.

Austin, G. (2008b). The "reversal of fortune" thesis and the compression of history: Perspectives from African and comparative economic history. *Journal of international Development*, *20*(8), 996–1027.

Austin, G. (2013a). Commercial agriculture and the end of slave-trading and slavery in West Africa, 1780s–1920s. In S. Schwarz, R. Law & S. Strickrodt (Eds.), *Commercial Agriculture, the Slave Trade and Slavery in Atlantic Africa* (pp. 243–265): Boydell & Brewer Ltd.

Austin, G. (2013b). Labour-intensity and manufacturing in West Africa, c. 1450–c. 2000. In G. Austin & K. Sugihara (Eds.), *Labour-intensive industrialization in global history* (pp. 201–230): Routledge.

Austin, G. (2015). African economic history in Africa. *Economic history of developing regions*, *30*(1), 79–94.

Balai, L. (2011). *Het slavenschip 'Leusden': slavenschepen en de West Indische Compagnie, 1720–1738*. Zutphen: Walburg Pers.

Bay, E. (1998). *Wives of the Leopard: Gender Politics, and Culture in the Kingdom of Dahomey* Charlottesville & London: University of Virginia Press.

Behrendt, S. (1997). Crew mortality in the transatlantic slave trade in the eighteenth century. *Slavery and Abolition*, *18*(1), 49–71.

Behrendt, S. (2001). Markets, transaction cycles, and profits: Merchant decision making in the British slave trade. *The William and Mary Quarterly*, *58*(1), 171–204.

Behrendt, S. (2007). Human capital in the British slave trade. In D. Richardson, S. Schwarz & A. Tibbles (Eds.), *Liverpool and transatlantic slavery* (pp. 66–97).

Behrendt, S., Eltis, D. & Richardson, D. (2001). The Costs of Coercion: African Agency in the Pre-Modern Atlantic World. *The Economic History Review*, *54*(3), 454–476.

Behrendt, S., Latham, A. & Northrup, D. (2010). *The Diary of Antera Duke, an Eighteenth-Century African Slave Trader*: Oxford University Press.

Bennett, N. & Brooks, G. (1965). *New England merchants in Africa: a history through documents, 1802 to 1865*: Africana Publishers.

Bergad, L. (2006). *Slavery and the demographic and economic history of Minas Gerais, Brazil, 1720–1888*: Cambridge University Press.

Bergad, L., García, F. & del Carmen Barcia, M. (1995). *The Cuban slave market, 1790–1880*: Cambridge University Press.

Brooks, G. (1970). *Yankee Traders, Old Coasters & African Middlemen: A History of American Legitimate Trade with West Africa in the nineteenth century*. Boston: Boston University Press Brookline, MA.

Byrd, A. (2010). *Captives and voyagers: black migrants across the eighteenth century British Atlantic World*. Baton Rouge: LSU Press.

Carney, J. (2001). African rice in the Columbian exchange. *The journal of African History, 42*(03), 377–396.

Carney, J. (2009). *Black rice: the African origins of rice cultivation in the Americas*. Cambridge MA: Harvard University Press.

Carney, J. & Rosomoff, R. (2011). *In the shadow of slavery: Africa's botanical legacy in the Atlantic world*. Oakland, California: University of California Press.

Carretta, V. (2005). *Equiano, the African: Biography of a self-made man*: University of Georgia Press.

Carter, S.B., Gartner, S.S., Haines, M.R., Olmstead, A.L., Sutch, R., & Wright, G. (2006). *Historical statistics of the United States: Earliest times to the present* (Vol. 5). New York: Cambridge University Press.

Chambers, D. (2002). Rejoinder-The Significance of Igbo in the Bight of Biafra Slave-Trade: A Rejoinder to Northrup's 'Myth Igbo'.

Chouin, G. & Decorse, C. (2010). Prelude to the Atlantic trade: new perspectives on southern Ghana's pre-Atlantic history (800–1500). *The Journal of African History, 51*(02), 123–145.

Chuku, G. (2015). *Igbo women and economic transformation in southeastern Nigeria, 1900–1960*: Routledge.

Curtin, P. (1972). *The Atlantic slave trade: a census*: University of Wisconsin Press.

Curtin, P. (1973). *Economic Change in Pre-colonial Africa: Senegambia in the Era of the Slave trade*: Madison.

Curtin, P. (1975). *Economic change in precolonial Africa (supplementary evidence)*: Madison.

Curto, J. (2004). *Enslaving spirits: the Portuguese-Brazilian alcohol trade at Luanda and its hinterland, c. 1550–1830*: Brill Academic Publishers.

Dalrymple-Smith, A., & Frankema, E. (2017) Slave ship provisioning in the long eighteenth century: A boost to West African commercial agriculture? *European Review of Economic History*, 21:2.

da Silva, F. & Sommerdyk, S. (2010). Reexamining the Geography and Merchants of the West Central African Slave Trade: Looking Behind the Numbers. *African Economic History*, 77–105.

Davis, D. (2006). *Inhuman bondage: The rise and fall of slavery in the New World*. Oxford: Oxford University Press.

Decorse, C. (1992). Culture contact, continuity, and change on the Gold Coast, AD 1400–1900. *African Archaeological Review, 10*(1), 163–196.

de Kok, G. (2016). Cursed capital: the economic impact of the transatlantic slave trade on Walcheren around 1770. *Tijdschrift voor Sociale en Economische Geschiedenis, 13*(3), 1–27.

Denzel, M. (2010). *Handbook of world exchange rates, 1590–1914*. Farnham: Ashgate Publishing Ltd.

den Heijer, H. (1997). *Goud, ivoor en slaven: scheepvaart en handel van de Tweede Westindische Compagnie op Afrika, 1674–1740*: Walburg.

De Vries, J. (1994). The industrial revolution and the industrious revolution. *Journal of Economic History, 54*(2), 249–270.

De Vries, J. (2015). Understanding Eurasian Trade in the Era of the Trading Companies. In M. Berg, F. Gottmann, H. Hodacs & C. Nierstrasz (Eds.), *Goods from the East, 1600–1800* (pp. 7–39): Pagrave Macmillan.

de Zwart, P. (2016). Globalization in the Early Modern Era: New Evidence from the Dutch-Asiatic Trade, c. 1600–1800. *The Journal of Economic History*, 76:2.

Dickson, K. (1969). *A historical geography of Ghana*: Cambridge University Press.

Dike, K. (1956). *Trade and politics in the Niger Delta, 1830–1885: an introduction to the economic and political history of Nigeria*. Oxford: Clarendon Press Oxford.

Dike, K. & Ekejiuba, F. (1990). *The Aro of south-eastern Nigeria, 1650–1980: a study of socio-economic formation and transformation in Nigeria*. Ibadan: University Press Limited.

Donnan, E. (1965). *Documents illustrative of the history of the slave trade to America* (Vol. 1): Octagon Books.

Drescher, S. (2004). *The mighty experiment: Free labor versus slavery in British emancipation*. Oxford: Oxford University Press.

Drescher, S. (2010). *Econocide: British slavery in the era of abolition*: University of North Carolina Press.

Dummett, R. (1998). *El Dorado in West Africa: the Gold-Mining Frontier, African Labor, and Colonial Capitalism on the Gold Coast* Ohio University Press.

Ejiogu, E. & Njoku, C. (2015). The Aru Igbo Trust Network and Slave-dealing in Igboland and the Lower Southeast Niger Basin: Assessing the Impacts and Consequences of Initial Abolitionary Efforts by Governments in the Atlantic World in the Period, 1787–1807. *Journal of Asian and African Studies*.

Eltis, D. (1984). Mortality and voyage length in the middle passage: new evidence from the nineteenth century. *The Journal of Economic History, 44*(02), 301–308.

Eltis, D. (1987). *Economic growth and the ending of the transatlantic slave trade*: Oxford University Press.

Eltis, D. (1989). Fluctuations in mortality in the last half century of the transatlantic slave trade. *Social Science History, 13*(03), 315–340.

Eltis, D. (1994). The relative importance of slaves and commodities in the atlantic trade of seventeenth-century Africa. *Journal of African History, 35*, 237–237.

Eltis, D. (2000). *The rise of African slavery in the Americas*: Cambridge University Press.

Eltis, D. (2009). Was Abolition of the US and British Slave Trade Significant in the Broader Atlantic Context? *The William and Mary Quarterly, 66*(4), 715–736.

Eltis, D. (2013). The Slave Trade and Commercial Agriculture in an African Context. In S. Schwarz, R. Law & S. Strickrodt (Eds.), *Commercial Agriculture, the Slave Trade and Slavery in Atlantic Africa*: Boydell & Brewer Ltd.

Eltis, D. & Jennings, L. (1988). Trade between Western Africa and the Atlantic world in the pre-colonial era. *The American Historical Review, 93*(4), 936–959.

Eltis, D., Lovejoy, P., Richardson, D., Law, R. & Strickrodt, S. (1999). *Ports of the Slave Trade (Bights of Benin and Biafra)*. University of Stirling: Centre of Commonwealth Studies.

Eltis, D., Lewis, F. & Richardson, D. (2005). Slave prices, the African slave trade, and productivity in the Caribbean, 1674–1807. *The Economic History Review, 58*(4), 673–700.

Eltis, D., Morgan, P. & Richardson, D. (2007). Agency and diaspora in Atlantic history: Reassessing the African contribution to rice cultivation in the Americas. *The American Historical Review, 112*(5), 1329–1358.

Eltis, D. A Brief Overview of the Trans-Atlantic Slave Trade. *Voyages: The Trans-Atlantic Slave Trade Database*, retrieved from http://www.slavevoyages.org. Accessed 16/07/2016.

Ehemann, C. (2007). Evaluating and adjusting for chain drift in national economic accounts. *Journal of Economics and Business*, 59:3.

Evans, C., & Rydén, G. (2018). 'Voyage iron': an Atlantic slave trade currency, its European origins, and West African impact. *Past and Present, 239*(1), 41–70.

Fage, J. (1980). A commentary on Duarte Pacheco Pereira's account of the Lower Guinea coastlands in his Esmeraldo de situ orbis, and on some other early accounts. *History in Africa, 7*, 47–80.

Feinberg, H. & Johnson, M. (1982). The West African Ivory Trade during the eighteenth century: The "… and Ivory" Complex. *International Journal of African Historical Studies*, 435–453.

Frankema, E. & Jerven, M. (2014). Writing history backwards or sideways: towards a consensus on African population, 1850–2010. *The Economic History Review, 67*(4), 907–931.

Frankema, E. & Waijenburg, M. (2012). Structural impediments to African Growth? New evidence from real wages in British Africa, 1880–1965. *The Journal of Economic History, 72*(04), 895–926.

Frankema, E., Williamson, J. & Woltjer, P. (2015). An economic rationale for the African scramble: the commercial transition and the commodity price boom of 1845–1885: National Bureau of Economic Research.

Garrard, T. (1980). *Akan Weights and the Gold Trade*: Longman.

Green, T. (2011). *The rise of the trans-Atlantic slave trade in Western Africa, 1300–1589* (Vol. 118). Cambridge University Press.

Green, T. (2016). Africa and the price revolution: currency imports and socioeconomic change in West and West-Central Africa during the seventeenth century. *The Journal of African History, 57*(1), 1–24.

Grindal, P. (2016). *Opposing the Slavers: The Royal Navy's Campaign of Suppression*: I.B.Tauris.

Haggerty, S. (2009). Risk and risk management in the Liverpool slave trade. *Business History, 51*(6), 817–834.

Hargreaves, S. (1987). *The political economy of nineteenth-century Bonny: a study of power, authority, legitimacy and ideology in a Delta trading community from 1790–1914*. The University of Birmingham.

Harms, R. (2008). *The Diligent: Worlds of the Slave Trade*: Basic Books.

Hawthorne, W. (2003). *Planting rice and harvesting slaves*. Heinemann.

Heglund, N., Willems, P., Penta, M. & Cavagna, G. (1995). Energy-saving gait mechanics with head-supported loads. *Nature, 375*(6526), 52.

Henrich, J., Boyd, R. & Richerson, P. (2012). The puzzle of monogamous marriage. *Philisophical Transactions of the Royal Society B, 367*(1589), 657–669.

Herbst, J. (2000). *States and power in Africa: comparative lessons in authority and control*: Princeton University Press.

Hernæs, P. (1998). *Slaves, Danes, and African Coast Society: The Danish Slave Trade from West Africa and Afro-Danish Relations on the eighteenth century Gold Coast*: Department of History, Norwegian University of Science and Technology (University of Trondheim).

Hilton, B. (2010). 1807 and All That: Why Britain Outlawed Her Slave Trade. In D. Peterson (Ed.), *Abolitionism and Imperialism in Britain, Africa, and the Atlantic* (pp. 63–83). Ohio: Ohio University Press.

Hogerzeil, S. & Richardson, D. (2007). Slave purchasing strategies and shipboard mortality: Day-to-day evidence from the Dutch African Trade, 1751–1797. *The Journal of Economic History, 67*(01), 160–190.

Hopkins, A. (1968). Economic Imperialism in West Africa: Lagos, 1880–921. *The Economic History Review, 21*(3), 580–606.

Hopkins, A. (1973). *An economic history of West Africa*. London: Longman.

Inikori, J. (1981). Market structure and the profits of the British African trade in the late eighteenth-century. *The Journal of Economic History, 41*(04), 745–776.

Inikori, J. (2002). *Africans and the Industrial Revolution in England: A study in international trade and economic development*: Cambridge University Press.

Inikori, J. (2007). Africa and the globalization process: Western Africa, 1450–1850. *Journal of Global History, 2*(1), 63.

Inikori, J. (2009). The economic impact of the 1807 British Abolition of the Transatlantic Slave Trade. In T. Falola & M. Childs (Eds.), *The changing worlds of Atlantic Africa: essays in honor of Robin Law*: Carolina Academic Press.

Inikori, J. (2011). Transatlantic Slavery and Economic Development in the Atlantic World: West Africa, 1450–1850. In D. Eltis & S. Engerman (Eds.), *The Cambridge World History of Slavery* (pp. 650–674). Cambridge: Cambridge University Press.

Inikori, J. & Daget, S. (1988). *The sources of supply for the Atlantic slave exports from the Bight of Benin and the Bight of Bonny (Biafra)*. Paper presented at the De la traite à l'esclavage: actes du colloque international sur la traite des noirs, Nantes.

Ipsen, P. (2015). *Daughters of the Trade: Atlantic Slavers and Interracial Marriage on the Gold Coast*: University of Pennsylvania Press.

Isichei, E. (1976). *A history of the Igbo people*: Macmillan.

Isichei, E. (1978). The Quest for Social Reform in the Context of Traditional Religion: A Neglected Theme of West African History. *African Affairs, 77*(309), 463–478.

Jennings, J. (2013). *The business of abolishing the British slave trade, 1783–1807*. London & New York: Routledge.

Jerven, M., Austin, G., Green, E., Uche, C., Frankema, E., Fourie, J., ... & Hillbom, E. (2012). *Moving forward in African economic history: Bridging the gap between methods and sources*. AEHN.

Johnson, M. (1966). The ounce in eighteenth-century West African trade. *The Journal of African History, 7*(02), 197–214.

Johnson, M. (1968). The nineteenth century gold 'Mithqal'in West and North Africa. *The Journal of African History, 9*(04), 547–569.

Johnson, M. (1986a). *Ivory and the nineteenth century Transformation in West Africa*. Paper presented at the Figuring African Trade: Proceedings of the Symposium on the Quantification and Structure of the Import and Export and Long Distance Trade in Africa, 1800–1913.

Johnson, M. (1986b) On Computerising Trade Statistics', in: G. Liesegang, H. Pasch and A. Jones (Eds.), *Figuring African Trade: Proceedings of the Symposium on the Quantification and Structure of the Import and Export and lone-distance Trade in Africa 1800–1913* (pp. 28–32): D. Reimer.

Johnson, M. (1986c). The slaves of Salaga. *The Journal of African History, 27*(02), 341–362.

Johnson, M., Lindblad, J. & Ross, R. (1990). *Anglo-African trade in the eighteenth century: English statistics on African trade 1699–1808*: Centre for the History of European Expansion.

Jones, A. (1983). From slaves to palm kernels: A history of the Galinhas Country (West Africa), 1730–1890. *Studien zur Kulturkunde Wiesbaden*, (68), 1–220.

Justesen, O., & Manley, J. (2005). *Danish sources for the history of Ghana 1657–1754. Vol. 1, 1657–1735*. Det Kongelige Danske Videnskabernes Selskab (The Royal Danish Academy of Sciences and Letters).

Kea, R. (1982). *Settlements, trade, and polities in the seventeenth century Gold Coast*. Baltimore: Johns Hopkins University Press.

Kelly, K.G. (1995). *Transformation and continuity in Savi, a West African trade town: an archaeological investigation of culture change on the coast of Bénin during the 17th and 18th centuries*.

Kiple, K.F. (1984). *The Caribbean slave: a biological history*: Cambridge University Press Cambridge.

Klein, H. (2010). *The Atlantic slave trade*. Cambridge: Cambridge University Press.

Klein, H.S., & Engerman, S.L. (1979). A note on mortality in the French slave trade in the eighteenth century. *The Uncommon Market: Essays in the Economic History of the Atlantic Slave Trade*, 261–272.

Klein, H. & Engerman, S. (1997). Long-term trends in African mortality in the transatlantic slave trade. *Slavery and Abolition, 18*(1), 36–48.

Klein, H., Engerman, S., Haines, R. & Shlomowitz, R. (2001). Transoceanic mortality: the slave trade in comparative perspective. *The William and Mary Quarterly, 58*(1), 93–118.

Klein, M. (2001). The slave trade and decentralized societies. *The Journal of African History, 42*(01), 49–65.

Kolapo, F. (2002). Nineteenth-century Niger River Trade and the 1844–1862 Aboh Interregnum. *African Economic History*(30), 1–29.

Kolapo, F. (2004). The Igbo and their Neighbours during the era of the Atlantic Slave-Trade. *Slavery & Abolition, 25*(1), 114–133.

Korieh, C. (2000). The nineteenth century commercial transition in West Africa: the case of the Biafra Hinterland. *Canadian Journal of African Studies/La Revue canadienne des études africaines, 34*(3), 588–615.

Last, M. (1967). *The Sokoto Caliphate*. London: Longman.

Latham, A. (1973). *Old Calabar, 1600–1891: The impact of the international economy upon a traditional society*. Oxford: Clarendon Press.

Law, R. (1976). Horses, firearms, and political power in pre-colonial West Africa. *Past & Present*(72), 112–132.

Law, R. (1977). *The Oyo empire, c. 1600–c. 1836: a West African imperialism in the era of the Atlantic slave trade*: Clarendon press Oxford.

Law, R. (1989a). Between the Sea and the Lagoons: The Interaction of Maritime and Inland Navigation on the Precolonial Slave Coast *Cahiers d'etudes africaines*, 209–237.

Law, R. (1989b). Slave-raiders and middlemen, monopolists and free-traders: The supply of slaves for the Atlantic trade in Dahomey c. 1715–1850. *The Journal of African History, 30*(01), 45–68.

Law, R. (1990a). "The Common People Were Divided": Monarchy, Aristocracy and Political Factionalism in the Kingdom of Whydah, 1671–1727. *The International Journal of African Historical Studies, 23*(2), 201–229.

Law, R. (1990b). The Gold Trade of Whydah in the Seventeenth and Eighteenth Centuries. In D. Henige & T. McCaskie (Eds.), *West African Economic and Social History: Studies in Memory of Marion Johnson* (pp. 105–I108).

Law, R. (1991). *The Slave Coast of West Africa, 1550–1750: the impact of the Atlantic slave trade on an African society*: Clarendon Press Oxford.

Law, R. (1992). Posthumous questions for Karl Polanyi: Price inflation in pre-colonial Dahomey. *The Journal of African History, 33*(03), 387–420.

Law, R. (1995a). *From Slave Trade to 'Legitimate' Commerce: The Commercial Transition in Nineteenth-century West Africa*. Cambridge: Cambridge University Press.

Law, R. (1995b). Introduction. In R. Law (Ed.), *From slave trade to 'legitimate' commerce: the commercial transition in nineteenth-century West Africa*. Cambridge: Cambridge University Press.

Law, R. (1995c). 'Legitimate' trade and gender relations in Yorubaland and Dahomey. In R. Law (Ed.), *From slave trade to 'legitimate' commerce: the commercial transition in nineteenth-century West Africa*. Cambridge: Cambridge University Press.

Law, R. (1997a). *The English in West Africa, 1681–1683: The Local Correspondence of the Royal African Company of England, 1681–1699: Parts 1, 2, 3*: Oxford University Press.

Law, R. (1997b). The politics of commercial transition: Factional conflict in Dahomey in the context of the ending of the Atlantic slave trade. *The Journal of African History, 38*(02), 213–233.

Law, R. (2004). *Ouidah: the social history of a West African slaving 'port', 1727–1892*: Ohio State University Press.

Law, R. (2010). Abolition and Imperialism: international law and the British suppression of the Atlantic slave trade. In D. Peterson (Ed.), *Abolitionism and Imperialism in Britain, Africa, and the Atlantic*: Ohio University Press.

Law, R. & Hair, P. (1998). The English in West Africa to 1700. In N. Canny (Ed.), *The Oxford History of the British Empire: Volume 1, The Origins of Empire: British Overseas Enterprise to the close of the seventeenth century*. Oxford: Oxford University Press.

Law, R., Schwarz, S. & Strickrodt, S. (2013). *Commercial agriculture, the slave trade and slavery in Atlantic Africa*: Boydell & Brewer Ltd.

Lawrence, A. (1963). *The Forts of West Africa*. London: Cape.

Lovejoy, P. (1978). Plantations in the Economy of the Sokoto Caliphate. *The Journal of African History, 19*(03), 341–368.

Lovejoy, P. (1980). *Caravans of Kola: the Hausa kola trade, 1700–1900*: Ahmadu Bello University Press.

Lovejoy, P. (1982). Polanyi's "Ports of Trade": Salaga and Kano in the nineteenth century. *Canadian Journal of African Studies/La Revue canadienne des études africaines, 16*(2), 245–278.

Lovejoy, P. (1985). The internal trade of West Africa before 1800. *History of West Africa, 1*, 648–690.

Lovejoy, P. (1986). *Salt of the desert sun: a history of salt production and trade in the Central Sudan*: Cambridge University Press.

Lovejoy, P. (1995). Kola nuts, the "coffee" of the central Sudan. In J. Goodman, P. Lovejoy & A. Sherratt (Eds.), *Consuming habits: Drugs in history and anthropology* (pp. 98–120). London: Routledge.

Lovejoy, P. (2011). *Transformations in slavery: a history of slavery in Africa* (Third ed.). Cambridge: Cambridge University Press.

Lovejoy, P. & Richardson, D. (1995a). British abolition and its impact on slave prices along the Atlantic coast of Africa, 1783–1850. *The Journal of Economic History, 55*(01), 98–119.

Lovejoy, P. & Richardson, D. (1995b). Competing markets for male and female slaves: prices in the interior of West Africa, 1780–1850. *International Journal of African Historical Studies*, 261–293.

Lovejoy, P. & Richardson, D. (1999). Trust, pawnship, and Atlantic history: the institutional foundations of the Old Calabar slave trade. *American Historical Review*, 333–355.

Lovejoy, P. & Richardson, D. (2004). 'This horrid hole': Royal Authority, Commerce and Credit at Bonny, 1690–1840. *The Journal of African History, 45*(03), 363–392.

Lovejoy, P. & Richardson, D. (2007). African agency and the Liverpool slave trade. In D. Richardson, S. Schwarz & A. Tibbles (Eds.), *Liverpool and transatlantic slavery* (pp. 43–65): Liverpool University Press.

Lynn, M. (1991). Bristol, West Africa and the nineteenth century Palm Oil Trade. *Historical Research, 64*(155), 359–374.

Lynn, M. (1992). The Profitability of the Early Nineteenth-Century Palm Oil Trade. *African Economic History* (20), 77–97.

Lynn, M. (1997). *Commerce and economic change in West Africa: The palm oil trade in the nineteenth century* (Vol. 93): Cambridge University Press.

Macdonald, J. (2004). *Feeding Nelson's Navy: The True Story of Food at Sea in the Georgian Era*: Frontline Books.

Maier, D. (1990). Military acquisition of slaves in Asante. In D. Henige & T. McCaskie (Eds.), *West African Economic and Social History: Studies in Memory of Marion Johnson* (pp. 119–132): University of Wisconson Press.

Maier, D. (2009). Precolonial Palm Oil Production and Gender Division of Labor in Nineteenth-Century Gold Coast and Togoland. *African Economic History, 37*(1), 1–32.

Mandelblatt, B. (2008). "Beans from Rochel and Manioc from Prince's Island": West Africa, French Atlantic Commodity Circuits, and the Provisioning of the French Middle Passage. *History of European Ideas, 34*(4), 411–423.

Mann, K. (2007). *Slavery and the Birth of an African City: Lagos, 1760–1900*: Indiana University Press.

Manning, P. (1982). *Slavery, Colonialism and Economic Growth in Dahomey 1640–1960*. Cambridge: Cambridge University Press.

Manning, P. (1986). Slave Trade,"Legitimate" Trade, and Imperialism Revisited: The Control of Wealth in the Bights of Benin and Biafra. In S. Lovejoy (Ed.), *Africans in Bondage. Studies in Slavery and the Slave Trade* (pp. 203–233). Madison.

Manning, P. (1990). *Slavery and African life: Occidental, Oriental, and African slave trades* (Vol. 67): Cambridge University Press.

Manning, P. (2012). Historical datasets on Africa and the African Atlantic. *Journal of Comparative Economics, 40*(4), 604–607.

Martin, P.M. (1972). *The external trade of the Loango Coast, 1576–1870: the effects of changing commercial relations on the Vili Kingdom of Loango* (pp. 73–92). Oxford: Clarendon Press.

Martin, P.M. (1986). Power, cloth and currency on the Loango coast. *African Economic History*, (15), 1–12.

Martin, S. (1988). *Palm oil and protest; An Economic History of the Ngwa Region*: Cambridge University Press.

Martinez, J. (2011). *The slave trade and the origins of international human rights law*: Oxford University Press.

Mattoso, K.M. de Queiros, Herbert S. Klein & Stanley L. Engerman (1986) "Research Note: Trends and Patterns in the Prices of Manumitted Slaves: Bahia, 1819–1888." *Slavery and Abolition, 7*(1), 59–67.

McCarthy, M. (1983). *Social change and the growth of British power in the Gold Coast: The Fante states, 1807–1874*: Rowman & Littlefield Publishers.

McCaskie, T.C. (2003). *State and society in pre-colonial Asante* (Vol. 79): Cambridge University Press.

McCaskie, T. (2007). Denkyira in the making of Asante c. 1660–1720. *The Journal of African History, 48*(01), 1–25.

McDade, K. (2011). Liverpool slave merchant entrepreneurial networks, 1725–1807. *Business History, 53*(7), 1092–1109.

McIntosh, S. (1999). Pathways to complexity: An African perspective. In S. McIntosh (Ed.), *Beyond chiefdoms: Pathways to complexity in Africa* (pp. 1–30). Cambridge: Cambridge University Press.

McPhee, A. (1926). *The Economic Revolution in British West Africa*. London: G. Routledge & Sons.

McSheffrey, G. (1983). Slavery, Indentured Servitude, Legitimate Trade and the Impact of Abolition in the Gold Coast, 1874–1901: A Reappraisal. *The Journal of African History, 24*(03), 349–368.

Metcalf, G. (1987). Gold, assortments and the trade ounce: Fante merchants and the problem of supply and demand in the 1770s. *The Journal of African History, 28*(01), 27–41.

Michon, B. (2007). La traite négrière nantaise au milieu du XVIIIe siècle (1748–1751),[w:] Les Ports et la traite négrière, Nantes. *Les Cahiers des Anneaux de la Mémoire, 10*, 34–63.

Miller, J. (1997). *Way of death: merchant capitalism and the Angolan slave trade, 1730–1830*: University of Wisconsin Press.

Miller, J.C. (1979). Some Aspects of the Commercial Organization of Slaving at Luanda, Angola—1760–1830. In H.A. Gemery & J.S. Hogendorn (Eds.), *The Uncommon Market: Essays in the Economic History of the Atlantic Slave Trade*: Academic Press New York, NY.

Miller, J.C. (1986). Slave Prices in the Portuguese Southern Atlantic, 1600–1830. In P.E. Lovejoy (Ed.), *Africans in Bondage: Studies in Slavery and the Slave Trade: essays in honor of Phillip D Curtin on the occasion of the twenty fifth anniversary of African Studies at the University of Wisconsin* (pp. 43–77): University of Wisconsin.

Monroe, J. & Ogundiran, A. (2012). *Power and landscape in Atlantic West Africa: Archaeological Perspectives*: Cambridge University Press.

Monroe, J.C. (2007). Continuity, revolution or evolution on the slave coast of West Africa? Royal architecture and political order in precolonial Dahomey. *The Journal of African History, 48*(03), 349–373.

Monroe, J.C. (2012). Building the state in Dahomey: power and landscape on the Bight of Benin. *Power and landscape in Atlantic West Africa: archaeological perspectives*, 191.

Monroe, J.C. (2015). Cities, Slavery, and Rural Ambivalence in Precolonial Dahomey. In L. Wilson Marshall (Ed.), *The Archaeology of Slavery: A Comparative Approach to Captivity and Coercion* (pp. 192): Southern Illinois University Press.

Morgan, K. (2003). James Rogers and the Bristol slave trade*. *Historical Research, 76*(192), 189–216.

Morgan, K. (2005). Remittance procedures in the eighteenth century British slave trade. *Business History Review, 79*(04), 715–749.

Morgan, K. (2007). Liverpool's Dominance in the British Slave Trade, 1740–1807. In D. Richardson, S. Schwarz & A. Tibbles (Eds.), *Liverpool and transatlantic slavery* (pp. 14–42). Liverpool: Liverpool University Press.

Newbury, C. (1965). *British Policy Towards West Africa: Select Documents 1786–1874*: Cambridge University Press.

Newson, L. (2007). *From Capture to Sale: The Portuguese Slave Trade to Spanish South America in the Early Seventeenth-century* (Vol. 12): Brill.

Noah, M.,E. & Ekpo, T. (1992). In T. Falola & M.R.S. Smith (Eds.), *Warfare and diplomacy in precolonial Nigeria: essays in honor of Robert Smith*: African Studies Program, University of Wisconsin.

Norman, N. (2009). Hueda (Whydah) country and town: archaeological perspectives on the rise and collapse of an African Atlantic kingdom. *The International Journal of African Historical Studies, 42*(3), 387–410.

Norman, N. (2012). From the shadow of an Atlantic citadel: An archaeology of the Huedan countryside. In J.C. Monroe & A. Ogundiran (Eds.), *Power and landscape in Atlantic West Africa: archaeological perspectives* (pp. 142–166). Cambridge: Cambridge University Press.

North, D., Wallis, J. & Weingast, B. (2009). *Violence and social orders: a conceptual framework for interpreting recorded human history*: Cambridge University Press.

Northrup, D. (1976). The compatibility of the slave and palm oil trades in the Bight of Biafra. *Journal of African History, 17*(3), 353–364.

Northrup, D. (1978). *Trade without rulers: pre-colonial economic development in southeastern Nigeria*. Oxford: Clarendon Press.

Northrup, D. (1979). Nineteenth-century patterns of slavery and economic growth in southeastern Nigeria. *The International Journal of African Historical Studies, 12*(1), 1–16.

Northrup, D. (2000). Igbo and Myth Igbo: Culture and ethnicity in the Atlantic world, 1600–1850. *Slavery and Abolition, 21*(3), 1–20.

Nunn, N. (2008). The long-term effects of Africa's slave trades. *The Quarterly Journal of Economics, 123*(1), 139–176.

Nwaubani, E. (1999). The Political Economy of Aboh, 1830–1857. *African Economic History*(27), 93–116.

Nwokeji, G. (2000). The Atlantic slave trade and population density: A historical demography of the Biafran hinterland. *Canadian Journal of African Studies/La Revue canadienne des études africaines, 34*(3), 616–655.

Nwokeji, G.U. (2006). Equiano the African: Biography of a Self-Made Man.

Nwokeji, G. (2010). *The Slave Trade and Culture in the Bight of Biafra: An African Society in the Atlantic World*: Cambridge University Press.

Ohadike, D. (1992). Igbo-Benin Wars. In T. Falola & R. Smith (Eds.), *Warfare and diplomacy in precolonial Nigeria: essays in honor of Robert Smith*: African Studies Program, University of Wisconsin.

Ohadike, D. (1994). *Anioma: a social history of the Western Igbo people*: Ohio University Press.

Ohadike, D. (1998). 'When slaves left, owners wept': Entrepreneurs and emancipation among the Igbo people. *Slavery and Abolition, 19*(2), 189–207.

Oriji, J. (1992). Ethical Ideals of Peace and the Concept of War in Igbo Society. In T. Falola & R.S. Smith (Eds.), *Warfare and diplomacy in precolonial Nigeria: essays in honor of Robert Smith*: African Studies Program, University of Wisconsin.

Osafo-Kwaako, P. & Robinson, J. (2013). Political centralization in pre-colonial Africa. *Journal of Comparative Economics, 41*(1), 6–21.

Pearson, R. & Richardson, D. (2008). Social capital, institutional innovation and Atlantic trade before 1800. *Business History, 50*(6), 765–780.

Perbi, A. (2004). *A history of indigenous slavery in Ghana: From the 15th to the 19th century*: Sub-Saharan Pub & Traders.

Posthumus, N.W. (1946). *Inquiry into the History of Prices in Holland* (Vol. 1, pp. 364–365). Leiden: EJ Brill.

Grenouilleau, P. (1995). Joseph Mosneron (1748–1833), armateur négrier nantais. Portrait culturel d'une bourgeoisie negociante au siècle des Lumières. Apogee.

Pomeranz, K. (2000). *The great divergence: China, Europe and the making of the modern world economy.* Princeton: Princeton University Press.

Postma, J. (1990). *The Dutch in the Atlantic slave trade, 1600–1815*: Cambridge University Press.

Radburn, N. (2009). *William Davenport, the Slave Trade, and Merchant Enterprise in Eighteenth-Century Liverpool.* (MA Thesis), University of Aukland.

Radburn, N. (2015). Keeping "the wheel in motion": Trans-Atlantic Credit Terms, Slave Prices, and the Geography of Slavery in the British Americas, 1755–1807. *The Journal of Economic History, 75*(03), 660–689.

Rediker, M. (2007). *The slave ship: A human history*. New York: Viking.

Reid, J. (1986). *Warrior aristocrats in crisis: the political effects of the transition from the slave trade to palm oil commerce in the nineteenth century kingdom of Dahomey.* (Phd), Stirling Univeristy, Stirling.

Reid, R. (2012). *Warfare in African history* (Vol. 6): Cambridge University Press.

Reynolds, E. (1974). *Trade and economic change on the Gold Coast, 1807–1874*: Longman.

Ribeiro, A. (2008). The Transatlantic Slave Trade to Bahia, 1582–1851. In D. Eltis & D. Richardson (Eds.), *Extending the frontiers: Essays on the new transatlantic slave trade database* (pp. 136–137): Yale University Press.

Richardson, D. (1986). *Bristol, Africa and the eighteenth century Slave Trade to America: Vol. 1 the Years of Expansion 1698–1729*. Bristol: Bristol Record Society.

Richardson, D. (1987). *Bristol and the eighteenth century Slave Trade to America Vol. 2 The Years of Ascendancy 1730–1745*. Bristol: Bristol Record Society.

Richardson, D. (1991). *Bristol and the eighteenth century Slave Trade to America Vol. 3 The Years of Decline 1746–1769*. Bristol: Bristol Record Society.

Richardson, D. (1996). *Bristol and the eighteenth century Slave Trade to America Vol. 3 The Final Year 1770–1807*. Bristol: Bristol Record Society.

Richardson, D. (1991). Prices of slaves in West and West Central Africa: Toward an annual series 1698–1807. *Bulletin of Economic Research, 43*(1), 21–56.

Richardson, D. (2001). Shipboard revolts, African authority, and the Atlantic slave trade. *The William and Mary Quarterly, 58*(1), 69–92.

Richardson, D., Tibbles, A. & Schwarz, S. (2007). *Liverpool and transatlantic slavery*: Liverpool University Press.

Rinchon, D. (1964). *Pierre-Ignace-Liévin van Alstein: capitaine négrier, Gand 1733-Nantes 1793* (Vol. 71): IFAN.

Rodney, W. (1972). How Europe underdeveloped Africa. *Beyond borders: Thinking critically about global issues*, 107–125.

Rönnbäck, K. (2014). Living standards on the pre-colonial Gold Coast: a quantitative estimate of African laborers' welfare ratios. *European Review of Economic History, 18*(2), 185–202.

Rönnbäck, K. (2015). *Labour and Living Standards in Pre-colonial West Africa: The Case of the Gold Coast*: Routledge.

Rönnbäck, K. & Oberg, S. (2016). *Mortality among European settlers in pre-colonial West Africa: The "White Man's Grave" revisited*. Goteborg Papers in Economic History. School of Business Economics and Law. Goteborg University. Goteborg.

Ross, D. (1971). Dahomey. In M. Crowder (Ed.), *West African Resistance: the military response to colonial occupation* (pp. 144–170). New York: Hutchinson & Co.

Ryan, M. (2011). The Price of Legitimacy in Humanitarian Intervention: Britain, the Right of Search, and the Abolition of the West African Slave Trade, 1807–1867. In B. Simms & D. Trim (Eds.), *Humanitarian Intervention: A History* (pp. 231–280). Cambridge: Cambridge University Press.

Sanders, J. (1982). Palm oil production on the Gold Coast in the aftermath of the slave trade: a case study of the Fante. *The International Journal of African Historical Studies, 15*(1), 49–63.

Schwarz, S. (2007). Commerce, Civilization and Christianity: The Development of the Sierre Leone Company. In D. Richardson, S. Schwarz & A. Tibbles (Eds.), *Liverpool and transatlantic slavery* (pp. 252–276): Liverpool University Press.

Searing, J. (2003). *West African Slavery and Atlantic Commerce: The Senegal River Valley, 1700–1860*. Cambridge: Cambridge University Press.

Segurola, B. & Rassinoux, J. (2000). *Dictionnaire fon-français*: Société des Missions Africaines.

Sheriff, A. (1987). *Slaves, spices and ivory in Zanzibar: Integration of an East African commercial empire into the world economy, 1770–1873*: Ohio University Press.

Sherratt, A. (1995). Alcohol and its alternatives: symbol and substance in pre-industrial cultures. In Goodman, J, Lovejoy, P & Sherratt, A (Eds), *Consuming habits: global and historical perspectives on how cultures define drugs*. London: Routledge.

Shumway, R. (2014). *The Fante and the transatlantic slave trade*: Boydell & Brewer.

Smith, R. (1989). *Warfare & diplomacy in pre-colonial West Africa*: Univ of Wisconsin Press.

Sommerdyk, S. (2012). *Trade and the Merchant Community of the Loango Coast in the Eighteenth Century* (Unpublished doctoral dissertation). University of the Hull, Hull.

Sommerdyk, S. (2015). Trans-Cultural Exchange at Malemba Bay: The Voyages of the Fregatschip Prins Willem v, 1755 to 1771. In D. Richardson & F.R. da Silva (Ed.), *Networks and Trans-Cultural Exchange in the South Atlantic 1590–1867*: Brill.

Soumonni, E. (1995). The Compatibility of the Slave and Palm Oil Trades in Dahomey, 1818–1858. In R. Law (Ed.), *From Slave Trade To 'Legitimate' Commerce: The Commercial Transition in Nineteenth-Century West Africa* (pp. 78–92): Cambridge University Press.

Sparks, R. (2014). *Where the Negroes are Masters: An African Port in the Era of the Slave Trade*: Harvard University Press.

Strickrodt, S. (2015). *Afro-European Trade in the Atlantic World: The Western Slave Coast, c. 1550–c. 1885*: Boydell & Brewer Ltd.

Svalesen, L. (2000). *The slave ship Fredensborg*: Indiana University Press.

Swanepoel, N. (2009). Every periphery is its own center: sociopolitical and economic interactions in nineteenth-century northwestern Ghana. *The International Journal of African Historical Studies*, 411–432.

Tachie-Obeng, E., Brown, E. & Brown, N. (2001). COLA NITIDA and COLA ACUMINATA A State of Knowledge Report undertaken for The Central African Regional Program for the Environment. Oxford Forestry Institute Department of Plant Sciences: University of Oxford.

Tadman, M. (2000). The demographic cost of sugar: debates on slave societies and natural increase in the Americas. *American Historical Review*, 1534–1575.

Taylor, C. (1952). *The vegetation zones of the Gold Coast*: Government Printing Department.

Thomas, H. (1999). *The slave trade: The story of the atlantic slave trade: 1440–1870*. London: Picador.

Thornton, J. (1998). *Africa and Africans in the Making of the Atlantic World, 1400–1800* (2nd ed.): Cambridge University Press.

Thornton, J. (1999). *Warfare in Atlantic Africa, 1500–1800*: UCL Press.

Van Den Boogaart, E. (1992). The trade between Western Africa and the Atlantic world, 1600–90: estimates of trends in composition and value. *The Journal of African History, 33*(03), 369–385.

Vos, J. (2009). The Slave Trade from the Windward Coast: The Case of the Dutch, 1740–1805. *African Economic History, 38*(1), 29–51.

Wariboko, W. (1998). A theory of the canoe house corporation. *African Economic History*(26), 141–172.

Wariboko, W. (2014). *Elem Kalabari of the Niger Delta: the transition from slave to produce trading under British imperialism*: Africa World Press.

Webb, J. (1985). The trade in gum Arabic: Prelude to French conquest in Senegal. *The Journal of African History, 26*(2–3), 149–168.

Whatley, W. (2014). *The Gun-Slave Cycle in the 18th Century British Slave Trade*. MPRA Paper No. 58741. Munich.

Wilks, I. (1975). *Asante in the 19th Century, The structure and evolution of a political order*. Cambridge.

Wilks, I. (1978). Land, Labour, Capital and the Forest Kingdom of Asante: A model of early change. In J. Freidman & M. Rowlands (Eds.), *The Evolution of Social Systems* (pp. 487–534). Pittsburgh.

Wilks, I. (1985). The State of the Akan and the Akan States: A Discursion (L'état des Akan et les États akan: discursion). *Cahiers d'etudes africaines, 22*, 231–249.

Wilks, I. (1993). *Forests of Gold: Essays on the Akan and the Kingdom of Asante*: Ohio University Press.

Wilks, I. (2001). *Akwamu 1640–1750: a study of the rise and fall of a West African empire*: Dept. of History, Norwegian University of Science and Technology.

Williams, E. (1944). *Slavery and capitalism*. Chapel Hill.

Wills, M. (2012). *The Royal Navy and the suppression of the Atlantic slave trade c. 1807–1867: anti-slavery, empire and identity.* University of Hull, Hull.

Wilson, L. (1991). *The Krobo people of Ghana to 1892: A political and social history*: Ohio University Center for International Studies.

Wrigley, E. (2007). English county populations in the later eighteenth-century. *The Economic History Review, 60*(1), 35–69.

Wyse, A. (1989). *The Krio of Sierra Leone: an interpretive history* (Vol. 2): C Hirst & Co.

Yarak, L. (1990). *Asante and the Dutch, 1744–1873*. Oxford: Clarendon Press.

Yarak, L. (1996). Slavery and the State in Asante History. In J. Hunwick & N. Lawler (Eds.), *The Cloth of Many Colored Silks: Papers on History and Society Ghanaian and Islamic in Honor of Ivor Wilks* (pp. 223–240): Northwestern University Press.

Yoder, J. (1974). Fly and Elephant parties: Political polarization in Dahomey, 1840–1870. *The Journal of African History, 15*(03), 417–432.

Online Sources

Allen, R. (2007). Prices and Wages in London and Southern England, 1259–1914, from http://www.iisg.nl/hpw/data.php. Retrieved 23rd June 2016.

Clark, G. (2006). England, Prices and Wages since 13th Century. *Global Price and Income History Group, University of California, Davis.,* from http://gpih.ucdavis.edu/Datafilelist.htm. Retrieved 15th July, 2015.

Officer, L. & Williamson, S. (2016). The Price of Gold 1257–2014. *Measuring Worth.*, from https://measuringworth.com/datasets/gold/result.php. Retrieved 20th May, 2016.

Voyages: The Trans-Atlantic Slave Trade Database, from http://www.slavevoyages.org/voyage/search. Retrieved 6th July, 2015.

Index

www.ingramcontent.com/pod-product-compliance
Lightning Source LLC
LaVergne TN
LVHW010641300926
849161LV00005B/1010
* 9 7 8 9 0 0 4 3 6 3 4 5 8 *